AL-RĀSHIDŪN

THE WAY OF THE RIGHTLY GUIDED CALIPHS

Ilm Forum

Foreword by Omar Suleiman

Al-Rāshidūn: The Way of the Rightly Guided Caliphs

First published in England by

Kube Publishing Ltd, Markfield Conference Centre, Ratby Lane, Markfield, Leicestershire LE67 9SY, United Kingdom.

Distributed by

Kube Publishing Ltd.
Tel: +44(0)1530 249230
Email: info@kubepublishing.com
Website: www.kubepublishing.com

Cataloguing-in-Publication Data is available from the British Library.

ISBN 978-1-84774-245-2 Casebound
ISBN 978-1-84774-246-9 Ebook

Cover design: Amaan Ansari
Typesetting: LiteBook Prepress Services
Printed by: Elma Basim, Turkey

Contents

Acknowledgements *v*

Foreword *vii*

Introduction *xi*

Al-Ṣiddīq: "Abū Bakr" ʿAbdullāh ibn Abī Quḥāfah *1*

Al-Fārūq: "Abū Ḥafṣ" ʿUmar ibn al-Khaṭṭāb *41*

Al-Ghanī: "Dhū al-Nūrayn" ʿUthmān ibn ʿAffān *95*

Al-Ḥaydar: "Abū Turāb" ʿAlī ibn Abī Ṭālib *143*

Acknowledgements

All gratitude is due to Allah ﷻ for graciously enabling us to bring forth this noble book and for inspiring the profound concept and idea within the visions of IlmForum. Any good found in this book and any accomplishments resulting from this effort are attributed solely to Allah ﷻ. We acknowledge that all goodness and purity emanate from Allah ﷻ.

We want to express our sincere thanks to all those who stood by us during the process of producing this book about the Four Caliphs. Numerous individuals have played a vital role in bringing this work to completion, and we sincerely pray that Allah ﷻ showers abundant blessings upon them for their unwavering support and valuable contributions.

A genuine heartfelt gratitude to Shamim Ahmed, AbdulHayy Salloo, Junaid Ahmed alongside Dr Salah Sharief and the entire Wordsmiths team. A special thanks to the dedicated team at IlmForum for their unwavering and sincere efforts behind the scenes. It is our sincere hope that this collective endeavour will not only enhance but profoundly deepen the understanding and appreciation of the remarkable legacies of the Four Caliphs. May this work serve as a source of genuine inspiration and enlightenment for all readers, touching hearts and minds with the richness of their words and actions.

– Saiful Alam, founder of IlmForum

Foreword

"Prophethood shall remain amongst you for as long as Allah wills it to remain, then Allah will remove it whenever He wishes to remove it... Then there shall be caliphate upon the methodology of prophethood and it shall remain for so long as Allah wishes it to remain, then Allah will remove it when He wishes to remove it... Then there shall be enforced monarchy and it shall remain for so long as Allah wishes it to remain, then Allah will remove it when He wishes to remove it... Then there shall be caliphate upon the methodology of prophethood..." Musnad Ahmad no. 18406

"There will come corrupt, tyrannous rulers: whoever confirms their lies and assists them in their oppression is not of me, nor I of him..." Musnad Ahmad no. 5669

While there remains much good within our Ummah and much that ought to inspire optimism, it is also a stark reality that there are few periods in our history, if any, as sunken in the darkness of tyranny and bereft of righteous leadership as that of our present moment.

From rampant corruption and brutal tyranny, to the betrayal and dereliction of duty, the deceit and deception on an industrial scale. It is because of this long chapter of darkness, however, that a work such as this is most timely and necessary.

For many, the names and stories of Al-Rashidun are not new. They are men whose names and lives are etched in the hearts and minds of Muslims the world over as being synonymous with the apex of virtue. The cream of the crop of that most revered and elite generation of humanity after the prophets themselves.

Our masajid, our centers of learning, and even our children and ourselves proudly bear their names, but the imperative and calling of our time - arguably more acutely needed today than at any other juncture in our Ummah's history

Thus far - is not *merely* to look to these great men to fuel a spiritual nostalgia as we pine for a bygone era. We must redouble our study of their lives and the lessons derived so that we may tread their footsteps. To take them not merely as namesakes and icons revered, but as guiding lights and exemplars to be followed in a time of immense darkness and rampant misguidance.

In Abū Bakr al-Siddiq ؓ we find the consummate embodiment of steadfastness, sincerity, and intense concern for the welfare of the believers.

In Omar ibn al-Khattab ؓ we witness a paragon of justice and living with fear of none but Allah alone.

In Uthman ibn Aan ؓ we find the example of one who ascended to the loftiest heights of nobility and might, but who remained unwaveringly devoted to self-service to the Ummah.

And in the intrepid person and life of Ali ibn Abi Talib ؓ we behold a comingling of immense courage and valour, but one tempered and anchored in wisdom and remarkable sagacity.

We would do well to recall and heed the instruction of our beloved Messenger : when he said صلى الله عليه وسل

I am leaving you upon a (path of) brightness whose night is like its day. No one will deviate from it after I am gone but one who is doomed. Whoever among you lives will see great conflict. I urge you to adhere to what you know of my way and the way of the Rightly Guided Caliphs, and cling stubbornly to it.

May we take the lives and legacies of these great men, not merely as namesakes or objects of lore, but as exemplars that inspire and guide us amidst confusion, and that light the way amidst the darkness. And may Allah use you, dear reader, as a means to revive and restore the rightly guided leadership our Ummah so desperately needs.

May Allah bless and reward the dedicated efforts of IlmForum for recognising the great importance of bringing forth this valuable book at such a critical time. I am hopeful and pray that *Al-Rashidun* will serve as a continuing source of inspiration and guidance, not only for today's readers but for future generations, reviving our connection to the legacy of the Rightly Guided Caliphs. I am confident that this book will illuminate the hearts and minds of all who seek to walk in the footsteps of these noble leaders, offering timeless lessons in leadership, justice, and compassion.

Omar Suleiman

Introduction

Adrift upon a storm-wracked sea of trials and doubts, in the long black night of a world without an Islamic caliphate, the *ummah* is confronted on all sides by mountainous wave after wave of test after test. Amongst it all, we look for hope, a light to lead us all once more to harbours safe, at which to moor and anchor ourselves against the tides and currents of the times, whichever seek to sweep us away. We shall only find it, as every generation of this Ummah ever has, in the great formative stories of the beginning of Islam.

For, too often, when we look to the celebrated scholars and academic sages of our time, and make them our heroes and models for success, we set ourselves up for heartbreak. Rarely in this age of ours do we find a guide who does not in some way fall short. Gazed upon from afar on the high pedestals of awe we have fashioned for them, they seem like the titans of old. Up close, we see them for what they are: as human as the rest of us, as much the victims of the vices of the time, and as equally prey to the world's temptations as we are. Many a celebrity scholar has found himself ensnared in scandal, his private vices made public and laid bare for all to see. Positions of trust are abused to sate an ego's lusts. Heterodox stances are taken simply for the sake of standing out. Even great minds become mired in petty politics or fall foul of the liberal zeitgeist of our age. Meanwhile, great scholars of the past are targeted without shame, for the sake of sheer spectacle, or to make a show of being an equal to gain stature and fame. As the old saying goes, 'If you wish to make a name for yourself, find a person of note and start a fight with him'.

Broken-hearted, we heed and appreciate the great wisdom in the words of Sayyidunā ʿAbdullāh ibn Masʿūd ﷺ:

مَن كانَ مُسْتَنًّا ، فَلْيَسْتَنَّ بِمَنْ قَدْ مَاتَ ، فَإِنَّ الْحَيَّ لا تُؤمَنُ عَلَيْهِ الْفِتْنَةُ ، أُولَئِكَ أَصْحَابُ مُحَمَّدٍ صَلَى اللهُ عَلَيهِ وَسَلَّمَ، كَانُوا أَفْضَلَ هَذِهِ الْأُمَّةِ: أَبَرَّهَا قُلُوبًا، وَأَعْمَقَهَا عِلْمًا، وَأَقَلَّهَا تَكَلُّفًا، اخْتَارَهُمُ اللهُ لِصُحْبَةِ نَبِيِّهِ، وَلِإِقَامَةِ دِينِهِ، فَاعْرِفُوا لَهُمْ فَضْلَهُمْ، وَاتَّبِعُوهُمْ عَلَى أَثَرِهِمْ، وَتَمَسَّكُوا بِمَا اسْتَطَعْتُمْ مِنْ أَخْلَاقِهِمْ وَسِيَرِهِمْ، فَإِنَّهُمْ كَانُوا عَلَى الْهُدَى الْمُسْتَقِيمِ.

Whosoever wishes to follow the way of another, then let him follow the way of one who has died, for one cannot be sure of the living not being led astray. The ones to follow are the Ṣaḥābah of Muhammad ﷺ who were the best of this Ummah, the purest of hearts, the most profound in knowledge, the most unassuming. Allah chose them to accompany His Prophet and to establish His religion. So recognise their excellence, follow their traces, and hold fast, as much as you are able, to their character and way of life. They were the ones who followed the right guidance.[1]

As Shaykh al-Islam Ibn Taymiyyah ﷺ explained,

Of that which is known necessarily to anyone who ponders on the Qur'an and Sunnah, and that which all groups of the Ahl al-Sunnah wa al-Jamāʿah have agreed upon, is that the best generation of this Ummah – in deed, word, and creed, and indeed every other virtue – are the very first generation, then those after them, and those after them, as is established and affirmed in many statements of the Prophet ﷺ. They are superior to their successors in every virtue, be it knowledge, action, faith, intellect, religion, speech, or worship. They are the ones most worthy of clarifying all issues or problems. This can only be refuted by one who ignores what is necessarily

---

1 Ibn ʿAbd al-Barr, *Jāmiʿ Bayān al-ʿIlm wa Faḍlihī*, Maktabah Nuʿmāniyyah, Peshawar (n.d), Vol. 2, p. 134.

known of the religion of Islam, and one whom God has allowed to be led astray by his knowledge.[2]

Just as stars have long gone but still gift their light to us so many aeons after their passing, guiding men across trackless deserts and seemingly endless seas, so too the light of the lives of the Ṣaḥābah ﷺ pierces through the passing ages and reaches us here and now. Above the nightly chaos of the world, their lives form a tapestry of constellations of guidance by which we may navigate through our own. It is said that Allah ﷻ informed His Messenger ﷺ,

يَا مُحَمَّدُ! إِنَّ أَصْحَابَكَ عِنْدِي بِمَنْزِلَةِ النُّجُومِ مِنَ السَّمَاءِ، بَعْضُهَا أَقْوَى مِنْ بَعْضٍ، وَلِكُلٍّ نُورٌ.

O Muhammad! Your Ṣaḥābah are to Me akin the stars in the heavens. Some are stronger than others, but each is a bearer of light.[3]

In another narration, we read that the Messenger of Allah ﷺ would look up at the night sky and say,

النُّجُومُ أَمَنَةٌ لِلسَّمَاءِ فَإِذَا ذَهَبَتِ النُّجُومُ أَتَى السَّمَاءَ مَا تُوعَدُ وَأَنَا أَمَنَةٌ لأَصْحَابِي فَإِذَا ذَهَبْتُ أَتَى أَصْحَابِي مَا يُوعَدُونَ وَأَصْحَابِي أَمَنَةٌ لأُمَّتِي فَإِذَا ذَهَبَ أَصْحَابِي أَتَى أُمَّتِي مَا يُوعَدُونَ.

The stars are a source of serenity for the heavens. When the stars are gone, the sky shall meet its appointed fate. I am a source of serenity for my Ṣaḥābah; when I am gone they shall meet theirs. And my Ṣaḥābah are a source of serenity for my Ummah; when they are gone my Ummah shall meet its appointed fate.[4]

---

2 Ibn Taymiyyah, *Majmūʿ al-Fatāwā*, Majmaʿ al-Mālik Fahd, Madinah (1425/2004), Vol. 4, pp. 157-158.

3 Muḥammad Ilyās al-Bārabankī, *Sharḥ Ḥayāt al-Ṣaḥābah*, Vol. 1, p. 65.

4 Muslim ibn al-Ḥajjāj al-Naysābūrī, *Ṣaḥīḥ Muslim*, 2531.

To find glory in the light of their lives and to exult in the memory of their virtues is a symbol of the faith we hold within us, for theirs were lives lived in the care and nurture of the noblest of all Prophets ﷺ, and theirs were deeds sincerely done to set precedents for all generations to come. It is as the Beloved Prophet ﷺ said,

لاَ تَسُبُّوا أَصْحَابِي، فَلَوْ أَنَّ أَحَدَكُمْ أَنْفَقَ مِثْلَ أُحُدٍ ذَهَبًا مَا بَلَغَ مُدَّ أَحَدِهِمْ وَلاَ نَصِيفَهُ

> None should revile my Ṣaḥābah. For if one amongst you were to spend as much gold as Mount Uḥud, it would not amount to so much as a single mudd⁵ of their spending, nor even half of it.⁶

All of the Ṣaḥābah ؓ were stars of guidance, but none shone so bright as the Four Friends (the *Chār Yār*, as they are known across the Indo-Persian world), the men who would become the Rightly Guided Caliphs (*al-Khulafā' al-Rāshidūn*). It is in their lives we see the extraordinary challenges that the early Muslim community faced, and how, under their leadership, the Ummah overcame them. It is in the study of this pivotal period of human history that we can find the successful application of the Qur'an and Sunnah, and practical answers and solutions to the problems that we face today. Imam Mālik ibn Anas ؒ once said,

لَا يَصْلُحُ آخِرُ هَذِهِ الْأُمَّةِ إِلَّا بِمَا صَلَحَ بِهِ أَوَّلُهَا.

> The last of this Ummah will not be rectified except by that which rectified the first of it.⁷

Furthermore, there can be no doubt that a study of the lives of the Ṣaḥābah ؓ and especially the lives of the Rightly Guided Caliphs ؓ is, in

---

5 A unit of measure equivalent to 775ml.
6 Muḥammad ibn Ismāʿīl al-Bukhārī, *Ṣaḥīḥ al-Bukhārī*, 3673; *Ṣaḥīḥ Muslim*, 2540, 2541a.
7 Ibn Taymiyyah, *Iqtiḍā' Ṣirāṭ al-Mustaqīm*, Vol. 2, p. 243.

fact, a completion of the study of the life and legacy of our Liege and Master Muhammad ﷺ, the Messenger of Allah. Though vastly different in type and temperament, each of these men had been refined and perfected by the teachings and company of the Messenger ﷺ as a jeweller shapes a diamond. Thus, each found a way to wholly pattern himself on the Sunnah of the Beloved Prophet ﷺ and to meticulously follow in his footsteps. Yet each did so in his distinct way. Each was a distinct beam in the spectrum of light shining forth from the prism of perfection. This is why the love, respect, and admiration for the Beloved Prophet ﷺ that is nurtured in the heart of one who studies their lives is unlike that of any other. Without a doubt, their stories are a source of inspiration and whenever we find our adherence to the covenants of our Prophet ﷺ beginning to weaken or wane or find our faith fading or diminished, we must return to this source to replenish ourselves once more.

Indeed, in the stories of their lives, Allah ﷻ has placed great strength. Shaykh ʿAbd al-Fattāḥ Abū Ghuddah ؒ described the stories of the righteous scholars and the Prophets ؑ as one of the best means of instilling virtue, of gaining strength to endure adversity for the sake of noble goals and sublime purposes, and of inspiring the courage and resolve to emulate those whose sacrifices raised them to the highest ranks and most honourable stations.'[8] It is said that the great Sufi saint Imam Junayd al-Baghdādī ؒ once proclaimed,

الحِكَايَاتُ جُنْدٌ مِنْ جُنُودِ اللهِ عَزَّ وَجَلَّ يُقَوِّي اللهُ بِهَا إِيمَانَ الْمُرِيدِينَ.

The stories of the pious are a troop from the troops of Allah, by which He bolsters the faith of devotees.[9]

8 ʿAbd al-Fattāḥ Abū Ghuddah, *Ṣafaḥāt min Ṣabr al-ʿUlamā*, Dār al-Salām, Cairo (1441/2020), p. 17.

9 Muḥammad Zakariyyā al-Kāndhlawī, *Ḥikāyāt al-Ṣaḥābah*, Idārah-e-Ishāʿat Dīniyāt, Delhi (n.d.), pp. 5-6.

When asked by what proof he made so bold a claim, the great Imam ﷺ recited the following verse in reply,

وَكُلًّا نَّقُصُّ عَلَيْكَ مِنْ أَنۢبَآءِ ٱلرُّسُلِ مَا نُثَبِّتُ بِهِۦ فُؤَادَكَ ۚ وَجَآءَكَ فِى هَٰذِهِ ٱلْحَقُّ وَمَوْعِظَةٌ وَذِكْرَىٰ لِلْمُؤْمِنِينَ

And all that We relate to you of tidings of the Messengers is so We may make firm your heart thereby. And herein has come to you the Truth, and good counsel, and a reminder for those who believe.[10]

What is more, not only do the stories of the pious strengthen our faith, but the mention of their lives and the very act of reviving their memories is a means of attracting Allah's ﷻ infinite mercy. Imam Sufyān ibn ʿUyaynah ﷺ, a scholar from the third generation of Islam, is cited as having said, 'Mercy descends at the mere mention of the pious.'[11]

It is imperative, then, that we return to the stories and statements of the Ṣaḥābah ﷺ again and again, for with each visit we shall find in them something new. This is because each time we return to a book, though the words contained within remain the same, the person reading them is not. As life moulds us with age and experience, we learn to appreciate details we had not previously considered and gain insight into aspects that were previously closed to us.

Further still, it is only through a constant and repeated study of the lessons of the lives and experiences of the Ṣaḥābah ﷺ, through examining and re-examining the wisdom of their words and statements, that we can hope to internalise and properly reap the benefits of this knowledge. Imam Muḥammad Zakariyyā al-Kāndhlawī ﷺ greatly stressed this point about reading any Islamic discourse, be it an epistle, biography, or Hadith, and

10 *al-Hūd*, 120.

11 Ibn al-Jawzī, *Ṣifah al-Ṣafwah*, Dār al-Kitāb al-ʿArabī, Beirut (1433/2012), p. 33.

noted that a cursory reading of such texts seldom, if ever, produces the desired effect.[12] This is reflected in the statement of Imam Abū Sulaymān al-Dārānī ﷺ who narrates, 'I attended the gathering of an orator, and his words affected my heart. Yet, when I stood to leave, none of its effects remained upon me. Hence, I returned a second time to listen to his talk, and his words remained etched upon my heart until I reached the streets, at which point I forgot them. Then I returned a third time, and this time his words remained with me until I reached home.'[13]

The scholars of the latter age were well cognisant of all this and gave much attention to writing works on the Ṣaḥābah ﷺ. Imam Muḥammad Zakariyyā al-Kāndhlawī, Shaykh ʿAlī al-Ṭanṭāwī, Shaykh Yūsuf al-Kāndhlawī, Shaykh ʿAbd al-Raḥmān Ra'fat al-Pāshā ﷺ and countless others have all written works around the lives, stories, and sayings of the Ṣaḥābah ﷺ. With this intent, *Ilmforum* came up with this concept, idea, and vision to elucidate the profound sayings and exemplary actions of the four Khalifas. This book aims to derive valuable lessons from their noble lives. We aspire to present a refined and insightful exploration of the wisdom encapsulated in the renowned statements and actions of these revered figures. Through their humble effort, Wordsmiths inspired by *Ilmforum* were able to also follow in their footsteps, to take some benefit from writing about the lives of the Ṣaḥābah ﷺ, to bask in the light of their guidance and be moved by the wisdom of their words, and perhaps move you, dear reader, in much the same way, if Allah wills.

---

12 Muḥammad Zakariyyā al-Kāndhlawī, *Ḥikāyāt al-Ṣaḥābah*, p. 6.

13 Ṣāliḥ Aḥmad al-Shāmī, *Mawāʿiẓ al-Imām Abī Sulaymān al-Dārānī*, al-Maktab al-Islāmī, Beirut (1419/1998), p. 63.

1

Al-Ṣiddīq: "Abū Bakr" ʿAbdullāh ibn Abī Quḥāfah

He was a man of remarkable moral excellence and character who shaped the world around him and who set it right and in motion toward a new and extraordinary direction. No other human being, short of the Prophets themselves, has ever faced challenges of the magnitude of those faced by Sayyidunā Abū Bakr ﵁. After all, what greater calamity and what greater challenge could there be than dealing with the loss of the Beloved Prophet ﷺ?

No greater catastrophe ever was, nor shall there ever be, than the death of the best of all creation. It was the greatest loss; a loss that made all other losses after it lighter to bear for every generation to come, and yet there was no time to mourn or to contemplate the sheer magnitude of it. Even as his funeral prayers were prayed, the message he had brought, the one that would transform all the world and all that was to come, was at its moment of greatest peril.

And so it was, at that most perilous hour when all political order imploded and every alliance collapsed; when apostasy spread like wildfire and the deserts of Arabia blazed with the flames of rebellion; when false Prophets emerged and rallied the weak of faith to their banners; and when the very light of Islam was in danger of being extinguished, that one man rose to save the Ummah.

There will never be another like Sayyidunā Abū Bakr ﵁, the man to whom all the Ummah owes an unpayable debt. Has there ever been another follower of the Prophet ﷺ to whom so many have owed so much? Without his guiding wisdom and steadying hand, it must honestly be said that by the end of his generation, Islam – and indeed the world itself – would have come to an end.

Name and Lineage

Like the Beloved, and indeed all the Rightly Guided Caliphs, our teacher Abū Bakr ﵁ was of the progeny of Prophets, being from the line of the Prophet Ismāʿīl ؑ. A son of the Quraysh and a Tamīmī, his lineage met that of the Beloved ﷺ at Murrah ibn Kaʿb. His full name was Abū Bakr ʿAbdullāh ibn Abī Quḥāfah ʿUthmān ibn ʿĀmir ibn ʿAmr ibn Kaʿb ibn Saʿd ibn Taym ibn Murrah ibn Kaʿb ibn Lu'ayy ibn Ghālib ibn Fihr ibn Mālik ibn al-Naḍr ibn Kinānah ibn Khuzaymah ibn Mudrikah ibn Ilyās ibn Muḍar ibn Nizār ibn Maʿd ibn ʿAdnān. His mother was known as Umm al-Khayr, literally the "Source of Good", her name being Salmā bint Sakhr ibn ʿĀmir ibn Kaʿb ibn Saʿd ibn Taym ibn Murrah.[1] Imam Ibn al-Athīr ؒ states that she was the cousin of Abū Quḥāfah, and thus the lineage of Abū Bakr ﵁ joined that of the Beloved ﷺ through both the paternal and maternal line.[2]

1 Ibn Saʿd al-Zuhrī, *Kitāb al-Ṭabaqāt al-Kubrā*, Maktabah al-Khānjī, Cairo (1421/2001), Vol. 3, p. 155.

2 Ibn al-Athīr: *Al-Nihāyah fī Gharīb al-Ḥadīth*, vol. 1 pg. 149.

Of his famed agnomen, it is said that it is taken from the word *bakr*, meaning "a young camel", which implies a youthful appearance among people.[3] It is also said that the agnomen Abū Bakr could possibly be literal,[4] as a Hadith in *Ṣaḥīḥ al-Bukhārī* mentions that he had married a woman from the tribe of Banū Kalb who was known as Umm Bakr, but divorced her before the migration (hijrah) to Medina.[5] Bakr was also the name of the leader of a great Arab tribe, which became known as the Banū Bakr, and thus it became synonymous with being the head of a great tribe, so Abū Bakr would mean "the patriarch of a great tribe."[6] Still more likely is what is hinted by Ibn Durayd in his book on etymology, in that it is derived from the verb and means to be early or to hasten in doing something.[7] No doubt Sayyidunā Abū Bakr ﵁ surpassed and overtook all others in performing good actions, always being the first to undertake all noble works. He was the first to ever suffer harm for the sake of Allah ﷻ and His Messenger ﷺ, the first to defend Allah's Messenger, and the first of this Ummah to call people towards Allah ﷻ.[8] Even the likes of Sayyidunā ʿUmar ibn al-Khaṭṭāb ﵁ would have to say,

وَلَا وَاللَّهِ مَا سَبَقْتُهُ إِلَى خَيْرٍ قَطُّ إِلَّا وَسَبَقَنِي إِلَيْهِ.

By Allah, I never raced him to any goodness, except that he superseded me.[9]

Al-ʿAtīq

عَنْ عَائِشَةَ، أَنَّ أَبَا بَكْرٍ، دَخَلَ عَلَى رَسُولِ اللَّهِ ﷺ فَقَالَ:

3 Ibn al-Athīr: *Al-Nihāyah fī Gharīb al-Ḥadīth*, vol. 1 pg. 149; al-Rāzī: *Mukhtār al-Ṣiḥāḥ*, pg. 39.

4 Mufti Raḍā' al-Ḥaqq, *Badr al-Layālī Sharḥ Bad' al-Amālī*, vol. 1, p. 481.

5 *Ṣaḥīḥ al-Bukhārī*, 3921.

6 ʿAlī al-Ṭanṭāwī, *Abū Bakr*, Dār al-Minārah, Jeddah (1402/1982), p. 46.

7 Ibn Durayd, *Al-Ishtiqāq*, Dar al-Jīl, Beirut (1411/1991), p. 49.

8 Dr ʿAlī M. Ṣallābī, *Abū Bakr as-Siddeeq*: His Life & Times, Dār al-ʿĀlamiyyah, Riyadh (1434/2013), p. 77.

9 Aḥmad ibn Ḥanbal, *Musnad Imām Aḥmad*, 175.

أَنْتَ عَتِيقُ اللّٰهِ مِنَ النَّارِ. فَيَوْمَئِذٍ سُمِّيَ عَتِيقًا.

Lady ʿĀ'ishah narrates that Abū Bakr entered upon the Messenger of Allah ﷺ who said, "Abū Bakr, you are the one whom Allah has freed from the Fire." From that day he was known as Al-ʿAtīq.[10]

One of the names by which he became renowned was al-ʿAtīq, which, as the Hadith indicates, was given to him by the Beloved Prophet ﷺ himself. Other narrations indicate that this was also a name he was known by before Islam, due to his handsomeness, his long history of good works, or because he was the first child in his family to survive.[11]

From the Hadith narrated above, we see that the Prophet ﷺ announced that Sayyidunā Abū Bakr ؓ was freed from the Fire. In fact, this was announced in the Qur'an when Allah ﷻ said,

وَسَيُجَنَّبُهَا ٱلْأَتْقَى

And the God-fearing one will be saved from it (the Fire).[12]

In a narration of Sayyidunā ʿUrwah ؓ, it is stated that seven enslaved Muslims were owned and persecuted by the Meccan disbelievers. Sayyidunā Abū Bakr ؓ spent a great amount of his own wealth to purchase and set them free. On this occasion, the last five verses of *Sūrah al-Layl* were revealed, beginning with the verse quoted above.[13]

---

10 Muḥammad ibn ʿĪsā al-Tirmidhī, *Jāmiʿ al-Tirmidhī*, 3679.

11 Jalāl al-Dīn al-Suyūṭī, *Tārīkh al-Khulafā'*, Wizārah al-Awqāf, Qatar (1434/2013), pp. 101-102

12 *al-Layl*, 17.

13 Muḥammad Thanā' Allāh Pānipatī, *Tafsīr Maẓharī*, Dār al-Ishāʿat, Karachi (1420/1999) Vol. 12, p. 384.

Accepting Islam

Abū Bakr ﵁ was the first man to respond and believe in Prophet Mohammad ﷺ. His deep friendship with the Prophet ﷺ led him to accept Islam without any hesitation. He knew the Prophet ﷺ as a truthful, honest, and noble man, so he knew that what his dear friend was telling him was the truth. His acceptance of Islam made the Prophet ﷺ very happy. Abū Bakr ﵁ becoming a Muslim was hugely significant for Islam as he was a noble man among the Quraish tribe. It was Abū Bakr Siddiq ﵁ who sought the Prophet's ﷺ permission to publicly call the people to Islam. He was severely beaten and became unconscious when the Muslims were preaching Islam in front of the Kaaba. However, as soon as he regained consciousness, he enquired about the wellbeing of the Prophet ﷺ despite severe pain of his own.

Al-Ṣiddīq

The most famed of his titles was al-Ṣiddīq, conferred to him owing to his absolute trust in and affirmation of the words of the Beloved Prophet ﷺ. Regarding this, the Mother of the Believers, Lady ʿĀ'ishah ﵂ narrates that when the Beloved Prophet ﷺ informed people of the Night Journey to al-Masjid al-Aqṣā, some of those who had embraced Islam and affirmed his Message apostatised. Meanwhile, the polytheists of Mecca rushed to Abū Bakr ﵁ and asked him if he believed his friend's claim that he had been taken to al-Masjid al-Aqṣā. He asked them to confirm that Allah's Messenger ﷺ had said this, and when they confirmed he replied,

لَئِنْ كَانَ قَالَ ذَلِكَ، لَقَدْ صَدَقَ.

If he has said this, then he has spoken the truth.

The polytheists were astonished and repeated their question again, asking whether he believed the Messenger of Allah ﷺ had travelled by night to al-Masjid al-Aqṣā and had returned before morning. Thus, Abū Bakr ﵁ replied,

نَعَمْ، إِنِّي لأُصَدِّقُهُ فِيمَا هُوَ أَبْعَدُ مِنْ ذَلِكَ أُصَدِّقُهُ بِخَبَرِ السَّمَاءِ فِي غُدْوَةٍ أَوْ رَوْحَةٍ.

Yes, I affirm him to be true in what is far more extraordinary than this.
I believe in the news he brings of the heavens each morn and eve.[14]

This is a testament to his absolute conviction and the firmness of his faith. He did not need to speak to the Prophet ﷺ before bearing witness to the Truth. If the Prophet ﷺ said it, then it was true. This is the reason why he earned the title of al-Ṣiddīq, the man of verity, a name by which he will be known forever.

Before Islam

He was born approximately two and a half to three years after the Year of the Elephant.[15] Regarding his appearance, it is said that he was a fair-skinned man, tall and slender, lean of flank and gaunt of face. His eyes were deep set beneath a prominent forehead, and he would dye his hair with henna and katam.[16] Most of his early years were spent in Mecca, which he only left for trade.[17] He was known to be amongst the most knowledgeable of people regarding genealogy and the history of the Arabs:

عَنْ عَائِشَةَ، أَنَّ رَسُولَ اللَّهِ ﷺ قَالَ:

فَإِنَّ أَبَا بَكْرٍ أَعْلَمُ قُرَيْشٍ بِأَنْسَابِهَا.

Lady ʿĀ'ishah reports that the Messenger of Allah ﷺ said, "Abū Bakr is the most knowledgeable of the Quraysh regarding their lineage."[18]

---

14 Al-Ḥākim al-Naysābūrī, *Mustadrak ʿalā al-Ṣaḥīḥayn*, Dār al-Kutub al-ʿIlmiyyah, Beirut (1422/2002), Vol. 3, p. 65. Hadith no. 4407.

15 Jalāl al-Dīn al-Suyūṭī, *Tārīkh al-Khulafā'*, p. 104.

16 Jalāl al-Dīn al-Suyūṭī, *Tārīkh al-Khulafā'*, p. 106.

17 Jalāl al-Dīn al-Suyūṭī, *Tārīkh al-Khulafā'*, p. 104.

18 *Ṣaḥīḥ Muslim*, 2490.

Even before Islam, he was renowned as a man of prominence and considered one of the leaders of the Quraysh.[19] He was a very successful merchant and was extremely generous with his wealth.[20] As well as this, he practised absolute teetotalism and never once drank alcohol. When he was asked about this by his fellow Ṣaḥābah ؓ, he explained,

كُنتُ أصُونُ عِرضِي وأحفَظُ مُرُوءَتِي؛ فإنَّ مَن شَرِبَ الْخَمرَ، كَانَ مُضِيعًا فِي عِرْضِه ومُرُوءَته.

I tried to protect my honour and guard my manliness, for whoever drinks wine will lose his honour and his manliness.[21]

Manliness, munificence, and courtesy were the traits he was well-known for, as attested to by Ibn al-Daghinah when Sayyidunā Abū Bakr ؓ intended to seek refuge in Abyssinia:

إِنَّ مِثْلَكَ لاَ يَخْرُجُ وَلاَ يُخْرَجُ، فَإِنَّكَ تَكْسِبُ الْمَعْدُومَ، وَتَصِلُ الرَّحِمَ، وَتَحْمِلُ الْكَلَّ، وَتَقْرِي الضَّيْفَ، وَتُعِينُ عَلَى نَوَائِبِ الْحَقِّ، وَأَنَا لَكَ جَارٌ فَارْجِعْ فَاعْبُدْ رَبَّكَ بِبِلَادِكَ.

The like of you should neither leave, nor be driven out. You earn for those without aid; you maintain good ties with kith and kin; you bear burdens for the disabled; you host guests generously; and you support every good work. I will be your protector! Return to your homeland and worship your Lord therein.[22]

The parallel and correspondence between Ibn al-Daghinah's description of Sayyidunā Abū Bakr ؓ and the words with which Umm al-Mu'minīn

---

19   Dr ʿAlī M. Ṣallābī, *Abū Bakr as-Siddeeq: His Life & Times*, International Islamic Publishing House, (2013), p. 60.
20   ʿAlī al-Ṭanṭāwī, *Abū Bakr*, p. 66.
21   Jalāl al-Dīn al-Suyūṭī, *Tārīkh al-Khulafā'*, pp. 105-106.
22   *Ṣaḥīḥ al-Bukhārī*, 2297; 3905.

Khadījah ؓ consoled the Beloved Prophet ﷺ on the day revelation began is startling:

كَلاَّ وَاللَّهِ مَا يُخْزِيكَ اللَّهُ أَبَدًا، إِنَّكَ لَتَصِلُ الرَّحِمَ، وَتَحْمِلُ الْكَلَّ، وَتَكْسِبُ الْمَعْدُومَ، وَتَقْرِي الضَّيْفَ، وَتُعِينُ عَلَى نَوَائِبِ الْحَقِّ

> Never! By Allah, Allah will never disgrace you. You maintain good ties with kith and kin, bear burdens for the disabled, earn for those without aid, host guests generously, and support every noble work.[23]

It shows how ably suited, well-prepared and well-equipped Sayyidunā Abū Bakr ؓ truly was for the companionship of Allah's Messenger ﷺ, as if he had been created for this purpose. His character and that of the Beloved Prophet ﷺ perfectly matched. There can be no greater praise than this, for the Beloved Prophet ﷺ was adorned with greatest attributes from his earliest age.

Abstinence from Worldly Wants

إِنَّه سَتُفْتَحُ لَكُمُ الشَّامُ، فَتَأْتُونَ أَرْضًا رَفِيعَةً حَيْثُ تَمَتَّعُونَ فِيهَا مِنَ الْخُبْزِ وَالزَّيْتِ، وَسَتُبْنَى لَكُمْ بِهَا مَسَاجِدُ، فَإِيَّاكُمْ أَنْ يَعْلَمَ اللَّهُ عَزَّ وَجَلَّ أَنَّكُمْ إِنَّمَا تَأْتُونَهَا تَلَهِّيًا! إِنَّمَا بُنِيَتْ لِلذِّكْرِ

> The Levant will be opened for you, and you will come upon a sublime land wherein you will enjoy bread and oil, and mosques will be built for you therein. Beware of Allah the Mighty and Majestic knowing that you are only coming to it to distract yourselves! It was only built for His remembrance.[24]

---

23   *Ṣaḥīḥ al-Bukhārī*, 3; *Ṣaḥīḥ Muslim*, 160a.
24   Aḥmad ibn Ḥanbal, *Al-Zuhd*, Dār al-Kutub al-ʿIlmiyyah, Beirut (1420/1999), pp. 93-94. Hadith no. 590.

In this sermon of Abū Bakr ﷺ, there is a warning that preoccupation with this world – or expansion in it – could either result in or be the result of neglecting divine remembrance (*dhikr*). When blessings simply become a means to pleasure and enjoyment and become a distraction from the remembrance of Allah ﷻ, then in reality they are a lure, a curse, and a temptation.[25] There is no blessing in anything which distracts you from Allah ﷻ. Having warned us of the dangers of becoming distracted by this world, our Master Abū Bakr ﷺ also advised us on how we may prevent ourselves from being affected by it. Sayyidunā Salmān al-Fārisī ﷺ visited him during his final illness when he was on his deathbed and humbly requested,

يَا خَلِيفَةَ رَسُولِ اللهِ، أَوْصِنِي.

O Caliph of Allah's Messenger, please do advise me.

فَقَالَ لَهُ أَبُو بَكرٍ: إِنَّ اللهَ عَزَّ وَجَلَّ فَاتِحٌ عَلَيْكُمُ الدُّنْيَا فَلَا تَأْخُذُوا مِنهَا إِلَّا بَلَاغَكُمْ، وَإِنَّ مَنْ صَلَّى صَلَاةَ الصُّبْحِ فَهُوَ فِي ذِمَّةِ اللَّهِ عَزَّ وَجَلَّ فَلَا تَخْفِرَنَّ اللَّهَ عَزَّ وَجَلَّ فِي ذِمَّتِهِ ، فَيُكِبَّكَ فِي النَّارِ عَلَى وَجْهِكَ.

Abū Bakr said to him, "Allah will soon open up the bounties of this world for you; take of it only what you need. The one who prays his morning prayer (Fajr) is under Allah's protection. Do not damage this protection by disobeying Him, lest He cast your face first into Hellfire."[26]

The world is not a goal in and of itself, but a test by which someone is measured and assessed. To take more than what is needed is failure. Obedience to Allah ﷻ is the only means of achieving success, all else is a distraction from the purpose of one's creation.

---

25 ʿUmar al-Muqbil, *Mawāʿiẓ al-Ṣaḥābah*, Dār al-Minhāj, Riyadh (1435/), p. 22.

26 Aḥmad ibn Ḥanbal, *Al-Zuhd*, 571.

Enjoining Good and Forbidding Evil

:قَالَ أَبُو بَكْرٍ بَعْدَ أَنْ حَمِدَ اللَّهَ وَأَثْنَى عَلَيْهِ

يَا أَيُّهَا النَّاسُ إِنَّكُمْ تَقْرَءُونَ هَذِهِ الآيَةَ وَتَضَعُونَهَا عَلَى غَيْرِ مَوَاضِعِهَا: ﴿عَلَيْكُمْ أَنْفُسَكُمْ لاَ يَضُرُّكُمْ مَنْ ضَلَّ إِذَا اهْتَدَيْتُمْ﴾ وَإِنَّا سَمِعْنَا النَّبِيَّ ﷺ يَقُولُ: إِنَّ النَّاسَ إِذَا رَأَوُا الظَّالِمَ فَلَمْ يَأْخُذُوا عَلَى يَدَيْهِ أَوْشَكَ أَنْ يَعُمَّهُمُ اللَّهُ بِعِقَابٍ.

Abū Bakr al-Ṣiddīq ◉ said,

After praising Allah and glorifying Him, Abū Bakr said, "O people, you recite the verse, 'take care of your selves. The one who has gone astray cannot harm you, if you are on the right path', and place it out of its proper context. We heard the Prophet saying, 'If the people see a transgressor oppressing and do not prevent his oppression, then Allah is certain to punish them all.'"[27]

In Imam Abū Dāwūd's ◉ transmission of this Hadith, two alternate wordings are given of the statement of Allah's Messenger ﷺ, which further clarify its meaning:

وَإِنِّي سَمِعْتُ رَسُولَ اللَّهِ ﷺ يَقُولُ: مَا مِنْ قَوْمٍ يُعْمَلُ فِيهِمْ بِالْمَعَاصِي ثُمَّ يَقْدِرُونَ عَلَى أَنْ يُغَيِّرُوا ثُمَّ لَا يُغَيِّرُوا إِلَّا يُوشِكُ أَنْ يَعُمَّهُمُ اللَّهُ مِنْهُ بِعِقَابٍ.

Indeed I heard Allah's Messenger say, 'No acts of disobedience are done among a people who are capable of preventing them but do not, except that it is certain that Allah will punish them all.'

وَقَالَ شُعْبَةُ فِيهِ: مَا مِنْ قَوْمٍ يُعْمَلُ فِيهِمْ بِالْمَعَاصِي هُمْ أَكْثَرُ مِمَّنْ يَعْمَلُهُ.

---

27   Aḥmad ibn Ḥanbal, *Musnad Imām Aḥmad*, 1, 29, 30, 53; Abū Dāwūd al-Sijistānī, *Sunan Abī Dāwūd*, 4338.

'No acts of disobedience are done among people more numerous than the perpetrators...'

Imam Khalīl Aḥmad al-Sahāranpūrī ؓ explains that placing the aforementioned verse "out of its proper context" means that you take it to apply to all people at all times, and thereby misinterpret it to mean that enjoining good and forbidding evil are no longer obligatory, which is clearly not true. The statement of the Beloved Messenger ﷺ reported immediately thereafter clearly indicates that enjoining good and forbidding evil is absolutely obligatory. As for the verse, it should be understood in the context of when people are unable to enjoin what is right and forbid what is wrong. This could be due to being weaker in strength, or the perpetrators greatly outnumbering those who seek to prevent them, as the alternate wordings of the Hadith indicate.[28]

Another similar statement of Sayyidunā Abū Bakr ؓ is also recorded by Imam al-Bayhaqī ؓ:

إِذَا عَمِلَ قَوْمٌ بِالْمَعَاصِي بَيْنَ ظَهْرَانَيْ قَوْمٍ هُمْ أَعَزُّ مِنْهُمْ فَلَمْ يُغَيِّرُوا عَلَيْهِمْ، أَنْزَلَ اللَّهُ عَلَيْهِمْ بَلَاءً، ثُمَّ لَمْ يَنْزِعْهُ مِنْهُمْ.

If a people commit sins in the presence of a people who are stronger than them, and the latter do not work to change them, Allah shall send down a calamity upon them and will not extract them from it.[29]

Both of Sayyidunā Abū Bakr's ؓ aforementioned statements are clearly reflected and indicated by the primary texts of the Qur'an and Sunnah. In the 78th and 79th verses of Sūrah al-Mā'idah, Allah ﷻ states:

---

28 Khalīl Aḥmad al-Sahāranpūrī, *Badhl al-Majhūd fī Ḥall Sunan Abī Dāwūd*, Dār al-Bashā'ir al-Islāmiyyah, Beirut (1427/2006), Vol. 12, p. 395.
29 Abū Bakr Aḥmad ibn al-Ḥusayn al-Bayhaqī, *Shuʿab al-Īmān*, Maktabah al-Rushd, Riyadh (1423/2003), Vol. 10, p. 50. Hadith no. 7145.

لُعِنَ ٱلَّذِينَ كَفَرُواْ مِنۢ بَنِىٓ إِسۡرَٰٓءِيلَ عَلَىٰ لِسَانِ دَاوُۥدَ وَعِيسَى ٱبۡنِ مَرۡيَمَۚ ذَٰلِكَ بِمَا عَصَواْ وَّكَانُواْ يَعۡتَدُونَ ٧٨ كَانُواْ لَا يَتَنَاهَوۡنَ عَن مُّنكَرٖ فَعَلُوهُۚ لَبِئۡسَ مَا كَانُواْ يَفۡعَلُونَ ٧٩

Those of the Children of Israel who disbelieved were cursed by the tongue of Dāwūd and ʿĪsā, Son of Maryam. That was because they rebelled and used to transgress. They did not restrain one another from the wickedness they did. How vile their deeds were!

These verses are explicit on their being cursed due to their disregard for forbidding evil. As for the Sunnah, we find it replete with exhortations, such as the Beloved Prophet's ﷺ statement,

وَالَّذِي نَفْسِي بِيَدِهِ، لَتَأْمُرُنَّ بِالْمَعْرُوفِ وَلَتَنْهَوُنَّ عَنِ الْمُنْكَرِ، أَوْ لَيُوشِكَنَّ اللهُ أَنْ يَبْعَثَ عَلَيْكُمْ عِقَابًا مِنْهُ، ثُمَّ تَدْعُونَهُ فَلاَ يُسْتَجَابُ لَكُمْ.

By the One Who holds my soul, you will enjoin good and forbid evil, or Allah will certainly send His punishment down on you. Then you will call out to Him, but will not be given a response.[30]

Indeed, one of the most profound parables found in the Sunnah is the Hadith of al-Nuʿmān ibn Bashīr رضي الله عنه, which amply demonstrates the importance of enjoining good and forbidding evil, as well as the danger of abandoning it or being negligent in this regard. The parable given of those who abide by Allah's Shariah and those who violate it is that of the passengers of a ship. Lots are drawn and each is assigned quarters, some are to reside in the lower decks and some are given places on the upper deck. To draw water, the residents of the lower deck must go above the deck. Yet, to save themselves time and avoid troubling the upper residents, they say, "Let's make a hole in our part of the ship, and not trouble those above us." If the people on the upper decks leave them to enact their intentions, they will all die; while if they prevent them, both parties are saved.[31]

30 *Jāmiʿ al-Tirmidhī*, 2169.

31 *Ṣaḥīḥ al-Bukhārī*, 2493.

As we read al-Ṣiddīq's sermons and this prophetic parable, it is only fitting that we strive to be the quickest to perform this virtuous act of enjoining good and forbidding evil according to our strength and ability, lest we allow our ship to sink and so perish along with those engaged in follies.

Umm al-Mu'minīn Umm Ḥabībah ؓ narrated that the Blessed Prophet ﷺ said,

كُلُّ كَلَامِ ابْنِ آدَمَ عَلَيْهِ لاَ لَهُ إِلاَّ أَمْرٌ بِمَعْرُوفٍ أَوْ نَهْيٌ عَنْ مُنْكَرٍ أَوْ ذِكْرُ اللهِ.

Every word of the son of Adam is against him, not for him, except for enjoining good or forbidding evil or the remembrance of Allah.[32]

The Dangers of the Tongue

حَدَّثَ زَيْدُ بْنُ أَسْلَمَ، عَنْ أَبِيهِ، أَنَّ عُمَرَ بْنَ الْخَطَّابِ دَخَلَ عَلَى أَبِي بَكْرٍ الصِّدِّيقِ وَهُوَ يَجْبِذُ لِسَانَهُ فَقَالَ لَهُ عُمَرُ:

مَهْ! غَفَرَ اللهُ لَكَ.

فَقَالَ أَبُو بَكْرٍ: إِنَّ هَذَا أَوْرَدَنِي الْمَوَارِدَ.

'Umar came upon Abū Bakr al-Ṣiddīq pulling his tongue and said, "Stop! May Allah forgive you!" Abū Bakr replied, "This tongue has led me to many pitfalls."[33]

These are the words of Al-Ṣiddīq ؓ regarding his tongue: how much more should we fear and chastise our own tongues? He said this out of piety and fear of Allah ﷻ, holding himself to account for even saying something unnecessary. Our tongues are prone to lies, are rarely safe from backbiting,

---

32 *Jāmi' al-Tirmidhī*, 2412.
33 Mālik ibn Anas, *Muwaṭṭa' Imām Mālik*, 1825.

and are ever quick to slander. Even when we do not backbite or slander ourselves, our ears are eager to listen and draw enjoyment from it, and our tongues fail to call it out for what it is.[34]

Sayyidunā Sahl ibn Saʿd ﷺ narrated that Allah's Messenger ﷺ said,

مَنْ يَضْمَنْ لِي مَا بَيْنَ لَحْيَيْهِ وَمَا بَيْنَ رِجْلَيْهِ أَضْمَنْ لَهُ الْجَنَّةَ.

Whoever guarantees me that he will control what is between his jaws (his tongue) and what is between his legs (his private parts), I guarantee him Paradise.[35]

Sayyidunā Abū Bakr ﷺ was very severe with himself due to his deep understanding of the Qur'an. He knew that even a harsh word would mean falling short of the excellence that Allah ﷻ Himself exhorts us toward:

وَقُل لِّعِبَادِى يَقُولُوا۟ ٱلَّتِى هِىَ أَحْسَنُ ۚ إِنَّ ٱلشَّيْطَـٰنَ يَنزَغُ بَيْنَهُمْ ۚ إِنَّ ٱلشَّيْطَـٰنَ كَانَ لِلْإِنسَـٰنِ عَدُوًّا مُّبِينًا

Tell My servants that they should speak that which is best. Surely, Satan sows discord among them. Indeed, Satan is an open enemy to mankind.[36]

Mufti Muḥammad Shafīʿ al-ʿUthmānī ﷺ explains that this verse discourages us against all foul or harsh talk, even against our enemies. He draws a comparison between when sometimes physically fighting and killing in the face of hostility becomes necessary as an inevitable measure of defence, and the use of harsh and foul language which is never necessitated. As he states, through the use of "foul language and harsh words,

34 ʿUmar al-Muqbil, *Mawāʿiẓ al-Ṣaḥābah*, p. 24.

35 *Ṣaḥīḥ al-Bukhārī*, 6474.

36 *Al-Isrā'*, 53.

neither a castle stands conquered nor anyone guided right, therefore, it has been prohibited."³⁷

Regarding the verse in Sūrah al-Rūm which states,

$$\text{ظَهَرَ ٱلْفَسَادُ فِى ٱلْبَرِّ وَٱلْبَحْرِ بِمَا كَسَبَتْ أَيْدِى ٱلنَّاسِ لِيُذِيقَهُم بَعْضَ ٱلَّذِى عَمِلُوا۟ لَعَلَّهُمْ يَرْجِعُونَ}$$

*Calamities have appeared on land and sea because of what the people's hands have earned, that He may make them taste a part of that which they have done, in order that they may return (to the right way).*³⁸

It is said that Sayyidunā Abū Bakr ؓ explained, 'The word 'land' refers to the tongue and the 'sea' to the heart. If the tongue becomes corrupt, the people cry over it; if the heart becomes corrupt, the Angels cry over it.'³⁹

Moreover, when Allah ﷻ describes the seven attributes of a perfect believer, He describes the second as,

$$\text{وَٱلَّذِينَ هُمْ عَنِ ٱللَّغْوِ مُعْرِضُونَ}$$

*Those who shun all vain things*⁴⁰

Abstention from *"laghw"*, i.e., all vain and frivolous things, includes abstention from things that are neither useful nor harmful, such as speech or actions that neither bring worldly good nor religious reward.⁴¹ If we hear

---

37 Muḥammad Shafīʿ al-ʿUthmānī, *Maʿārif al-Qurʾān*, Maktabah Dār al-ʿUlūm, Karachi (1440/2019), Vol. 5, pp. 516-517.

38 *Al-Rūm*, 41.

39 Aḥmad ibn Muḥammad al-Ḥijjī, *Al-Istiʿdād li Yawm al-Mīʿād*, Dār al-Tarbiyyah, Damascus (n.d.), p. 29.

40 *Al-Muʾminūn*, 3.

41 Muḥammad Shafīʿ al-ʿUthmānī, *Maʿārif al-Qurʾān*, Vol. 6, p. 302.

others engaged in unprofitable or shameful talk, then we should withdraw ourselves from that situation also, as is indicated elsewhere in the Qur'an.[42]

Sayyidunā Abū Bakr al-Ṣiddīq ﵁ was the most careful of people with regards to the words he spoke, and the most knowledgeable of people about the status of a man's words, his chivalry, and his honour, and so his words were few. In fact, his first commandment to his governors and generals, and all public servants, was to limit their speech. To Sayyidunā Khālid ibn al-Walīd ﵁, he advised,

أَقِلَّ مِنَ الْكَلَامِ فَإِنَّمَا لَكَ مَا وُعِيَ عَنْكَ.

Speak less, for you only have reward for what is retained from you.[43]

To Yazīd ibn Abī Sufyān ﵁, he advised,

إِذَا وَعَظْتَهُمْ فَأَوْجِزْ، فَإِنَّ كَثِيرَ الْكَلَامِ يُنْسِي بَعْضُهُ بَعْضًا.

When you preach to them, be brief, for lots of speech will mean parts of it are forgotten.[44]

In another statement attributed to Sayyidunā Abū Bakr ﵁, he said,

إِنَّ الْبَلَاءَ مُوَكَّلٌ بِالْمَنْطِقِ.

Trials are authorised by speech.[45]

---

42 *Al-Qaṣaṣ*, 55.

43 ʿAbbās Maḥmūd al-ʿAqqād, *ʿAbqariyyah al-Ṣiddīq*, Mu'assasah Hindāwī, Windsor (1435/2014), p. 119.

44 Ibid.

45 Abū al-Faḍl Aḥmad ibn Muḥammad al-Maydānī, *Majmaʿ al-Amthāl*, Dār al-Kutub al-ʿIlmiyyah, Beirut (1443/2021) Vol. 1, p. 47.

This was part of a verse of poetry by Ṣāliḥ ibn ʿAbd al-Quddūs which Abū Bakr ؓ was known to frequently cite.⁴⁶ The full verse is,

إِنَّ الْبَلَاءَ مُوَكَّلٌ بِالْمَنْطِقِ   اِحْذَرْ لِسَانَكَ أَنْ يَّقُولَ فَتُبْتَلَى

Protect your tongue, in case it speaks

And you be put on trial.

Indeed all trials are authorised

By speech of wit and guile.

The meaning of these verses is that a person may say something bad, or criticise others for a mistake, and then become afflicted by the very same thing. Although some things are predetermined, Allah ﷻ has created causes for such decrees, one of which is that a person speaks about it. Muslims should accustom their tongue to saying only that which is good, to never speak ill of themselves or others, and to ask Allah ﷻ for well-being. This is because speaking ill or cursing oneself or one's kinsfolk at a moment of acceptance could lead to dire consequences.⁴⁷

Moreover, its meaning is attested to by the words of the Beloved Prophet ﷺ when he went to visit a Bedouin Arab who was ill. Whenever the Beloved Prophet ﷺ visited someone who was ill, he would say, 'No harm will come; it is a purification, if Allah wills'.

Yet, when he spoke this benediction on this occasion, the man replied, 'A purification! No, rather it is a fever which boils an old man and will send him to visit the cemetery'.

---

46 Ibn Qayyim al-Jawziyyah, *Tuḥfah al-Mawdūd bi Aḥkām al-Mawlūd*, Dār ʿĀlam al-Fawāʾid, Makkah (1436/ 2015), p. 179.

47 Ibn Rajab al-Ḥanbalī, *Jāmiʿ al-ʿUlūm wa al-Ḥikam*, Dār al-Fārūq, Mansourah (1436/2015), Vol. I, p. 411.

To which the Beloved Prophet SA replied, 'Very well, then'.[48]

The Beloved Prophet's ﷺ reply to the Bedouin's pessimistic statement indicated that Allah ﷻ would do just as the old man had said, and according to other narrations it happened just so.[49]

Imam Ibn al-Qayyim ؒ states, 'We have seen lessons from this in our own lives and the lives of others, and what we have seen is a mere drop in the ocean'.[50] He further states that safeguarding the tongue and choosing good names is a part of Allah's blessings on His servants.[51]

Sayyidunā Abū Hurayrah ؓ narrated that the Messenger of Allah ﷺ warned,

إِنَّ الْعَبْدَ لَيَتَكَلَّمُ بِالْكَلِمَةِ مِنْ رِضْوَانِ اللَّهِ لاَ يُلْقِي لَهَا بَالاً، يَرْفَعُ اللَّهُ بِهَا دَرَجَاتٍ، وَإِنَّ الْعَبْدَ لَيَتَكَلَّمُ بِالْكَلِمَةِ مِنْ سَخَطِ اللَّهِ لاَ يُلْقِي لَهَا بَالاً يَهْوِي بِهَا فِي جَهَنَّمَ.

A slave of Allah utters a word indifferently which is pleasing to Allah, by which Allah raises his status; another slave of His utters a word which is displeasing to Allah without considering its gravity, due to which he will be thrown into Hell.[52]

Forgive and Forego

رُوِيَ عَنْ أَبِي بَكْرٍ:

48 *Ṣaḥīḥ al-Bukhārī*, 3616, 5656, 5662, 7470.

49 Muḥammad Yūnus al-Jaunpūrī, *Anwār al-Mishkāh*, Dār al-Ḥamd, Surat (1445/2023) Vol. 3, p. 330.

50 Ibn Qayyim al-Jawziyyah, *Tuḥfah al-Mawdūd bi Aḥkām al-Mawlūd*, Dār ʿĀlam al-Fawā'id, Makkah (1436/ 2015), p. 179.

51 Ibid.

52 *Ṣaḥīḥ al-Bukhārī*, 3478.

بَلَغَنَا أَنَّ اللَّهَ تَبَارَكَ وَتَعَالَى يَأْمُرُ يَوْمَ الْقِيَامَةِ مُنَادِيًا فَيُنَادِي: أَلا مَنْ كَانَ لَهُ عِنْدَ اللَّهِ عَزَّ وَجَلَّ
شَيْءٌ فَلْيَقُمْ، فَيَقُومُ أَهْلُ الْعَفْوِ، فَيُكَافِئُهُمُ اللَّهُ عَزَّ وَجَلَّ بِمَا كَانَ مِنْ عَفْوِهِمْ عَنِ النَّاسِ.

Abū Bakr al-Ṣiddīq ﵁ said,

It has reached us that on the Day of Resurrection, Allah will command a caller to call out, "Whoever has a matter with Allah Almighty, let him rise." Then the people of Forgiveness will rise, and Allah Almighty will reward them for their pardoning of people.[53]

One of the greatest examples of forgiveness is indeed that of Sayyidunā Abū Bakr ﵁ himself, on the occasion when he had sworn to cut off maintenance from his cousin, Sayyidunā Misṭaḥ ibn Uthāthah ﵁. When we contemplate this event, we find that it gives even greater weight and significance to the aforementioned statement.

When the great tribulation of the slander (*ifk*) afflicted the Muslims and the hypocrites spread malicious slander against the Mother of the Believers Lady ʿĀ'ishah ﵂, two of the Ṣaḥābah ﵃ were also embroiled in the slandering. Ḥassān ibn Thābit ﵁ and Misṭaḥ ibn Uthāthah ﵁, two illustrious Ṣaḥābīs who were both veterans of Badr, were swept along in this tribulation and became involved in the slander. After the verses of exoneration were revealed, they were meted punishment for false accusation according to the Shariah. However, they were sincere in their repentance and sorrow over what had occurred and what they had become part of. In the same way, Lady ʿA'ishah's ﵂ innocence was declared through revelation, and so too was their pardon and the acceptance of their repentance.

Misṭaḥ ﵁ was in a state of poverty, and due to his benevolence and the tie of kinship they shared, Sayyidunā Abū Bakr ﵁ had long been his patron and had supported him financially. It doubly hurt Sayyidunā Abū Bakr ﵁

---

53 Abū Bakr al-Marwazī, *Musnad Abī Bakr al-Ṣiddīq*, Maktab al-Islāmī, Beirut (1406/1986), p. 62. Hadith no. 21.

then when he learned of Misṭaḥ's involvement in the spread of lies and slander against his innocent daughter. He swore an oath that he would never give financial aid to Misṭaḥ ﵁ again. His philanthropy was vast and he helped so many others, and had no obligation to help any single specific poor person, but Allah ﷻ held al-Ṣiddīq ﵁ to a higher standard and wanted to make him a model for all Muslims to come. Allah ﷻ wished for him to rise above his personal hurt and natural grief, and to reach for a rank of supreme ethics. And so, the following verse was revealed:

وَلَا يَأْتَلِ أُو۟لُوا۟ ٱلْفَضْلِ مِنكُمْ وَٱلسَّعَةِ أَن يُؤْتُوٓا۟ أُو۟لِى ٱلْقُرْبَىٰ وَٱلْمَسَـٰكِينَ وَٱلْمُهَـٰجِرِينَ فِى سَبِيلِ ٱللَّهِ ۖ وَلْيَعْفُوا۟ وَلْيَصْفَحُوٓا۟ ۗ أَلَا تُحِبُّونَ أَن يَغْفِرَ ٱللَّهُ لَكُمْ ۗ وَٱللَّهُ غَفُورٌ رَّحِيمٌ

The men of grace and wealth among you should not swear against giving [their charitable gifts] to kinsmen, to the poor, and to refugees in the way of Allah. They should forgive and forego. Do you not like that Allah forgives you? Allah is Ever-Forgiving, Ever-Merciful.[54]

He was encouraged to break his oath and expiate for it. It was beneath his dignity, knowledge, and excellence that he should halt his aid and what Allah ﷻ had bestowed upon him. Rather, his godly honour meant he should forgive and forego, just as Allah ﷻ had forgiven them.[55] Upon hearing this revelation, Sayyidunā Abū Bakr ﵁ declared,

.وَاللَّهِ إِنِّي لَأُحِبُّ أَنْ يَغْفِرَ اللَّهُ لِي

By Allah, I do indeed love that Allah forgives me.[56]

54 *Al-Nūr*, 22.

55 Muḥammad Shafīʿ al-ʿUthmānī, *Maʿārif al-Qurʾān*, Vol. 6, pp. 588-390.

56 *Ṣaḥīḥ al-Bukhārī*, 2661, 4141, 4750, 4757; *Ṣaḥīḥ Muslim*, 2770a.

He immediately continued his financial aid and support to Misṭaḥ ﵁, and further assured him, stating, "I will never withhold it from him again."[57]

Love for the Ahl al-Bayt

قَالَ أَبُو بَكْرٍ:

وَالَّذِي نَفْسِي بِيَدِهِ، لَقَرَابَةُ رَسُولِ اللَّهِ ﷺ أَحَبُّ إِلَيَّ أَنْ أَصِلَ مِنْ قَرَابَتِي.

Abū Bakr al-Ṣiddīq ﵁ said,

By the One Who holds my soul, the relatives of Allah's Messenger are dearer to me than my own relatives.[58]

These were words of reassurance he spoke to Sayyidunā ʿAlī ibn Abī Ṭālib ﵁, and he swore an oath to prove it. Often, when preaching from the pulpit of the Prophet's Masjid, he would remind people of the great status and worth that the family of the Prophet ﷺ held with him, saying,

ارْقُبُوا مُحَمَّدًا ﷺ فِي أَهْلِ بَيْتِهِ.

Look after Muhammad by looking after his family.[59]

Imam Ibn Ḥajar al-ʿAsqalānī ﵀ explains that Sayyidunā Abū Bakr ﵁ would address and advise the people with these words, and that "looking after" a thing (*murāqabah*) means protecting it (*muḥāfaẓah*).[60] Out of reverence

57 Ibid.

58 *Musnad Imām Aḥmad*, 55; *Ṣaḥīḥ al-Bukhārī*, 3711, 3712, 4035, 4036, 4240, 4241; *Ṣaḥīḥ Muslim*, 1759a.

59 *Ṣaḥīḥ al-Bukhārī*, 3713, 3751.

60 Ibn Ḥajar al-ʿAsqalānī, *Fatḥ al-Bārī bi Sharḥ Ṣaḥīḥ al-Bukhārī*, al-Risālah al-ʿĀlamiyyah, Damascus (1434/2013), Vol. 11, p. 153.

for the Messenger of Allah ﷺ, we should ensure that we honour his family, avoid troubling them, and ward off harm from them.

Another example of Sayyidunā Abū Bakr's ؓ love for the family of the Prophet ﷺ is given in *Ṣaḥīḥ al-Bukhārī*, when having led the ʿAṣr prayer that day, he went out walking and saw al-Ḥasan ؓ playing among other boys. He lifted him onto his shoulders and said, "My father be ransomed for your sake! You resemble the Prophet ﷺ and not ʿAlī", while Sayyidunā ʿAlī ؓ stood smiling.[61]

Yet, still greater is the story of his father Sayyidunā Abū Quḥāfah's ؓ coming into Islam:

عَنْ أَنَسٍ فِي قِصَّةِ إِسْلَامِ أَبِي قُحَافَةَ، قَالَ: فَلَمَّا مَدَّ يَدَهُ يُبَايِعُهُ بَكَى أَبُو بَكْرٍ، فَقَالَ النَّبِيّ صَلَّى اللَّهُ عَلَيْهِ وَسَلَّمَ:

مَا يُبْكِيكَ؟

قَالَ: لَأَنْ تَكُونَ يَدُ عَمِّكَ مَكَانَ يَدِهِ وَيُسَلِّمُ وَيُقِرُّ اللَّهُ عَيْنَكَ أَحَبَّ إِلَيَّ مِنْ أَنْ يَكُونَ.

When Abū Quḥāfah extended his hand to pledge allegiance to the Prophet, Abū Bakr began to cry. The Prophet asked, "What makes you cry?" He replied, "Would that it was your uncle's hand (Abū Ṭālib) in place of my father's hand, that it was he embracing Islam and Allah brought comfort to your eyes by it, that would have been still more beloved to me than this.[62]

Only someone who has embraced Islam rather than been born into it can understand the immensity of this statement. The father to whom he had preached Islam for decades, whose guidance he had prayed for every night, whose salvation was finally at hand, what could have been more beloved to

61 *Ṣaḥīḥ al-Bukhārī*, 3542.

62 Ibn Ḥajar al-ʿAsqalānī, *Al-Iṣābah fī Tamyīz al-Ṣaḥābah*, Dār al-Kutub al-ʿIlmiyyah, Beirut (1415/ 1995), vol. 7 p. 199.

his heart, dearer to his soul, than for him to embrace Islam? And yet... our Teacher Abū Bakr ﷺ would have gladly given up this joy if it meant that the Beloved Prophet ﷺ experienced this joy instead. Abū Quḥāfah's ﷺ Islam was the answer to a lifetime of prayers, but Abū Ṭālib's would have been a balm for the Beloved ﷺ. What greater sign of love for the Ahl al-Bayt can there be than this?

Avoidance of Sin

رُوِيَ عَنْ أَبِي بَكْرٍ:

أَطْوَعُ النَّاسِ لله أَشَدُّهُمْ بُغْضًا لِمَعْصِيَتِهِ.

Abū Bakr al-Ṣiddīq ﷺ said,

The most obedient of people to Allah are those who hate disobeying Him the most.[63]

Many people may carry out multiple acts of obedience and engage in good works, yet when the opportunity to sin arises, they have very little resistance. Such a person's claim to obedience is deficient, and their self-perception of piety false.[64] This is why the great saint Sahl ibn ʿAbdullāh al-Tustarī ﷺ declared, "Deeds of righteousness are done by the righteous and the ungodly alike: only a *ṣiddīq* avoids sins."[65] The Ṣaḥābah were extremely scrupulous in this regard. Sayyidunā Abū Bakr ﷺ states,

كُنَّا نَتْرُكُ سَبْعِينَ بَاباً مِنَ الْحَلَالِ مَخَافَةَ بَابٍ وَاحِدٍ مِنَ الْحَرَامِ.

63 Aḥmad Zakī Ṣafwat, *Jamharah Khuṭub al-ʿArab fī ʿUṣūr al-ʿArabiyyah al-Zāhirah*, Maktabah al-ʿIlmiyyah, Beirut (1352/1933), Vol. 2, p. 466.

64 ʿUmar al-Muqbil, *Mawāʿiẓ al-Ṣaḥābah*, p. 25.

65 Abū Nuʿaym al-Aṣfahānī, *Ḥilyah al-Awliyāʾ wa Ṭabaqāt al-Aṣfiyāʾ*, Dār al-Fikr, Beirut (1416/1996), Vol. 10, p. 211.

We would leave off seventy doors of the lawful (halal), out of fear that we may enter into one door of the unlawful (haram).[66]

At the pinnacle of scrupulousness, to avoid even those lawful things that bring one close to the unlawful shows how serious a matter this was for the Ṣaḥābah. The Prophet ﷺ himself gave the most perfect analogy for this:

إنَّ الْحَلَالَ بَيِّنٌ، وَإنَّ الْحَرَامَ بَيِّنٌ، وَبَيْنَهُمَا أُمُورٌ مُشْتَبِهَاتٌ لَا يَعْلَمُهُنَّ كَثِيرٌ مِنْ النَّاسِ، فَمَنْ اتَّقَى الشُّبُهَاتِ فَقْد اسْتَبْرَأَ لِدِينِهِ وَعِرْضِهِ، وَمَنْ وَقَعَ فِي الشُّبُهَاتِ وَقَعَ فِي الْحَرَامِ، كَالرَّاعِي يَرْعَى حَوْلَ الْحِمَى يُوشِكُ أَنْ يَرْتَعَ فِيهِ، أَلَا وَإِنَّ لِكُلِّ مَلِكٍ حِمًى، أَلَا وَإِنَّ حِمَى اللهِ مَحَارِمُهُ، أَلَا وَإِنَّ فِي الْجَسَدِ مُضْغَةً إذَا صَلَحَتْ صَلَحَ الْجَسَدُ كُلُّهُ، وَإِذَا فَسَدَتْ فَسَدَ الْجَسَدُ كُلُّهُ، أَلَا وَهِيَ الْقَلْبُ.

That lawful is clear and the unlawful is clear, and between the two are doubtful matters about which many people do not know. Thus he who avoids doubtful matters clears himself regarding his religion and honour, but he who falls into doubtful matters will fall into the unlawful. It is like the shepherd who pastures around a sanctuary, all but grazing therein. Indeed every king has a sanctuary, and Allah's sanctuary is His prohibitions. Indeed in the body, there is a morsel of flesh, which, if it is whole the body is whole, and if it is diseased all the body is diseased. Indeed it is the heart.[67]

Pious Leadership

قَالَ أَبُو بَكْرٍ:

اعْلَمُوا أَنَّ أَكْيَسَ الْكَيْسِ التَّقْوَى، وَأَنَّ أَحْمَقَ الْحُمْقِ الْفُجُورُ، وَأَنَّ أَقْوَاكُمْ عِنْدِي الضَّعِيفُ

66 Abū Ṭālib al-Makkī, *Qūt al-Qulūb*, Dār al-Kutub al-ʿIlmiyyah, Beirut (1426/2005) Vol. 2, pp. 486-487.

67 *Ṣaḥīḥ al-Bukhārī*, 52, 2051; *Ṣaḥīḥ Muslim*, 1599a.

حَتَّى آخُذَ لَهُ بِحَقِّهِ، وَأَنَّ أَضْعَفَكُمْ عِنْدِي الْقَوِيُّ حَتَّى آخُذَ مِنْهُ الْحَقَّ، أَيُّهَا النَّاسُ، إِنَّمَا أَنَا مُتَّبِعٌ، وَلَسْتُ بِمُبْتَدِعٍ، فَإِنْ أَحْسَنْتُ فَأَعِينُونِي، وَإِنْ زُغْتُ فَقَوِّمُونِي.

Abū Bakr al-Ṣiddīq ﵁ said,

Know that the best intelligence is piety, and the worst stupidity is immorality. The strongest of you in my sight is the weak until I fulfil his rights; the weakest of you in my sight is the strong until I take what rights are due from him. O people, I am only a follower and not an innovator. If I do well, then help me; if I deviate, straighten me.[68]

Three distinct points are being made in this statement: (1) that the binary of both the nature and outcome of deeds is linked to true intelligence; (2) that rights are both owed to people and due upon them; (3) and that each of us as followers of the Prophet ﷺ should be supported or challenged based upon our adherence to his Sunnah.

In Sūrah al-Layl, after establishing the binary nature of night and day, and of male and female, Allah ﷻ makes a comparison with human action and the results of that action,

إِنَّ سَعْيَكُمْ لَشَتَّىٰ

Your effort is indeed dispersed toward diverse ends.[69]

The following verses in the chapter further unpack this, explaining that those who accept the truth, fear Allah ﷻ, and strive towards good will be rewarded with eternal bliss, while those who reject the truth, are unmindful of Allah ﷻ, and behave immorally will be punished with eternal despair. The actions themselves are diverse, in that some do good deeds and others commit evil

68 Ibn Saʿd al-Zuhrī, *Kitāb al-Ṭabaqāt al-Kubrā*, Vol. 3, p. 167.

69 *al-Layl*, 4.

acts; and the results of the actions are thus naturally diverse too.[70] As Allah ﷻ says in Sūrah al-Inshiqāq,

يَـٰٓأَيُّهَا ٱلۡإِنسَـٰنُ إِنَّكَ كَادِحٌ إِلَىٰ رَبِّكَ كَدۡحٗا فَمُلَـٰقِيهِ

O man, you strive tirelessly to reach your Lord, and you shall meet Him.[71]

The Prophet ﷺ summarised this concept succinctly in the Hadith narrated by Abū Mālik al-Ashʿarī ؓ, in which the Prophet ﷺ said,

كُلُّ النَّاسِ يَغْدُو فَبَائِعٌ نَفْسَهُ فَمُعْتِقُهَا أَوْ مُوبِقُهَا

All men awaken and conduct their business, thereby emancipating themselves or destroying themselves.[72]

This is why the first generations would strive and toil to "set their necks free". It is said some would glorify Allah ﷻ through *tasbīḥ* 12,000 times a day as a measure of their blood money as if they had killed themselves and so were bound to pay a wergild to set themselves free.[73] Secondly, Sayyidunā Abū Bakr al-Ṣiddīq ؓ explained that rights are owed by those in positions of advantage towards those who are in positions of weakness or disadvantage. In this way, the roles become reversed: the weak have a sort of power over the strong for it is the responsibility of each of us to fulfil the rights of the other, and the weakest are owed more rights than the strong. Abū Hurayrah ؓ narrated that the Prophet ﷺ said,

لَيْسَ مِنَّا مَنْ لَمْ يَرْحَمْ صَغِيرَنَا وَيُوَقِّرْ كَبِيرَنَا وَيَأْمُرْ بِالْمَعْرُوفِ وَيَنْهَ عَنِ الْمُنْكَرِ.

---

70 Mufti Muḥammad ibn Mawlānā Sulaymān Hafizji Bardolī, *Taysīr al-Qur'ān*, Noorani Makatib, Dabhel, (1440/2019) Vol. 2, p. 699.

71 *al-Inshiqāq*, 6.

72 *Ṣaḥīḥ Muslim*, 223.

73 Ibn Rajab al-Ḥanbalī, *Jāmiʿ al-ʿUlūm wa al-Ḥikam*, Vol. 2, p. 602.

He is not one of us who does not have mercy upon our young, respect our elders, and command good and forbid evil.[74]

Fulfilling these rights are a moral duty upon us, and failure to comply with one's duty is not the action of a Muslim.

Thirdly, it is incumbent upon us to remember that a Muslim leader is only our leader insofar as he acts upon the Sunnah of the Prophet ﷺ. Abū Hurayrah ؓ narrated that the Prophet ﷺ said,

نَحْنُ الآخِرُونَ السَّابِقُونَ. مَنْ أَطَاعَنِي فَقَدْ أَطَاعَ اللَّهَ، وَمَنْ عَصَانِي فَقَدْ عَصَى اللَّهَ، وَمَنْ يُطِعِ الأَمِيرَ فَقَدْ أَطَاعَنِي، وَمَنْ يَعْصِ الأَمِيرَ فَقَدْ عَصَانِي، وَإِنَّمَا الإِمَامُ جُنَّةٌ يُقَاتَلُ مِنْ وَرَائِهِ وَيُتَّقَى بِهِ، فَإِنْ أَمَرَ بِتَقْوَى اللَّهِ وَعَدَلَ، فَإِنَّ لَهُ بِذَلِكَ أَجْرًا، وَإِنْ قَالَ بِغَيْرِهِ، فَإِنَّ عَلَيْهِ مِنْهُ.

We are the last but will be the foremost to enter Paradise. He who obeys me obeys Allah, and he who disobeys me disobeys Allah. He who obeys the leader obeys me, and he who disobeys the leader disobeys me. The leader is like a shelter for whose safety the Muslims should fight and where they should seek protection. If the leader orders people with righteousness and rules justly, then he will be rewarded for that, and if he does the opposite, he will be responsible for it.[75]

As Allah ﷻ explains in Sūrah al-Nisā':

يَـٰٓأَيُّهَا ٱلَّذِينَ ءَامَنُوٓا۟ أَطِيعُوا۟ ٱللَّهَ وَأَطِيعُوا۟ ٱلرَّسُولَ وَأُو۟لِى ٱلْأَمْرِ مِنكُمْ ۖ فَإِن تَنَـٰزَعْتُمْ فِى شَىْءٍ فَرُدُّوهُ إِلَى ٱللَّهِ وَٱلرَّسُولِ إِن كُنتُمْ تُؤْمِنُونَ بِٱللَّهِ وَٱلْيَوْمِ ٱلْـَٔاخِرِ ۚ ذَٰلِكَ خَيْرٌ وَأَحْسَنُ تَأْوِيلًا

O believers! Obey Allah and obey the Messenger and those in authority among you. Should you disagree on anything, then refer it to Allah and His

---

74 *Jāmiʿ al-Tirmidhī* 1921.

75 *Ṣaḥīḥ al-Bukhārī*, 2956-2957.

Messenger, if you truly believe in Allah and the Last Day. This is the best and fairest resolution.[76]

Whenever a leader makes a decision, it should be compared and contrasted against the Qur'an and the Sunnah of the Prophet ﷺ; if the leader falls short, he must be corrected. Too often we find people following "the rulers" without holding them up to this standard. A Muslim ruler is only our ruler so long as he acts by the Qur'an and Sunnah. Leadership is a necessity, but the responsibility upon the leader is great – it is not something to be sought, nor coveted, for failure to fulfil the duties of leadership can have the direst of consequences. The Prophet ﷺ is reported to have said,

إِنَّ الْعِرَافَةَ حَقٌّ وَلاَ بُدَّ لِلنَّاسِ مِنَ الْعُرَفَاءِ وَلَكِنَّ الْعُرَفَاءَ فِي النَّارِ.

The rank of chief is necessary, for people must have chiefs, but the chiefs are in the Fire.[77]

The understood meaning here is that chiefs are ever in danger of damnation and destruction due to the slightest unfairness or miscarriage of justice.[78] The Prophet ﷺ is also reported to have said,

إِنَّ أَحَبَّ النَّاسِ إِلَى اللَّهِ يَوْمَ الْقِيَامَةِ وَأَدْنَاهُمْ مِنْهُ مَجْلِسًا إِمَامٌ عَادِلٌ وَأَبْغَضَ النَّاسِ إِلَى اللَّهِ وَأَبْعَدَهُمْ مِنْهُ مَجْلِسًا إِمَامٌ جَائِرٌ.

Indeed the most beloved to Allah from amongst the people on the Day of Judgement, and the nearest to Him, is the just leader; and the most hated of people to Allah, and the furthest from Him, is the oppressive leader.[79]

---

76 *al-Nisā'*, 59.

77 *Sunan Abī Dāwūd*, 2934.

78 Khalīl Ahmad Sahāranpūrī, *Badhl al-Majhūd fī Ḥall Sunan Abī Dāwūd*, Vol. 10, p. 114.

79 *Jāmiʿ al-Tirmidhī*, 1329.

During the reign of Sayyidunā ʿUmar ibn al-Khaṭṭāb ﵁, people began to erect tall buildings, and ʿUmar ﵁ warned them against pride and delivered the following message with regards to pious, learned, and intelligent leadership,

يَا مَعْشَرَ الْعُرَيْبِ، الْأَرْضَ الْأَرْضَ، إِنَّهُ لَا إِسْلَامَ إِلَّا بِجَمَاعَةٍ، وَلَا جَمَاعَةَ إِلَّا بِإِمَارَةٍ، وَلَا إِمَارَةَ إِلَّا بِطَاعَةٍ، فَمَنْ سَوَّدَهُ قَوْمُهُ عَلَى الْفِقْهِ، كَانَ حَيَاةً لَهُ وَلَهُمْ، وَمَنْ سَوَّدَهُ قَوْمُهُ عَلَى غَيْرِ فِقْهٍ، كَانَ هَلَاكًا لَهُ وَلَهُمْ.

O Arabs, to the ground, to the ground![80] There is no Islam without community, and there is no community without leadership, just as there is no leadership without compliance. Thus, whoever has been made a leader by his people while he has a deep understanding will bring prosperity to himself and his people. And whoever has been made a leader by his people while he has no deep understanding, he shall destroy himself and destroy them.[81]

Taqwā, Faith, and Humility

رُوِيَ عَنْ أَبِي بَكْرٍ:

وَجَدْنَا الْكَرَمَ فِي التَّقْوَى، وَالْغِنَى فِي الْيَقِينِ، وَالشَّرَفَ فِي التَّوَاضُعِ.

Abū Bakr al-Ṣiddīq ﵁ said,

We found honour in piety, independence in belief, and nobility in humility.[82]

80 Meaning: "Humble yourselves to the ground!"

81 Abū Muḥammad al-Dārimī, *Sunan al-Dārimī*, 257.

82 Abū Ḥāmid al-Ghazālī, *Iḥyā ʿUlūm al-Dīn*, Dār al-Maʿrifah, Beirut (1302/1982), Vol. 3, p. 343.

Sayyidunā Abū Bakr al-Ṣiddīq ﷺ was exemplary in all of these qualities and more. The first of these qualities is *taqwā*, which loosely translates as piety or the quality of being God-fearing (it is interesting to note that the English language does not have an equivalent word). Shāh ʿAbd al-ʿAzīz Muḥaddith Dehlawī ﷺ defined a person who has *taqwā* as one who protects himself from disbelief and all manners of sin, great or small, and that, should he commit a sin, he will immediately turn away from it and seek Allah's forgiveness.[83] Allah ﷻ Himself actually refers to Sayyidunā Abū Bakr al-Ṣiddīq ﷺ as *al-Atqā*, the most God-fearing, in Sūrah al-Layl.[84] Shāh Dehlawī ﷺ further defines *al-Atqā* as a person who does not miss out even a single etiquette of the Shariah, who is constantly concerned with avoiding sin, and whose mind is averse to even the *thought* of sin. In short, his outward self and inward self are the same.[85]

Allah ﷻ Himself describes our Master Abū Bakr ﷺ in Sūrah al-Ḥujurāt thus,

إِنَّ أَكْرَمَكُمْ عِندَ ٱللَّهِ أَتْقَىٰكُمْ

Surely the noblest of you in the sight of Allah is the most God-fearing amongst you.[86]

When Allah ﷻ describes him thus in the Qur'an, when his name is eternally tied to that of the noble Prophet ﷺ, what greater honour can be bestowed on the man who is called *al-Atqā*?

Taqwā is a quality that must be instilled in the believer and then maintained and protected. Complacency in this regard will lead to moral and

---

83 Shāh ʿAbd al-ʿAzīz Muḥaddith Dehlawī, *Tafsīr ʿAzīzī: Pārah ʿAmma*, Idarah Islamiyat, Karachi (1423/2002), p. 487.

84 *al-Layl*, 17.

85 Shāh ʿAbd al-ʿAzīz Muḥaddith Dehlawī, *Tafsīr ʿAzīzī: Pārah ʿAmma*, p. 487.

86 *al-Ḥujurāt*, 13.

spiritual decline, so much so that the believer's heart will be indistinguishable from that of a nonbeliever and will be afflicted with anxiety and depression. One only needs to undertake a quick self-assessment to see that this rot has already taken hold of us. Once we have established the problem, we can then look to remedy it through spiritual self-development and prayer. The Prophet ﷺ advised,

مَنْ كَثُرَ هَمُّهُ فَلْيَقُلْ: اللَّهُمَّ إِنِّي عَبْدُكَ وَابْنُ عَبْدِكَ وَابْنُ أَمَتِكَ وَفِي قَبْضَتِكَ نَاصِيَتِي بِيَدِكَ مَاضٍ فِيَّ حُكْمُكَ عَدْلٌ فِيَّ قَضَاؤُكَ أَسْأَلُكَ بِكُلِّ اسْمٍ هُوَ لَكَ سَمَّيْتَ بِهِ نَفْسَكَ أَوْ أَنْزَلْتَهُ فِي كِتَابِكَ أَوْ عَلَّمْتَهُ أَحَدًا مِنْ خَلْقِكَ أَوْ أَلْهَمْتَ عِبَادَكَ أَوِ اسْتَأْثَرْتَ بِهِ فِي مَكْنُونِ الْغَيْبِ عِنْدَكَ أَنْ تَجْعَلَ الْقُرْآنَ رَبِيعَ قلبِي وجِلاء هَمِّي وغَمِّي مَا قَالَهَا عَبْدٌ قَطُّ إِلَّا أَذْهَبَ اللَّهُ غَمَّهُ وَأَبْدَلَهُ فَرَحًا.

Whoever is afflicted by anxiety should say, "O Allah, I am Your servant, the son of Your servant and Your handmaid. I am at Your disposal, and my forelock is in Your possession. Only Your judgement affects me and only Your decree concerns me. I beseech You by Your every name You gave Yourself, sent down in Your Book, taught any of Your creations, or kept to Yourself in the Unseen, to make the Qur'an the spring of my heart and the means of clearing away my anxiety and depression." No one had ever said it without Allah removing his grief and granting him joy in its place.[87]

Returning to the topic at hand, with regards to Sayyidunā Abū Bakr's ﵁ faith and belief, we have already discussed how and why he was renowned by the name al-Ṣiddīq due to the strength and completeness in belief in Allah ﷻ and his Prophet ﷺ. In fact, the Prophet ﷺ described the completeness of his faith when he said, "If the faith of Abū Bakr was weighed against the faith of the world, his faith would outweigh it."[88]

Finding independence in the certainty of belief is finding freedom in knowing Who one belongs to and upon Whom one is reliant. Sayyidunā Abū

---

87 Al-Khaṭīb al-Tibrīzī, *Mishkāt al-Maṣābīḥ*, 2452.

88 Ibn ʿAsākir ʿAlī ibn al-Ḥasan, *Tārīkh Madīnah Dimashq*, Dār al-Fikr, Syria (1415/1995), Vol. 30, p. 126.

Bakr's ﷺ faith in Allah ﷻ was so complete that nothing in this world could distract him from the worship of Allah ﷻ and the service of the Prophet ﷺ. His wealth was spent entirely in the path of Allah ﷻ. Muḥammad Mālik ibn Idrīs Kāndhlawī ﷺ states that before accepting Islam, Sayyidunā Abū Bakr ﷺ was known as one of the wealthiest amongst the Quraysh, owning a fortune of 40,000 dinars[89] which he spent freely and sincerely to aid the Prophet ﷺ and his Ṣaḥābah. Yet, when he became the Caliph (having spent all of his wealth in the service of the Muslims) he set himself a wage from the public treasury (*bayt al-māl*) of just 2 dirhams[90] a day.[91] In fact, Abū Hurayrah ﷺ narrated that the Prophet ﷺ said,

مَا لأَحَدٍ عِنْدَنَا يَدٌ إِلاَّ وَقَدْ كَافَيْنَاهُ مَا خَلاَ أَبَا بَكْرٍ فَإِنَّ لَهُ عِنْدَنَا يَدًا يُكَافِئُهُ اللَّهُ بِهَا يَوْمَ الْقِيَامَةِ وَمَا نَفَعَنِي مَالُ أَحَدٍ قَطُّ مَا نَفَعَنِي مَالُ أَبِي بَكْرٍ وَلَوْ كُنْتُ مُتَّخِذًا خَلِيلاً لاَتَّخَذْتُ أَبَا بَكْرٍ خَلِيلاً أَلاَ وَإِنَّ صَاحِبَكُمْ خَلِيلُ اللَّهِ.

There is no favour due upon us from anyone, except that we have repaid it, except for Abū Bakr. He has a due over us, which Allah will repay on the Day of Judgement. No one's wealth has benefited me as much as Abū Bakr's wealth has. And were I to take a khalīl, then I would have taken Abū Bakr as a khalīl, but indeed your companion is Allah's khalīl.[92]

The nobility in humility is apparent to those who have spent time with the truly humble believers amongst us. ʿIyāḍ ibn Ḥimār ﷺ narrated that the Prophet ﷺ advised the believers,

وَإِنَّ اللَّهَ أَوْحَى إِلَيَّ أَنْ تَوَاضَعُوا حَتَّى لاَ يَفْخَرَ أَحَدٌ عَلَى أَحَدٍ وَلاَ يَبْغِي أَحَدٌ عَلَى أَحَدٍ.

89 A dinar was a gold coin, 4.25 grams in weight.

90 A Dirham was a silver coin, 3 grams in weight.

91 Muḥammad Mālik ibn Idrīs al-Kāndhlawī, *Maʿārif al-Qurʾān (Idrīsī)*, Maktabah al-Maʿārif, Shāhdādpur (1422/2001), Vol. 8, p. 474.

92 *Jāmiʿ al-Tirmidhī*, 3661.

Indeed Allah has revealed to me that you should adopt humility so that no one may wrong another and no one may be disdainful towards another.[93]

This is an inherent quality of the believer: he is humble, regardless of his status in this life or the next, and he guards himself against pride and haughtiness. In fact, in another Hadith, the Prophet ﷺ explained this very concept by saying,

مَنْ شَرِبَ بِيَدِهِ وَهُوَ يَقْدِرُ عَلَى إِنَاءٍ يُرِيدُ التَّوَاضُعَ كَتَبَ اللَّهُ لَهُ بِعَدَدِ أَصَابِعِهِ حَسَنَاتٍ وَهُوَ إِنَاءُ عِيسَى ابْنِ مَرْيَمَ عَلَيْهِمَا السَّلاَمُ إِذْ طَرَحَ الْقَدَحَ فَقَالَ أُفٍّ هَذَا مَعَ الدُّنْيَا

Whoever drinks from his hand while he is able to drink from a vessel, intending humility by it, Allah will record good deeds for him equivalent to the number of his fingers. The hand was ʿĪsā ibn Maryam's drinking vessel when he threw away the cup and said, "Uff! This belongs to the world."[94]

Sayyidunā Abū Bakr ﵁, the best of all men after the Prophets themselves,[95] was likewise the pinnacle of humility. Despite being promised Paradise, despite being the Prophet's closest and dearest companions, and despite Allah ﷻ Himself specifically highlighting His Divine Pleasure upon him,[96] he would say, "I wish I was a simple hair on the body of a believer."[97]

Such was the humility of Sayyidunā Abū Bakr ﵁. In fact, his *taqwā* and humility were so refined that he would do great deeds in secret. On one occasion, Abū Ṣāliḥ ﵁ narrates that Sayyidunā ʿUmar ibn al-Khaṭṭāb ﵁, who was renowned for his anonymous acts of charity and kindness, was committed to the care of an old, disabled blind woman who lived on the outskirts of

93 *Ṣaḥīḥ Muslim*, 2865d.

94 Ibn Mājah, Muḥammad ibn Yazīd, *Sunan Ibn Mājah*, 3431.

95 *Tafsīr ʿAzīzī: Pārah ʿAmma*, p. 488.

96 *al-Layl*, 21.

97 Muḥammad Zakariyyā al-Kāndhlawī, *Faḍāʾil al-Aʿmāl*, Farid Book Depot, Delhi (1421/2000), p.41.

Medina, secretly going at night to draw water for her and manage her daily affairs. One evening, he arrived to find that someone else had preceded him and taken care of all she needed. Sayyidunā ʿUmar ibn al-Khaṭṭāb ﷺ began to increase his visits and came earlier, lest someone come to help her before him again, and he lay in wait to see who it was that was also helping her. He found that it was Sayyidunā Abū Bakr al-Ṣiddīq ﷺ, who was the Caliph at the time.[98]

What greater example of sincerity and *taqwā* can there be than that of the first and second Caliphs of the Prophet ﷺ secretly aiding an old blind woman, who would have been of no consequence and beneath the notice of anyone else? They cared deeply for every Muslim and went out of their way to help each of them individually, despite their status or position, doing so in secret such that no one would attribute the good deed to them.

ʿUmar ibn al-Khaṭṭāb ﷺ stated with regard to Sayyidunā Abū Bakr ﷺ,

مَا اسْتَبَقْنَا خَيْرًا قَطُّ إِلَّا سَبَقَنَا إِلَيْهَا أَبُو بَكْرٍ.

Never did we ever compete in doing good, except that Abū Bakr beat us all to it.[99]

In fact, just as Sayyidunā Abū Bakr ﷺ hid his good deeds, his sincerity extended to hiding the bad deeds of others. Sayyidunā Zubayd ibn al-Ṣalt ﷺ reported that he heard Sayyidunā Abū Bakr al-Ṣiddīq ﷺ say,

لَوْ أَخَذْتُ شَارِبًا لَأَحْبَبْتُ أَنْ يَسْتُرَهُ اللَّهُ وَلَوْ أَخَذْتُ سَارِقًا لَأَحْبَبْتُ أَنْ يَسْتُرَهُ اللَّهُ

98 Ibn ʿAsākir ʿAlī ibn al-Ḥasan, *Tārīkh Madīnah Dimashq*, Vol. 30, p. 322.

99 *Musnad Imām Aḥmad*, 265.

Were I to take hold of a drinker of wine, I would prefer for Allah to cover his sin; and were I to take hold of a thief, I would prefer for Allah to cover his sin.

In another narration,

لَوْ لَمْ أَجِدْ لِلسَّارِقِ وَالزَّانِي وَشَارِبِ الْخَمْرِ إِلا ثَوْبِي لأَحْبَبْتُ أَنْ أَسْتُرَهُ عَلَيْهِ.

If I found nothing with the thief, the adulterer, and the drinker of wine but my robe, I would prefer to cover them with it.[100]

Preparation for the Grave

رُوِيَ عَنْ أَبِي بَكْرٍ:

مَنْ دَخَلَ الْقَبَرَ بِلَا زَادٍ، فَكَأَنَّمَا رَكِبَ الْبَحْرَ بِلَا سَفِينَةٍ.

Abū Bakr al-Ṣiddīq ﷺ said,

Whoever enters the grave without provision is one who tries to sail the sea without a ship.[101]

Death comes suddenly. We plan and prepare and strive to amass. We measure our success by profit margins, corporate positions, and public perceptions of us. We work hard to be successful. But death comes suddenly, and compared to the pond of now, the ocean of the Hereafter is vast and endless. Sayyidunā Abū Bakr's ﷺ aphorism reminds us that true provision is not that of this

100 Ibn Abī Shaybah, Abū Bakr ʿAbdullāh ibn Muḥammad, *Muṣannaf Ibn Abī Shaybah*, 3958.

101 Ibn Ḥajar al-ʿAsqalānī, *al-Istiʿdād li-Yawm al-Miʿād*, Dār al-Tarbiyyah, Damascus (n.d.), pg. 26

fleeting world. True provision is in repentance, in righteous deeds, and in awareness of the nearness of our demise. For death comes suddenly.

Sayyidunā Abū Bakr ؓ advised Khālid ibn al-Walīd ؓ, "Flee from honour and it will follow you; desire death and you will be given abundant life."[102]

The meaning is clear: honour is given to those who shun it and are sincere in their deeds, and death is not a thing to be feared but welcomed. The righteous ones who are sincere in their deeds desire to meet Allah ﷻ. At the time of his passing, the Prophet ﷺ was given the option of staying in this world and then meeting Allah ﷻ, or to meet Allah ﷻ in death at that moment.

'Ā'ishah al-Ṣiddīqah ؓ stated that "When the Prophet ﷺ was healthy, he would say, 'No soul of a Prophet is taken until he is shown his place in Paradise and then he is given the option.' When death approached him, while his head was on my lap, he became unconscious and then recovered consciousness. He then looked at the ceiling of the house and said, 'O Allah, with the Highest Companion!' I said to myself, 'He is not going to choose us', and I realised that this is what he had said to us when he was healthy. The last words he spoke were,

$$\text{اللّٰهُمَّ الرَّفِيقَ الأَعْلَى.}$$

O Allah, with the Highest Companion!"[103]

As death approached Sayyidunā Abū Bakr ؓ, and his time in this world drew to a close, he called the man he would choose as his successor, Sayyidunā 'Umar ibn al-Khaṭṭāb ؓ, and bestowed upon him the following advice:

---

102 Aḥmad ibn Muḥammad ibn 'Abd Rabbih, *Al-ʿIqd al-Farīd (The Unique Necklace)*, Garnet Publishing, Reading (2006), Vol. 1, p. 74.
103 *Ṣaḥīḥ al-Bukhārī*, 4463.

I appoint you as my successor and advise you to fear Allah. Know that certain deeds are done for Allah during the day, which He will not accept during the night; and certain deeds must be done during the night, which He will not accept during the day. What is more, Allah will not accept an optional deed until the obligatory is fulfilled.

The ones whose Scale of Deeds will be heavy on the Day of Requital will be so due to their following of the Truth in this world and the seriousness with which they took it. When Truth is placed on the Scale tomorrow, it will surely be heavy. As for those whose Scale of Deeds will be light on the Day of Requital, it will be so due to their following of Falsehood in this world and their considering it paltry. When Falsehood is placed on the Scale tomorrow, it will surely be light.

When Allah described the inhabitants of the Garden, He spoke about their most virtuous deeds, and He overlooked their evils. When I think of them, I say to myself, 'I fear I will not be able to join them.' When Allah described the inmates of the Fire, He spoke of their vilest deeds and rejected their good. When I think of these people, I say to myself, 'I hope I am not placed with them.' He mentions verses of Mercy with verses of Punishment to make one a God-fearing slave, hoping for nothing but good from Allah and not being thrown into despair.

If you remember and uphold my advice, there will be nothing of the Unseen more beloved to you than death, which will inevitably come to you. If you disregard my advice, there will be nothing of the Unseen more detestable than death, and you will not escape it.[104]

The first portion of his advice to Sayyidunā ʿUmar ibn al-Khaṭṭāb ﷺ was to ensure that everything is performed within its allotted time. This is

104 Abū ʿUthmān ʿAmr ibn Baḥr al-Jāḥiẓ, *Bayān wa al-Tabyīn*, Maktabah al-Khānjī, Cairo (1418/1998), Vol. 2, p. 45.

a fundamental principle in Islam, and a believer must ensure that his duties towards Allah ﷻ are fulfilled when they are due and not delayed or missed due to procrastination. However, this was some advice from one Caliph to another, and therefore this also serves as an advice in dealing with the day-to-day tasks related to the affairs of statecraft. Every task one has to complete must be triaged, appointed a time according to necessity and importance, and then completed expeditiously without unnecessary delays. Failing to do so is a failure of leadership, and the leader will have to answer to Allah ﷻ.

The second principle that Sayyidunā Abū Bakr ؓ highlighted to Sayyidunā ʿUmar ibn al-Khaṭṭāb ؓ is that of self-assessment and reflection. Our deeds are to be weighed – of this, there is no doubt. If that is the case, every deed must be scrutinised and checked for sincerity of intention, correctness of action, and any inkling of pride which may form as a result of it. If our deeds are to be weighed, it is the height of folly not to check them beforehand and ensure that they will have weight. Sayyidunā ʿUmar ibn al-Khaṭṭāb ؓ would later advise the people in a sermon, 'Take yourselves to the task before you are called to account; assess yourselves before you are assessed; and prepare yourselves for the Grand Assembly. Nothing will be concealed about you when your record is presented.'[105]

Thirdly, Sayyidunā Abū Bakr ؓ reminded his friend that a Muslim should be suspended between hope in Allah's Divine Mercy and fear of His Divine Wrath. If Sayyidunā Abū Bakr ؓ himself feared he would not be amongst the people of Paradise and hoped that he would not be punished for his actions, then we Muslims of today must also strive to achieve such a state, suspended between hope and fear.

Sayyidunā Abū Bakr ؓ concluded by saying that whoever adhered to these three principles had nothing to be fearful of death, but would rather yearn for it.

105 *Muṣannaf Ibn Abī Shaybah*, 37178.

And so it was, the final moments of Abū Bakr ﷺ came, and as per his last wish, he was buried alongside his Beloved ﷺ. It is said that on the day he died an earthquake shook the city of Medina. Sayyidunā Abū Bakr's father, who was by then a very old man, sat bewildered. "What is this?" he asked the men who had come to speak to him.

"Your son has died", they told him.

"A great misfortune!" he – the only father to ever see his son become a Caliph; the only father to ever inherit from one – replied. "Who has undertaken the duty of command after him?"

"'Umar", they said.

"His companion", he replied.[106]

106 Jalāl al-Dīn al-Suyūṭī, *Tārīkh al-Khulafā'*, p. 174.

2

Al-Fārūq: "Abū Ḥafṣ" ʿUmar ibn al-Khaṭṭāb

One of the greatest rulers the world has ever seen, Sayyidunā ʿUmar ibn al-Khaṭṭāb ﵁ became the second of the Rightly Guided Caliphs, and the first to carry the title of Amīr al-Mu'minīn, the Leader of the Believers. Famed for his astute foresight and formidable nature, he was given the epithet of al-Fārūq, the Discerner, by the Beloved Prophet ﷺ himself.

Under his farsighted leadership, Islam spread in all directions, akin to the unstoppable surge of a flood unchecked. The great powers of the age, the ancient and mighty empire of Persia and its enduring rival, the continent-spanning Imperium of Rome, were felled and swept away with a speed and swiftness unmatched in history. Islamic institutions of governance were formed, and Muslim armies marched to liberate every land and establish Allah's Law in every region. Yet the man himself was the very paradigm of humble asceticism.

No great palaces were built for him, nor were monuments raised to honour his name and maintain his fame. He sat on no throne and bore none of the accoutrements of power projection seen upon the figures and heads of the rulers of Rome and Ctesiphon. Instead, he kept to the humble life and style of his predecessors. He kept aloof of all temporary, worldly pleasures, and remained a man devoted to prayer and fasting.

Among his many achievements was the introduction of countless new and necessary concepts and ideas to the governance of the fledgling Islamic Caliphate. He established an official public treasury, the official *hijrah* calendar, a payrolled reserve army, military barracks in key locations across the Caliphate, and taxation for customs and importation, while also setting up an official police force. He organised jails and guest houses in various cities, schools, as well as waystations for travellers between the two Holy Cities, and founded several cities including Kufa and Basra. He set up stipends for teachers, introduced wages for imams and muezzins, employed official emissaries, and even built canals.[1]

Name and Lineage

His full title, name, and lineage read thus: the Amīr al-Mu'minīn Abū Ḥafṣ al-Fārūq ʿUmar ibn al-Khaṭṭāb ibn Nufayl ibn ʿAbd al-ʿUzzā ibn Riyāḥ ibn Qurṭ ibn Razāḥ ibn ʿAdiyy ibn Kaʿb ibn Lu'ayy al-Qurashī al-ʿAdawī.[2] A man of noble Qurayshī lineage through its Banū ʿAdiyy strand, his family line converges with that of the Beloved Prophet ﷺ in Kaʿb ibn Lu'ayy ibn Ghālib.

The Remarkable Story of his Acceptance of Islam

Prophet Mohammad ﷺ used to pray saying, 'O Allah honour Islam through Abu Jahl bin Hisham or through Umar bin Al-Khattab.'[3] Allah accepted his du'a enabling Umar ؓ by, to accept Islam and become one of the biggest

1 Ibn Jarīr al-Ṭabarī, *Tārīkh al-Rusul wa al-Mulūk*; Abū Hilāl al-Ḥasan al-ʿAskarī, *al-Awāʾil*.

2 Jalāl al-Dīn al-Suyūṭī, *Tārīkh al-Khulafā'*, p. 174.

3 *Tirmidhi: 3683*

companions of the Prophet ﷺ. The story of his conversion is one of the most remarkable stories that we can think of.

As an arch enemy of Islam, Umar ؓ became angry when a small group of Muslims migrated to Abyssinia as he thought this would affect the future unity of the Quraish. Hence, he decided to kill the Prophet ﷺ himself. On his way, he met his friend Nuaim bin Abdullah ؓ who had secretly become a Muslim. Seeing Umar ؓ so enraged and determined to kill the Prophet ﷺ, he wanted to divert his attention and told him that Umar's own sister and her husband also converted to Islam. Hearing this, Umar ؓ went to his sister's house and found them reciting verses from Surah Taha. Umar ؓ started beating up his brother-in-law, and even attacked his sister when she tried to rescue her husband. Upon hearing his sister's determination about her faith even after she fell to the ground bleeding, Umar ؓ calmed down, felt guilty, and asked his sister to let him read from what she was reciting. His sister asked him to be clean first before touching the Holy Scripture, which he complied with. As he was reading from the Qur'an, he felt overwhelmed and his heart melted with repentance. He immediately went to the Prophet ﷺ and accepted Islam. This happened in 616 AD, one year after the Migration to Abyssinia.

On the Battlefield

عَنْ يَحْيَى بْنِ سَعِيدٍ، أَنَّ عُمَرَ بْنَ الْخَطَّابِ، قَالَ:

كَرَمُ الْمُؤْمِنِ تَقْوَاهُ وَدِينُهُ حَسَبُهُ وَمُرُوءَتُهُ خُلُقُهُ وَالْجُرْأَةُ وَالْجُبْنُ غَرَائِزُ يَضَعُهَا اللَّهُ حَيْثُ شَاءَ فَالْجَبَانُ يَفِرُّ عَنْ أَبِيهِ وَأُمِّهِ وَالْجَرِيءُ يُقَاتِلُ عَمَّا لاَ يَؤُوبُ بِهِ إِلَى رَحْلِهِ وَالْقَتْلُ حَتْفٌ مِنَ الْحُتُوفِ وَالشَّهِيدُ مَنِ احْتَسَبَ نَفْسَهُ عَلَى اللَّهِ.

Sayyidunā ʿUmar ibn al-Khaṭṭāb ؓ said:

The nobility of the believer is his God-consciousness. His dīn is the measure of his pedigree. His manliness is his good character. Boldness and cowardice are but instincts that Allah places wherever He wills. The coward shrinks from defending even his father and mother; the bold one fights for the sake of the combat, not the spoils. Being slain is but one way of meeting death, and the martyr is the one who gives himself, expectant of reward from Allah.[4]

Even during the Age of Ignorance, Sayyidunā ʿUmar ﵁ was known for his fearlessness and masculine virtue. He was feared by the people, known for his courage and his immense physical strength. In the above narration, he clarified what true courage is. It is a willingness to give everything, even one's life, in the cause of Allah ﷻ, seeking only to participate in the cause and not to gain spoils. A sincerity of intention is required in true courage, and Sayyidunā ʿUmar ﵁ would prove his embodiment of this quality throughout his life. Sayyidunā ʿUmar ﵁, having drank from the wellspring of knowledge that was the company of the Prophet ﷺ for decades, in fact narrated a similar sentiment from the Prophet ﷺ,

الشُّهَدَاءُ ثَلَاثَةٌ رَجُلٌ مُؤْمِنٌ جَيِّدُ الْإِيمَانِ لَقِيَ الْعَدُوَّ فَصَدَقَ اللهَ حَتَّى قُتِلَ فَذَلِكَ الَّذِي يَرْفَعُ إِلَيْهِ النَّاسُ أَعْنَاقَهُمْ يَوْمَ الْقِيَامَةِ، وَرَفَعَ رَسُولُ اللهِ صَلَّى اللهُ عَلَيْهِ وَسَلَّمَ رَأْسَهُ حَتَّى وَقَعَتْ قَلَنْسُوَتُهُ أَوْ قَلَنْسُوَةُ عُمَرَ، وَرَجُلٌ مُؤْمِنٌ جَيِّدُ الْإِيمَانِ لَقِيَ الْعَدُوَّ فَكَأَنَّمَا يُضْرَبُ جِلْدُهُ بِشَوْكِ الطَّلْحِ أَتَاهُ سَهْمٌ غَرْبٌ فَقَتَلَهُ هُوَ فِي الدَّرَجَةِ الثَّانِيَةِ وَرَجُلٌ مُؤْمِنٌ جَيِّدُ الْإِيمَانِ خَلَطَ عَمَلًا صَالِحًا وَآخَرَ سَيِّئًا لَقِيَ الْعَدُوَّ فَصَدَقَ اللهَ حَتَّى قُتِلَ فَذَلِكَ فِي الدَّرَجَةِ الثَّالِثَةِ.

'Martyrs are of three kinds; the first is a believing man, strong in faith, who meets the enemy and shows sincerity to Allah until he is killed. He is the one to whom people will raise their heads on the Day of Resurrection.' At this, the Messenger of Allah raised his head until his hat or ʿUmar's hat fell off. 'The second is a believing man, strong in faith, who meets the enemy and it is as if his skin was beaten with the thorns of an acacia tree, then a stray arrow kills him – he will be in the second rank. The third is a believing man, strong in faith, who mixes good deeds with bad, who meets

4 *Muwaṭṭa' Imām Mālik*, 996.

the enemy and shows sincerity to Allah until he is killed – he will be in the third rank'.[5]

Sayyidunā 'Umar ﷺ participated in every conflict by the side of the Prophet ﷺ and did not miss a single battle.[6] There are Hadiths concerning him about every major military event that the Prophet ﷺ participated in. Sayyidunā 'Umar's moral virtue and steadfastness in the religion were displayed again and again in the fields of war, such as when he slew his maternal uncle on the Day of Badr. He would later refer to this often as a badge of honour to show his commitment to the faith.[7] Despite the softness of his heart and care for those in positions of weakness, his will was iron and his bravery in battle unmatched. Amīr al-Mu'minīn 'Umar ﷺ referred to this quality in others when he said, 'I am amazed that a man can be with his family like a child, but if he is called forth he is found to be a true man.[8]

He was nevertheless deeply concerned with upholding correct battlefield etiquette and would not allow the commission of war crimes on the field. As the Amīr al-Mu'minīn, he decreed, 'Do not steal the spoils, do not be treacherous with the enemy, do not mutilate the dead, and do not kill children. Fear Allah regarding the farmers who do not wage war against you.'[9] It was this extreme uprightness and manly virtue that made the Devil himself fear him. He could not be deterred from what was right and true, and he would willingly give everything to uphold it. The Prophet ﷺ once famously said to him,

---

5 *Musnad Imām Aḥmad*, 146.

6 Ibn al-Jawzī 'Abd al-Raḥmān ibn 'Alī, *Manāqib Amīr al-Mu'minīn 'Umar ibn al-Khaṭṭāb*, p. 89.

7 'Alī M. Ṣallābī, *'Umar ibn al-Khaṭṭāb: His Life and Times*, Riyadh, International Islamic Publishing House (1428/2007), Vol. 1, p. 94.

8 Abū Bakr Aḥmad ibn Ḥusayn ibn 'Alī ibn Mūsā al-Khusrawjirdī al-Bayhaqī, *Shu'ab al-Īmān*, 7851.

9 Abū 'Uthmān Sa'īd ibn Manṣūr, *Sunan Sa'īd ibn Manṣūr*, 2466.

وَالَّذِي نَفْسِي بِيَدِهِ، مَا لَقِيَكَ الشَّيْطَانُ قَطُّ سَالِكًا فَجًّا إِلاَّ سَلَكَ فَجًّا غَيْرَ فَجِّكَ.

By the One who holds my life in His Hand, the Shayṭān never meets you on a path except that he takes another path![10]

Keeping Good Company

عَنْ مُحَمَّدِ بْنِ شِهَابٍ، قَالَ: قَالَ عُمَرُ:

لَا تَعْتَرِضْ فِيمَا لَا يَعْنِيكَ، وَاعْتَزِلْ عَدُوَّكَ، وَاحْتَفِظْ مِنْ خَلِيلِكَ إِلَّا الْأَمِينَ، فَإِنَّ الْأَمِينَ لَا يُعَادِلُهُ شَيْءٌ، وَلَا تَصْحَبِ الْفَاجِرَ فَيُعَلِّمُكَ مِنْ فُجُورِهِ، وَلَا تَفْشِ إِلَيْهِ بِسِرِّكَ، وَاسْتَشِرْ فِي أَمْرِكَ الَّذِينَ يَخْشَوْنَ اللَّهَ.

Sayyidunā ʿUmar ibn al-Khaṭṭāb ﷺ said:

Do not get involved in that which does not concern you; stand apart from your enemy; and only take a trustworthy person as a bosom friend, for a trustworthy person has no equal. Do not keep the company of an immoral person, lest he teaches you his immorality, and do not divulge your secrets to him. Consult in your affairs with only those who greatly fear Allah.[11]

Keeping good company is the surest way to ensure that we do not fall into evil and immorality. Spending time with criminals will naturally lead us to crime, whilst spending time with the pious will naturally lead us to goodness. We should thus maintain a healthy distance from our enemies, which is not restricted to the most literal sense of the word, but also extends to those who may unwittingly be our enemies by leading us into crime and sin and becoming the ultimate means of our downfall. Sayyidunā ʿUmar ﷺ advised solitude over bad company, as Ismāʿīl ibn Umayyah ﷺ narrates that Sayyidunā ʿUmar ﷺ said,

---

10 *Ṣaḥīḥ Muslim*, 2396.

11 *Muṣannaf Ibn Abī Shaybah*, 27180.

إِنَّ فِي الْعُزْلَةِ رَاحَةً مِنْ خِلَاطِ السُّوءِ.

Indeed in solitude is ease and freedom from evil company.[12]

No company at all is superior to keeping bad company. Each of us should reflect on who we spend our time with, and whether the company we keep is good or bad. If it is beneficial, then it should be sought out; if it is ultimately detrimental, it should be cut off; and if it is not directly beneficial but not detrimental, then it should be limited. This is why Sayyidunā ʿUmar ﷺ advised his own children,

إِذَا أَصْبَحْتُمْ فَتَبَدَّدُوا، وَلاَ تَجْتَمِعُوا فِي دَارٍ وَاحِدَةٍ. فَإِنِّي أَخَافُ عَلَيْكُمْ أَنْ تَقَاطَعُوا، أَوْ يَكُونَ بَيْنَكُمْ شَرٌّ.

When you awake in the morning, separate; and do not meet together in the same house. Indeed I fear that you may split or that some evil may occur between you.[13]

Sayyidunā ʿUmar's advice to keep the company of the trustworthy is advice born from personal experience. For whose company did he benefit from the most, and who did he spend time with? Al-Ṣādiq al-Amīn ﷺ (The Honest and Trustworthy) and al-Ṣiddīq ﷺ (the Affirmer). As Sayyidunā ʿUmar ﷺ himself narrates,

كَانَ رَسُولُ اللهِ صَلَّى اللهُ عَلَيْهِ وَسَلَّمَ يَسْمُرُ عِنْدَ أَبِي بَكْرٍ رَضِيَ اللهُ عَنْهُ اللَّيْلَةَ كَذَاكَ فِي الْأَمْرِ مِنْ أَمْرِ الْمُسْلِمِينَ وَأَنَا مَعَهُ.

The Messenger of Allah stayed up late one night with Abū Bakr, discussing an issue from the issues of the Muslims, and I was with him.[14]

---

12 Wakīʿ ibn al-Jarrāḥ, *Kitāb al-Zuhd*, 250.

13 *Al-Adab al-Mufrad*, 415.

14 *Musnad Imām Aḥmad*, 228.

He was ever the third in their noble company as countless Hadiths bear testimony to, and he would constantly advise people to keep good company, as he had seen and reaped the benefits of spending his days and nights in the best of company. He loved their company deeply, and would actively seek it out whenever he could, and would advise others to do the same, saying,

إِذَا رَزَقَكَ اللَّهُ وُدَّ امْرِئٍ مُسْلِمٍ، فَتَشَبَّثْ بِهِ مَا اسْتَطَعْتَ.

When Allah bestows upon you the love of a dignified fellow Muslim, cling to it as much as you can.[15]

He would also advise to keep the company of those who were constantly repentant, as this is another sure sign of a person whose company should be sought, saying,

جَالِسُوا التَّوَّابِينَ فَإِنَّهُمْ أَرَقُّ شَيْءٍ أَفْئِدَةً.

Keep the company of the repentant ones, for they have the softest hearts.[16]

Indeed, for Sayyidunā ʿUmar ﷺ, good company was one of the few joys of life. He would state that,

لَوْلَا أَنْ أَسِيرَ فِي سَبِيلِ اللَّهِ، أَوْ أَضَعَ جَبِينِي لِلَّهِ فِي التُّرَابِ، أَوْ أُجَالِسَ قَوْمًا يَلْتَقِطُونَ طَيِّبَ الْكَلَامِ كَمَا يُلْتَقَطُ التَّمْرُ، لَأَحْبَبْتُ أَنْ أَكُونَ قَدْ لَحِقْتُ بِاللَّهِ.

Were it not for journeying in the path of Allah, placing my forehead on the dirt, and sitting in the company of those who pluck the best of speech like the plucking of dates, then I would have wished to join Allah.[17]

15 Wakīʿ ibn al-Jarrāḥ, *Kitāb al-Zuhd*, 334.
16 *Muṣannaf Ibn Abī Shaybah*, 37184.
17 *Muṣannaf Ibn Abī Shaybah*, 34466.

Through keeping good company and frequenting good places, people protect their outward image. This too is essential for a Muslim, as carelessness in this regard will lead others to see us as bad company and cause the righteous to shun us. During his time as the Commander of the Faithful, Sayyidunā ʿUmar ibn al-Khaṭṭāb ﷺ stated,

إِنَّ أُنَاسًا كَانُوا يُؤْخَذُونَ بِالْوَحْيِ فِي عَهْدِ رَسُولِ اللَّهِ ﷺ، وَإِنَّ الْوَحْيَ قَدِ انْقَطَعَ، وَإِنَّمَا نَأْخُذُكُمُ الْآنَ بِمَا ظَهَرَ لَنَا مِنْ أَعْمَالِكُمْ. فَمَنْ أَظْهَرَ لَنَا خَيْرًا أَمِنَّاهُ وَقَرَّبْنَاهُ، وَلَيْسَ إِلَيْنَا مِنْ سَرِيرَتِهِ شَيْءٌ، اَللَّهُ يُحَاسِبُهُ فِي سَرِيرَتِهِ. وَمَنْ أَظْهَرَ لَنَا سُوءًا لَمْ نَأْمَنْهُ وَلَمْ نُصَدِّقْهُ، وَإِنْ قَالَ إِنَّ سَرِيرَتَهُ حَسَنَةٌ.

In the time of Allah's Messenger, people were judged by Revelation. Now that Revelation has ceased, we judge by what is apparent of your outward actions. Whoever shows us good, we shall trust and favour. It is not for us to take account of what one does in secret; Allah will judge him for that. And whosoever presents to us an evil deed, we shall neither trust nor believe him, even if he claims that his intentions were good.[18]

In another statement, he said,

مَنْ عَرَّضَ نَفْسَهُ لِلتُّهْمَةِ فَلَا يَلُومَنَّ مَنْ أَسَاءَ بِهِ الظَّنَّ.

He who puts himself in a compromising position should not blame those who think ill of him.[19]

Despite this, he would nevertheless warn people to temper their feelings towards others, to neither become infatuated and therefore misguided, nor become spiteful due to their poor company. Aslam ﷺ stated that Sayyidunā ʿUmar ﷺ once said to him,

18 *Ṣaḥīḥ al-Bukhārī*, 2641.

19 Abū Dāwūd al-Sijistānī, *Kitāb al-Zuhd*, 83.

.لاَ يَكُنْ حُبُّكَ كَلَفًا، وَلاَ بُغْضُكَ تَلَفًا

Do not let your love become infatuation, nor your anger become destruction.

When Aslam ﷺ asked him to elaborate, he said,

.إِذَا أَحْبَبْتَ كَلِفْتَ كَلَفَ الصَّبِيِّ، وَإِذَا أَبْغَضْتَ أَحْبَبْتَ لِصَاحِبِكَ التَّلَف

When you love, you are infatuated like a child. When you hate, you desire destruction for your companion.[20]

Noble Character

:قَالَ عُمَرُ

.حَسَبُ الرَّجُلِ دِينُهُ، وَمُرُوءَتُهُ خُلُقُهُ، وَأَصْلُهُ عَقْلُهُ

Sayyidunā ʿUmar ibn al-Khaṭṭāb ﷺ said:

A man's honour is in his religion, his chivalry is his good character, and his foundation is his intellect.[21]

Keeping the company of the noble and good is only possible when one is of noble character himself. The good flock to the good, just as the sinful flock to the evil. One is only as good as One's character, and mere possession of strength and courage alone cannot label one chivalrous. Likewise, nobility of blood alone does not make someone noble; rather it is nobility of thought and deed that makes a person noble.

---

20 *Al-Adab Al-Mufrad*, 1322.

21 *Muṣannaf Ibn Abī Shaybah*, 26975.

Sayyidunā ʿUmar ibn al-Khaṭṭāb ﷺ was a jewel of nobility and from whichever aspect one looked at him, they would find in him goodness of character, nobility of deeds, high thought, and deep concern for others. The Prophet of Allah ﷺ explained this far more clearly when he stated,

.النَّاسُ مَعَادِنُ كَمَعَادِنِ الْفِضَّةِ وَالذَّهَبِ، خِيَارُهُمْ فِي الْجَاهِلِيَّةِ خِيَارُهُمْ فِي الإِسْلاَمِ

People are like mines of gold and silver; those who were excellent in the Age of Ignorance are excellent in Islam.[22]

This was ʿUmar ﷺ, an ambassador for the Quraysh in the Age of Ignorance and the Commander of the Faithful in the Age of Islam.

At another time, Sayyidunā ʿUmar ibn al-Khaṭṭāb ﷺ stated,

إِنْ كَانَ لَكَ دِينٌ فَإِنَّ لَكَ حَسَبًا، وَإِنْ كَانَ لَكَ عَقْلٌ فَإِنَّ لَكَ أَصْلًا، وَإِنْ كَانَ لَكَ خُلُقٌ فَلَكَ مُرُوءَةٌ، وَإِلَّا فَأَنْتَ شَرٌّ مِنْ حِمَارٍ.

If you have religion, then you have nobility; if you have intelligence, then you have a foundation; and if you have good character, then you have chivalry. Or else, you are worse than a donkey.[23]

A donkey lacks nobility, stock, and chivalry, but the donkey has not been given the tools and faculty of a human being, and thus, a human being who lacks these qualities (religion, sound mind, and good character) must be considered worse.

Good character is not only inherently beneficial to the possessor, but it is also a means of attaining rewards and benefits from Allah ﷻ. Sayyidunā ʿUmar ibn al-Khaṭṭāb ﷺ states,

22 *Ṣaḥīḥ Muslim*, 2638.

23 Ibn ʿAbd Rabbih al-Andalūsī, *al-ʿIqd al-Farīd*, Vol. 2, p. 110.

مَنْ أُعْطِيَ الدُّعَاءَ لَمْ يُحْرَمِ الإِجَابَةَ، وَمَنْ أُعْطِيَ الشُّكْرَ لَمْ يُحْرَمِ الزِّيَادَةَ، وَمَنْ أُعْطِيَ الاسْتِغْفَارَ لَمْ يُمْنَعَ الْقَبُولَ.

Whoever is granted the grace to supplicate will not be deprived of the answer, whoever is granted gratefulness will not be denied plentifulness, and whoever is granted atonement will not be withheld of absolution.[24]

The Divine Words of Allah ﷻ attest to this, as He has stated in His Qur'an,

ٱدْعُونِىٓ أَسْتَجِبْ لَكُمْ

Call upon me, I will respond to you.[25]

لَئِن شَكَرْتُمْ لَأَزِيدَنَّكُمْ

If you are grateful, I will certainly give you more.[26]

ٱسْتَغْفِرُوا۟ رَبَّكُمْ إِنَّهُۥ كَانَ غَفَّارًا

Seek your Lord's forgiveness, for He is truly Most Forgiving.[27]

It should be borne in mind that certain good qualities are only considered good in the correct situations; if relied upon at the wrong time, they may lead to loss instead of gain. Sayyidunā ʿUmar ؓ has given us one such example in the following saying,

التُّؤَدَةُ فِي كُلِّ شَيْءٍ خَيْرٌ، إِلَّا مَا كَانَ فِي أَمْرِ الْآخِرَةِ.

---

24 Aḥmad ibn Yaḥyā ibn Jābir al-Balādhurī, *Ansāb al-Ashrāf*, Vol. 10, p. 303.

25 *Al-Ghāfir*, 60.

26 *Ibrāhīm*, 7.

27 *Al-Nūḥ*, 10.

Deliberation is good in all matters except when it comes to the Hereafter.²⁸

When doing good works, one should hasten toward what is right and good. There should be no hesitation in the giving of alms, in praying *ṣalāh*, in the call for the defence of the weak, and in standing against oppression. In other situations, such as when confronted with something that enrages us, or when making financial investments, etc., we should deliberate and be certain that the intended action is the correct response. Sayyidunā 'Umar ؓ also said,

أَجْوَدُ النَّاسِ مَنْ جَادَ عَلَى مَنْ لَا يَرْجُو ثَوَابَهُ، وَإِنَّ أَحْلَمَ النَّاسِ مَنْ عَفَا بَعْدَ الْقُدْرَةِ، وَإِنَّ أَبْخَلَ النَّاسِ الَّذِي يَبْخَلُ بِالسَّلَامِ، وَإِنَّ أَعْجَزَ النَّاسِ الَّذِي يَعْجِزُ فِي دُعَاءِ اللهِ.

The most open-handed person is the one who gives to those whose reward he does not expect, the most clement is he who forgives when he can retaliate, the most miserly is the one who withholds the greeting of peace, and the most incapable is the one who cannot supplicate to Allah.²⁹

As an example of the first of the qualities listed by Sayyidunā 'Umar ؓ, giving without expectation of reward, it would be remiss of us not to refer back the first Caliph of Islam, Sayyidunā Abū Bakr al-Ṣiddīq ؓ, whom Allah ﷻ Himself described thus,

وَسَيُجَنَّبُهَا ٱلْأَتْقَى ١٧ ٱلَّذِى يُؤْتِى مَالَهُۥ يَتَزَكَّىٰ ١٨ وَمَا لِأَحَدٍ عِندَهُۥ مِن نِّعْمَةٍ تُجْزَىٰٓ ١٩ إِلَّا ٱبْتِغَآءَ وَجْهِ رَبِّهِ ٱلْأَعْلَىٰ ٢٠ وَلَسَوْفَ يَرْضَىٰ ٢١

*But the righteous will be spared from it (the Raging Fire) – those who donate of their wealth only to purify themselves, not in return for someone's favours, but seeking the pleasure of their Lord, the Most High. They will certainly be pleased.*³⁰

---

28 *Muṣannaf Ibn Abī Shaybah*, 35619.
29 *Muṣannaf Ibn Abī Shaybah* 38337.
30 *Al-Layl*, 17-21.

As mentioned, these verses were revealed about Sayyidunā Abū Bakr رضي الله عنه.[31] The key point for the current discussion, however, lies in verses 18 and 19, in which Sayyidunā Abū Bakr رضي الله عنه is described as giving his wealth away 'only to purify' himself and 'not in return for someone's favours'.[32] Such qualities are the peak of a noble character, for one cannot challenge such a man's intentions for giving, nor can those intentions be called into question. His outward and his inward selves are proven by Allah ﷻ to be one and the same, and this is why Sayyidunā Abū Bakr رضي الله عنه is the greatest man in the history of the world outside of the Prophets.[33]

Forgiveness at the time of retaliation when the means are present and one has the power to exact revenge is also a sign of greatness. When Waḥshī ibn Ḥarb رضي الله عنه, the slayer of Sayyidunā Ḥamzah ibn ʿAbd al-Muṭṭalib رضي الله عنه, went to the Prophet ﷺ following the Victory of Mecca, the following exchange took place, as narrated by Waḥshī ibn Ḥarb رضي الله عنه himself,

فَلَمَّا رَآنِي، قَالَ: آنْتَ وَحْشِيٌّ؟ قُلْتُ: نَعَمْ. قَالَ: أَنْتَ قَتَلْتَ حَمْزَةَ؟ قُلْتُ: قَدْ كَانَ مِنَ الأَمْرِ مَا بَلَغَكَ. قَالَ: فَهَلْ تَسْتَطِيعُ أَنْ تُغَيِّبَ وَجْهَكَ عَنِّي؟ فَخَرَجْتُ.

When he saw me, he said, "Are you Waḥshī?" I said, "Yes." He said, "Was it you who killed Ḥamzah?" I replied, "What happened is what has reached you." He said, "Can you hide your face from me?" And so I left.[34]

At this point, the entire Arabian Peninsula was under the control of the Prophet ﷺ and he had the power to do as he wished to whomever he wished. The killer of his dear and beloved uncle, his uncle who had fought so valiantly for the cause of Islam, who had protected the Prophet ﷺ so fiercely, was standing before him. Had he wished, he could have slain him in the same manner and none could oppose him in doing so. Instead, the Prophet ﷺ

31 Shāh ʿAbd al-ʿAzīz Muḥaddith Dehlawī, *Tafsīr ʿAzīzī: Pārah ʿAmma*, p.487.

32 *Al-Layl*, 18-19.

33 Shāh ʿAbd al-ʿAzīz Muḥaddith Dehlawī, *Tafsīr ʿAzīzī: Pārah ʿAmma*, p.488.

34 *Ṣaḥīḥ al-Bukhārī*, 4072.

forgave him and asked Waḥshī ﵁ to remove himself from his sight, due to the pain that the constant reminder of his uncle's death caused. Can there be a greater example of forgiveness in all the history of the world? It would later be Waḥshī ibn Ḥarb ﵁ who slew Musaylimah the Liar, a false prophet who had risen following the passing away of the Prophet of Allah ﷺ.

Sayyidunā ʿUmar ﵁ warned against low qualities and bad character traits in his letter to Abū Mūsā al-Ashʿarī ﵁, writing,

إِنَّ الْحِكْمَةَ لَيْسَتْ عَنْ كِبَرِ السِّنِّ، وَلَكِنَّهُ عَطَاءُ اللَّهِ يُعْطِيهِ مَنْ يَشَاءُ. فَإِيَّاكَ وَدَنَاءَةَ الْأُمُورِ وَمِرَاقَ الْأَخْلَاقِ.

Wisdom does not come with old age, rather it is a gift that Allah bestows on whoever He wills. So beware of vileness and low character.[35]

Asceticism and *Zuhd*

قَالَ عُمَرُ بْنُ الْخَطَّابِ رَضِيَ اللَّهُ عَنْهُ:

وَاللَّهِ مَا الدُّنْيَا فِي الْآخِرَةِ إِلَّا كَنَفْجَةِ أَرْنَبٍ.

Sayyidunā ʿUmar ibn al-Khaṭṭāb ﵁ said

By Allah, compared to the Hereafter, this world is nothing but a rabbit's hop.[36]

Such is the brevity of our time in this transitory world – a duration as short as a rabbit's hop, encompassing the time it takes for the tiny animal to make the jump. Sayyidunā ʿUmar ibn al-Khaṭṭāb ﵁ understood this point completely and had internalised the thought. His asceticism was complete, and

35 Ibn Abī al-Dunyā, *Al-Ishrāf fī Manāzil al-Ashrāf*, 236.

36 Ibn Abī al-Dunyā, *Kitāb al-Zuhd*, 13.

he took account of every second he spent in this world, scrutinising it for a hint of wastefulness. He understood that though our time in this world is short, the judgement at the end of it will be long. Every moment given to us is a means for our success or failure. He would advise the Muslims,

اتَّزِرُوا وَارْتَدُوا وَانْتَعِلُوا وَأَلْقُوا الْخِفَافَ وَالسَّرَاوِيلَاتِ وَأَلْقُوا الرُّكُبَ وَانْزُوا نَزْوًا، وَعَلَيْكُمْ بِالْمَعَدِّيَّةِ وَارْمُوا الْأَغْرَاضَ وَذَرُوا التَّنَعُّمَ وَزِيَّ الْعَجَمِ، وَإِيَّاكُمْ وَالْحَرِيرَ فَإِنَّ رَسُولَ اللَّهِ صَلَّى اللَّهُ عَلَيْهِ وَسَلَّمَ قَدْ نَهَى عَنْهُ، وَقَالَ لَا تَلْبَسُوا مِنْ الْحَرِيرِ إِلَّا مَا كَانَ هَكَذَا، وَأَشَارَ رَسُولُ اللَّهِ صَلَّى اللَّهُ عَلَيْهِ وَسَلَّمَ بِإِصْبَعَيْهِ.

Wear izārs,[37] cloaks, and shoes, but not boots and trousers, and throw away your stirrups and mount your steeds. Wear rough clothes and practise archery; keep away from luxury and the dress of the non-Arabs. Beware of silk, for the Messenger of Allah forbade it and said, "Do not wear silk except this much", and the Messenger of Allah gestured with two fingers.[38]

This was the advice he would give to his governors and generals. Abū ʿUthmān ﷺ narrated a similar Hadith in which he stated that a letter came to the Muslim troops in Azerbaijan in which the following words were written:

يَا عُتْبَةَ بْنَ فَرْقَدٍ وَإِيَّاكُمْ وَالتَّنَعُّمَ وَزِيَّ أَهْلِ الشِّرْكِ وَلَبُوسَ الْحَرِيرِ، فَإِنَّ رَسُولَ اللَّهِ صَلَّى اللَّهُ عَلَيْهِ وَسَلَّمَ نَهَانَا عَنْ لَبُوسِ الْحَرِيرِ، وَقَالَ إِلَّا هَكَذَا، وَرَفَعَ لَنَا رَسُولُ اللَّهِ صَلَّى اللَّهُ عَلَيْهِ وَسَلَّمَ إِصْبَعَيْهِ.

O ʿUtbah ibn Farqad, beware of luxury, the garb of the polytheists (mushrikīn), and the wearing of silk, for the Messenger of Allah forbade us from wearing silk and said, "Except this much", and the Messenger of Allah held up two fingers to us.[39]

---

37 An *izār* is a voluminous outer garment that covers the whole body.

38 *Musnad Imām Aḥmad*, 301; *Ṣaḥīḥ al-Bukhārī*, 5829; *Ṣaḥīḥ Muslim*, 2069.

39 *Musnad Imām Aḥmad*, 92.

ʿAbdullāh ibn al-Zubayr ﵁ narrated,

سَمِعَتْ عُمَرَ بْنَ الْخَطَّابِ، رَضِيَ اللَّهُ عَنْهُ يَقُولُ فِي خُطْبَتِهِ إِنَّهُ سَمِعَ مِنْ رَسُولِ اللَّهِ صَلَّى اللَّهُ عَلَيْهِ وَسَلَّمَ يَقُولُ:

مَنْ يَلْبَسِ الْحَرِيرَ فِي الدُّنْيَا فَلَا يُكْسَاهُ فِي الْآخِرَةِ.

I heard Sayyidunā ʿUmar ibn al-Khaṭṭāb say in his sermon that he heard the Messenger of Allah say, "Whoever wears silk in this world will not be clothed with it in the Hereafter."[40]

He thus advocated for an intentionally hard life for the Muslims and warned against becoming used to the soft luxuries of the world, despite the many successes that the Muslims were accomplishing during his reign, such as the conquests of Persia and the Levant. He himself showed complete adherence to this principle, to the point that even when he arrived in the Levant as a victorious conqueror, he did so without a hint of pride or pomp. Ṭāriq ibn Shihāb ﵁ narrates,

لَمَّا قَدِمَ عُمَرُ الشَّامَ أَتَتْهُ الْجُنُودُ وَعَلَيْهِ إِزَارٌ وَخُفَّانِ وَعِمَامَةٌ، وَأَخَذَ بِرَأْسِ بَعِيرِهِ يَخُوضُ الْمَاءَ، فَقَالُوا لَهُ: يَا أَمِيرَ الْمُؤْمِنِينَ، تَلَقَّاكَ الْجُنُودُ وَبَطَارِقَةُ الشَّامِ وَأَنْتَ عَلَى هَذَا الْحَالِ؟ قَالَ: فَقَالَ عُمَرُ:

إِنَّا قَوْمٌ أَعَزَّنَا اللَّهُ بِالإِسْلَامِ، فَلَنْ نَلْتَمِسَ الْعِزَّ بِغَيْرِهِ.

When Sayyidunā ʿUmar came to the Levant, the Muslim army came out to meet him and found him wearing a wraparound garment, leather socks, and a turban, holding his camel's head as it was treading water. They said, "O Amīr al Mu'minīn, will you meet the army and patriarchs of the Levant in this state?" Sayyidunā ʿUmar replied, "Indeed, we are a people whom

---

40 *Musnad Imām Aḥmad*, 123.

Allah honoured Islam, and we will not seek honour through anything other than it."[41]

In another narration during that time, Qays ﷺ narrates,

لَمَّا قَدِمَ عُمَرُ الشَّامَ اسْتَقْبَلَهُ النَّاسُ وَهُوَ عَلَى بَعِيرِهِ فَقَالُوا: يَا أَمِيرَ الْمُؤْمِنِينَ، لَوْ رَكِبْتَ بِرْذَوْنًا يَلْقَاكَ عُظَمَاءُ النَّاسِ وَوُجُوهُهُمْ، فَقَالَ عُمَرُ:

لَا أَرَاكُمْ هَاهُنَا، إِنَّمَا الْأَمْرُ مِنْ هَاهُنَا وَأَشَارَ بِيَدِهِ إِلَى السَّمَاءِ.

When Sayyidunā ʿUmar came to the Levant, he was welcomed by the people while he was riding a camel. They beseeched, "Amīr al-Mu'minīn, if only you would ride upon a horse, as you are going to meet the leaders of the people and their chiefs?" He said, "I do not look to you people here. Rather the matter is from there", and he gestured with his hand to the heavens.[42]

Sayyidunā ʿUmar ibn al-Khaṭṭāb ﷺ could only behave in such a way, because he had spent a lifetime in close proximity with the beloved Prophet of Allah ﷺ and had witnessed him live through hardest years, enduring oppression and boycott, siege and hunger. Nuʿmān ibn Bashir ﷺ once delivered a sermon in which he stated,

ذَكَرَ عُمَرُ رَضِيَ اللَّهُ عَنْهُ مَا أَصَابَ النَّاسُ مِنَ الدُّنْيَا فَقَالَ لَقَدْ رَأَيْتُ رَسُولَ اللَّهِ صَلَّى اللَّهُ عَلَيْهِ وَسَلَّمَ يَظَلُّ الْيَوْمَ يَلْتَوِي مَا يَجِدُ دَقَلًا يَمْلَأُ بِهِ بَطْنَهُ.

Sayyidunā ʿUmar mentioned what the people had acquired of the world and said, "I saw the Messenger of Allah spend the day curled up in hunger, unable to find even the worst dates with which to fill his stomach."[43]

41 *Muṣannaf Ibn Abī Shaybah*, 36114.

42 *Muṣannaf Ibn Abī Shaybah*, 36111.

43 *Musnad Imām Aḥmad*, 353.

What he witnessed clearly affected him, as he continued to strive throughout his life to achieve the impossible levels of asceticism exhibited by his Beloved ﷺ. Abū Sinān al-Du'alī ؓ stated that he once entered upon Sayyidunā 'Umar ibn al-Khaṭṭāb ؓ, who was surrounded by a group of the earliest Muhājirīn. Sayyidunā 'Umar ؓ sent for a basket that had been brought to him from Iraq. Within it there was a ring. One of Sayyidunā 'Umar's ؓ sons took the ring and put it in his mouth. Sayyidunā 'Umar ؓ took it from him and then wept. The people sitting with him asked, "Why do you weep when Allah has granted you victory, caused you to prevail over your enemies, and granted you joy? Sayyidunā 'Umar ؓ then explained,

إِنِّي سَمِعْتُ رَسُولَ اللَّهِ صَلَّى اللَّهُ عَلَيْهِ وَسَلَّمَ يَقُولُ لَا تُفْتَحُ الدُّنْيَا عَلَى أَحَدٍ إِلَّا أَلْقَى اللَّهُ عَزَّ وَجَلَّ بَيْنَهُمْ الْعَدَاوَةَ وَالْبَغْضَاءَ إِلَى يَوْمِ الْقِيَامَةِ وَأَنَا أُشْفِقُ مِنْ ذَلِكَ.

I heard the Messenger of Allah say, "Accumulation of worldly luxuries does not become available to a people except that Allah stirs up among them enmity and hatred until the Day of Resurrection, and I am greatly concerned by this."[44]

Despite all of this, and his sincere advice to the Muslims to choose hardship over ease, he did not expect or command others to live their life to the standards he held himself to. He was quoted to have said,

إِذَا أَوْسَعَ اللَّهُ عَلَيْكُمْ فَأَوْسِعُوا عَلَى أَنْفُسِكُمْ جَمَعَ رَجُلٌ عَلَيْهِ ثِيَابَهُ.

When Allah has been generous to you, be generous to yourselves. Let a man wear a combination of his garments.[45]

In fact, he would teach that it was okay for others to enjoy what they have been blessed with in this world, though he would stress the caveat that one

44 *Musnad Imām Aḥmad*, 93.

45 *Muwaṭṭa' Imām Mālik*, 1656.

does not allow love for the world to enter his heart at the expense of the Hereafter. He once wrote,

إِنَّ الدُّنْيَا خَضْرَةٌ حُلْوَةٌ، فَمَنْ أَخَذَهَا بِحَقِّهَا كَانَ قَمِنًا أَنْ يُبَارِكَ لَهُ فِيهَا، وَمَنْ أَخَذَهَا بِغَيْرِ ذَلِكَ كَانَ كَالْآكِلِ الَّذِي لَا يَشْبَعُ.

The world is verdant and sweet. Whoever takes it while observing its rights shall be blessed in it, and whoever takes from it without doing so will be like one who eats without ever being satiated.[46]

On another occasion, he is reported to have said,

لَا تَحْزَنْ أَنْ يُعَجَّلَ لَكَ كَثِيرٌ مِمَّا تُحِبُّ مِنْ أَمْرِ دُنْيَاكَ إِذَا كُنْتَ ذَا رَغْبَةٍ فِي أَمْرِ آخِرَتِكَ.

Do not be saddened by the hastening to you of the affairs you wish for in this world, so long as you long for the rewards of the Hereafter.[47]

The constant awareness of the Hereafter and its superiority over this worldly life is an essential part of protecting oneself from the trap of falling in love with the false beauty of this world. A Muslim should never be in a situation where he forgets his ultimate duty of pleasing Allah ﷻ and the ultimate reward (or punishment) that awaits humanity in the Hereafter. One should therefore remain in a state of complete humility and never think too highly of himself. ʿUbaydullāh ibn ʿAdiyy ibn al-Khiyār ؓ reported that Sayyidunā ʿUmar ibn al-Khaṭṭāb ؓ said,

إِنَّ الْعَبْدَ إِذَا تَوَاضَعَ لِلَّهِ رَفَعَ اللَّهُ حِكْمَتَهُ، وَقَالَ: انْتَعِشْ نَعَشَكَ اللَّهُ، فَهُوَ فِي نَفْسِهِ صَغِيرٌ وَفِي أَنْفُسِ النَّاسِ كَبِيرٌ، وَإِنَّ الْعَبْدَ إِذَا تَعَظَّمَ وَعَدَا طَوْرَهُ وَهَصَّهُ اللَّهُ إِلَى الْأَرْضِ وَقَالَ: اخْسَأْ أَخْسَأَكَ اللَّهُ، فَهُوَ فِي نَفْسِهِ كَبِيرٌ، وَفِي أَنْفُسِ النَّاسِ صَغِيرٌ، حَتَّى لَهُوَ أَحْقَرُ عِنْدَهُ مِنْ خِنْزِيرٍ.

46 *Muṣannaf Ibn Abī Shaybah*, 37164.

47 Ibn Abī al-Dunyā, *Kitāb al-Zuhd*, 174.

When the servant humbles himself before Allah, He raises him in wisdom and says, "Rise, may Allah raise you!" And so, though he feels small within himself, in the hearts of the people he is great. When the servant becomes haughty and exceeds his limits, Allah casts him to the Earth and says, "Be disgraced, may Allah disgrace you!" And so, though he feels great within himself, in the hearts of the people he is small until he is lower in His eyes than a pig.[48]

Allah ﷻ rewards the humble one with the respect of the people in this world and His blessings in the Hereafter. The haughty one, however, is treated with disdain by his peers in this world and will be questioned on his behaviour in the Hereafter. Allah ﷻ says in the Qur'an,

فَلَا تُزَكُّوٓاْ أَنفُسَكُمْۖ هُوَ أَعْلَمُ بِمَنِ ٱتَّقَىٰٓ

So do not falsely elevate yourselves. He knows best who is truly righteous.[49]

It is for this reason that Sayyidunā ʿUmar ibn al-Khaṭṭāb رضي الله عنه advised Abū Mūsā al-Ashʿarī رضي الله عنه in a letter with the following words,

إِنَّكَ لَنْ تَنَالَ الْآخِرَةَ بِشَيْءٍ أَفْضَلَ مِنَ الزُّهْدِ فِي الدُّنْيَا

You will not find the Hereafter with anything better than detachment from the world.[50]

However, one should be mindful that detachment from this world itself can become a source of pride, for such is the weakness of human beings and the trickery of Shayṭān. One should therefore follow the limits that the Prophet ﷺ himself advised, detaching one's heart from the world, but

48 *Muṣannaf Ibn Abī Shaybah*, 37180.

49 *Al-Najm*, 32.

50 *Muṣannaf Ibn Abī Shaybah*, 37189.

accepting the gifts of Allah ﷻ when they come. It was narrated from ʿAbdullāh ibn al-Saʿdī ﵁ that he once came to Sayyidunā ʿUmar ibn al-Khaṭṭāb ﵁ during his caliphate and the following exchange took place:

قَالَ لَهُ عُمَرُ: أَلَمْ أُحَدَّثْ أَنَّكَ تَلِي مِنْ أَعْمَالِ النَّاسِ أَعْمَالًا فَإِذَا أُعْطِيتَ الْعُمَالَةَ كَرِهْتَهَا؟ قَالَ فَقُلْتُ: بَلَى. فَقَالَ عُمَرُ رَضِيَ اللَّهُ عَنْهُ: فَمَا تُرِيدُ إِلَى ذَلِكَ؟ قَالَ قُلْتُ: إِنَّ لِي أَفْرَاسًا وَأَعْبُدًا، وَأَنَا بِخَيْرٍ وَأُرِيدُ أَنْ تَكُونَ عُمَالَتِي صَدَقَةً عَلَى الْمُسْلِمِينَ. فَقَالَ عُمَرُ رَضِيَ اللَّهُ عَنْهُ: فَلَا تَفْعَلْ فَإِنِّي قَدْ كُنْتُ أَرَدْتُ الَّذِي أَرَدْتَ، فَكَانَ النَّبِيُّ صَلَّى اللَّهُ عَلَيْهِ وَسَلَّمَ يُعْطِينِي الْعَطَاءَ فَأَقُولُ أَعْطِهِ أَفْقَرَ إِلَيْهِ مِنِّي حَتَّى أَعْطَانِي مَرَّةً مَالًا فَقُلْتُ أَعْطِهِ أَفْقَرَ إِلَيْهِ مِنِّي، قَالَ فَقَالَ لَهُ النَّبِيُّ صَلَّى اللَّهُ عَلَيْهِ وَسَلَّمَ: خُذْهُ فَتَمَوَّلْهُ وَتَصَدَّقْ بِهِ، فَمَا جَاءَكَ مِنْ هَذَا الْمَالِ وَأَنْتَ غَيْرُ مُشْرِفٍ وَلَا سَائِلٍ فَخُذْهُ وَمَا لَا فَلَا تُتْبِعْهُ نَفْسَكَ.

Sayyidunā ʿUmar said to him, "Have I not been told that you do work for people, but then when you are given your wages you do not accept them?"

I said, "Indeed."

Sayyidunā ʿUmar asked, "Why do you do that?"

I said, "I have horses and slaves, and I am well. I want my work to be an act of charity towards the Muslims."

Sayyidunā ʿUmar said, "Do not do that, for I once wished to do the same as you now wish to do. The Prophet ﷺ would give me some payment and I would say, 'Give it to one who is more in need of it than I.' One day he gave me something and I said, 'Give it to one who is more in need of it than I.' The Prophet ﷺ said, 'Take it, keep it, and give it in charity. Whatever of this worldly wealth comes to you, when you are neither hoping for it nor asking for it, accept it; but, if it does not come to you, do not hope for it.'"[51]

51 *Musnad Imām Aḥmad*, 100.

Thus, one should not be so inclined towards asceticism that they deny themselves an opportunity to do further good in the form of acting upon the advice of the Prophet ﷺ by actively giving in charity themselves, if that is what they wish to do with their wealth. By extension, one should avoid anything that plants the seeds of pride in their heart, for therein lies the gravest danger for any practising, sincere Muslim. Ibrāhīm al-Taymī ﵀ has narrated from his father, who stated,

كُنَّا قُعُودًا عِنْدَ عُمَرَ بْنِ الْخَطَّابِ، فَدَخَلَ عَلَيْهِ رَجُلٌ فَسَلَّمَ عَلَيْهِ، فَأَثْنَى عَلَيْهِ رَجُلٌ مِنَ الْقَوْمِ فِي وَجْهِهِ، فَقَالَ عُمَرُ: عَقَرْتَ الرَّجُلَ عَقَرَكَ اللهُ، تُثْنِي عَلَيْهِ فِي وَجْهِهِ فِي دِينِهِ.

We were sitting in the company of Sayyidunā ʿUmar when a man entered, presented his greetings, and then praised a man from the tribe to his face. Sayyidunā ʿUmar said, "You have destroyed the man, may Allah destroy you, for you have praised him to his face about his religion."[52]

Such an act may on the surface seem good and fine, yet it can destroy the sincerity within the God-fearing person's heart, just as the smallest of leaks can destroy the sturdiest house.

On Speech

عَنْ حُمَيْدٍ، أَنَّهُ سَمِعَ أَنَسًا يَقُولُ: خَطَبَ رَجُلٌ عِنْدَ عُمَرَ فَأَكْثَرَ الْكَلَامَ، فَقَالَ عُمَرُ:

إِنَّ كَثْرَةَ الْكَلَامِ فِي الْخُطَبِ مِنْ شَقَاشِقِ الشَّيْطَانِ.

Anas ﵁ said, "A man gave a speech in the presence of ʿUmar and spoke at length. ʿUmar said, 'Superfluous words in oration are from the tricks of Shayṭān.'"[53]

52 *Muṣannaf Ibn Abī Shaybah*, 27954.

53 *Al-Adab al-Mufrad*, 876.

The tongue is a dangerous tool that, much like a double-edged sword, can be turned on the speaker should they become careless in its use. Sayyidunā ʿUmar ﷺ succinctly describes the problem and the solution in eight words, demonstrating a perfect example of how good speech should be.

One should limit their speech to only that which is beneficial, such that: (1) if the words are false, they are not said; (2) if the subject matter is not beneficial, it is avoided; and (3) if the words do not add benefit, they are omitted.

It is common knowledge that it is better to not speak at all than say something that causes harm, but the wise one considers their words for the benefit they can provide, and thus useless speech is also cancelled out. Any speech that contains a morsel of falsehood within it has been corrupted and should be left unsaid. Sayyidunā ʿUmar ﷺ advised,

لَيْسَ فِي مَا دُونَ الصِّدْقِ مِنَ الْحَدِيثِ خَيْرٌ.

There is no good in anything less than truthful speech.[54]

Even if every word said is truthful, it should be checked again to see if it is beneficial before being spoken. A person may believe that they speak only the truth and still be considered by their peers to be a liar, as not everything one reads, sees, or hears is necessarily true. Sayyidunā ʿUmar ﷺ said,

حَسْبُ امْرِئٍ مِنَ الْكَذِبِ أَنْ يُحَدِّثَ بِكُلِّ مَا سَمِعَ.

A man is reckoned a liar when he voices all he hears.[55]

This concept of checking one's speech for truth before speaking should also be utilised when joking and jesting with one's friends and family. Even in

---

54 Abū Dāwūd, *Kitāb al-Zuhd*, 48.

55 *Al-Adab Al-Mufrad*, 884.

mirth, we must be careful not to cut ourselves on the sharpness of our lying tongues. Sayyidunā 'Umar ؓ advised,

$$\text{لَا تَبْلُغُ حَقِيقَةَ الْإِيمَانِ حَتَّى تَدَعَ الْكِذْبَ فِي الْمِزَاحِ.}$$

You will not achieve true faith until you refrain from lying in jest.[56]

With all this said, the bladed tongue still has a front edge, which can, and indeed *should*, be used when the situation is called for. Zayd ibn Ṣawḥān ؓ states that,

$$\text{قَالَ عُمَرُ: مَا يَمْنَعُكُمْ إِذَا رَأَيْتُمُ الرَّجُلَ يَخْرِقُ أَعْرَاضَ النَّاسِ لَا تُغيرُوا عَلَيْهِ؟ قَالُوا: نَتَّقِي لِسَانَهُ، قَالَ: ذَاكَ أَدْنَى أَنْ تَكُونُوا شُهَدَاءَ}$$

Sayyidunā 'Umar said, "What prevents you from stopping a man when you witness him violating the honour of others?" The people said, "We fear his tongue will be turned on us." He replied, "It is the least you can do, for you are witnesses."[57]

When people are being oppressed, by words or by actions, it is incumbent upon a Muslim to interject and oppose the oppressor. One cannot stand silently whilst another is wrongfully mocked and ridiculed, or when falsehood is being spread. In such situations, a Muslim must stand and be heard. The famous Hadith of the Prophet ﷺ reminds us how important this is:

$$\text{مَنْ رَأَى مِنْكُمْ مُنْكَرًا فَلْيُغَيِّرْهُ بِيَدِهِ فَإِنْ لَمْ يَسْتَطِعْ فَبِلِسَانِهِ فَإِنْ لَمْ يَسْتَطِعْ فَبِقَلْبِهِ وَذَلِكَ أَضْعَفُ الْإِيمَانِ.}$$

Whoever amongst you sees an evil should change it with his hand, and if he lacks the strength then he should do so with his tongue, and if he [still]

---

56   *Muṣannaf Ibn Abī Shaybah*, 27263.
57   *Muṣannaf Ibn Abī Shaybah*, 27188.

lacks the strength then he should [abhor it] with his heart,
and that is the weakest of faith.[58]

Therefore, in all situations where physical intervention is either disproportionate, likely to cause harm, or not possible because of one's weakness due to strength, skill, or lack of numbers, it is necessary to weaponise one's tongue against tyrants and wrongdoers. Silent rage in such situations is the weakest level of faith.

Thereafter, if our words are to be used as weapons to oppose evil, then we should train both our tongues and our minds to utilise our chosen language with great skill and laser precision. Every word should be correct, every turn of phrase should be appropriate, and every analogy or example given is exact and to the point. ʿAbd al-Raḥmān ibn ʿAjlān ﷺ narrates,

مَرَّ عُمَرُ بْنُ الْخَطَّابِ رَضِيَ اللَّهُ عَنْهُ بِرَجُلَيْنِ يَرْمِيَانِ، فَقَالَ أَحَدُهُمَا لِلْآخَرِ: أَسَبْتَ، فَقَالَ عُمَرُ: سُوءُ اللَّحْنِ أَشَدُّ مِنْ سُوءِ الرَّمْيِ.

Sayyidunā ʿUmar ibn al-Khaṭṭāb passed by two men who were shooting.
One man said to another, "Hit [the target]."[59] Sayyidunā ʿUmar said,
"Poor grammar is worse than poor marksmanship."[60]

Soft-Heartedness and Caring for Others

حَدَّثَنَا شُعْبَةُ قَالَ: أَخْبَرَنِي عَبْدُ الْمَلِكِ قَالَ: سَمِعْتُ قَبِيصَةَ بْنَ جَابِرٍ قَالَ: سَمِعْتُ عُمَرَ، أَنَّهُ قَالَ:

مَنْ لاَ يَرْحَمُ لاَ يُرْحَمُ، وَلاَ يُغْفَرُ مَنْ لاَ يَغْفِرُ، وَلاَ يُعْفَ عَمَّنْ لَمْ يَعْفُ، وَلاَ يُوقَّ مَنْ لا يَتَوَقَّ.

58 *Ṣaḥīḥ Muslim*, 49a.

59 He used a س instead of a ص, the correct phrase would be أَصَبْتَ.

60 *Al-Adab Al-Mufrad*, 881.

Qabīṣah ibn Jābir ﷺ narrated that he heard Sayyidunā ʿUmar ﷺ say:

"The one who shows no mercy will be shown no mercy, the one who does not forgive will not be forgiven, and the one who does not pardon will not be pardoned."[61]

Sayyidunā ʿUmar ibn al-Khaṭṭāb ﷺ was a man of many qualities, but one of the qualities he was most known for was his soft-heartedness towards the weak and downtrodden, and his deep desire to always do what is right. We see these sentiments echo throughout his life. He did not rest on his laurels and wait for others to come and ask for help, but actively sought out opportunities to find the people in need of his aid to provide it to them.

One such occasion is narrated by Aslam ﷺ. He explains that he went out patrolling with Sayyidunā ʿUmar ibn al-Khaṭṭāb ﷺ one night beyond the outskirts of the city when they came upon a campfire. As they approached the camp, they found a woman with small children who were quarrelling with one another whilst a pot boiled over the campfire. Sayyidunā ʿUmar ibn al-Khaṭṭāb ﷺ approached and sought permission to draw closer and then asked why the children were upset. She explained that they were cold and hungry and that the pot was filled with only water which she was boiling so they would fall asleep as they waited while believing that there was food to eat, adding that Allah ﷻ would judge between Sayyidunā ʿUmar ﷺ and them.[62]

Sayyidunā ʿUmar ibn al-Khaṭṭāb ﷺ returned to the city with Aslam ﷺ where they gathered flour and animal fat. Aslam ﷺ offered to carry the supplies, but Sayyidunā ʿUmar ﷺ ordered him to place it on the back of the Amīr al-Mu'minīn, as Aslam ﷺ would not bear his burden on the Day of Requital. They came back to the family with Sayyidunā ʿUmar ﷺ carrying

61 *Al-Adab al-Mufrad*, 371.

62 Sayyidunā ʿUmar ibn al-Khaṭṭāb had not named himself and she did not know who he was.

the supplies the entire way. On arrival, he cooked for the family and ordered the woman to feed her children, and did not stop until they had all eaten with fulfilment. The woman thanked him, saying, "May Allah reward you, you are more deserving to rule than the Commander of the Faithful!" He left advising her to come to the court of the Commander of the Faithful. He walked a short distance away, and sat down on his knees, facing the fire and did not speak for some time, watching the children play until they had fallen asleep. When Aslam ؓ asked as to why he had done this, Sayyidunā 'Umar ؓ replied,

يَا أَسْلَمُ، إِنَّ الْجُوعَ أَسْهَرَهُمْ وَأَبْكَاهُمْ، فَأَحْبَبْتُ أَنْ لَا أَنْصَرِفَ حَتَّى أَرَى مَا رَأَيْتُ.

> O Aslam, hunger had kept them wakeful and made them weep. I did not wish to leave until I saw what I saw.[63]

On another occasion when Sayyidunā 'Umar ؓ was out on patrol, he came across an unfamiliar tent and heard someone groaning in pain from within. He approached and spoke to a man who was sitting outside the tent. After some encouragement from Sayyidunā 'Umar ؓ the man explained that his wife was suffering from labour pains inside the tent, and there was no one to attend to her. Sayyidunā 'Umar ؓ returned home and explained the situation to his wife, Sayyidah Umm Kulthūm bint 'Alī ibn Abī Ṭālib ؓ. She was the granddaughter of the Prophet ﷺ and thus prepared at once and left with him to help these strangers, taking some food with them. On arrival, his wife entered the tent to act as a midwife whilst he busied himself preparing food for the expectant parents. A short while later, Sayyidah Umm Kulthūm ؓ called out, "O Amīr al-Mu'minīn, congratulate your friend on the birth of his son!"

The man was naturally extremely embarrassed to learn that the Commander of the Faithful had been cooking for them whilst his wife was

---

63 Abū 'Abdillāh Aḥmad Ibn Muḥammad Ibn Ḥanbal al-Dhuhalī, *Faḍā'il al-Ṣaḥābah*, 382.

acting as their midwife. Sayyidunā ʿUmar ﵁ allayed his worries with kind words, fed the couple, and then asked them to attend his court in the morning for further help.[64]

In a third example, Amīr al-Mu'minīn ʿUmar ibn al-Khaṭṭāb ﵁ once passed a group of people who were eating whilst their servants stood nearby. Sayyidunā ʿUmar ﵁ asked,

مالي لا أرى خُدَّامَكم يأكلون معكم، أترغبون عنهم؟

Why do I not see your servants eating with you? Do you not like them?

One of the men said, "No, by Allah, O Leader of the Faithful. Rather, we have preference over them." Sayyidunā ʿUmar ﵁ was greatly angered by this and said,

ما لقومٍ يستأثرون على خُدَّامهم، فَعَلَ الله تعالى به، وفَعَلَ.

What is the matter with people who prefer themselves over their servants? Allah will deal with them, and it is done!

Then Sayyidunā ʿUmar ﵁ said to the servants,

اجلِسوا، فكُلُوا.

Sit down and eat.

The servants sat to eat, though the Amīr al-Mu'minīn did not.[65]

64 Muḥammad Zakariyyā al-Kāndhlawī, *Faḍā'il al-Aʿmāl*, Waterval Islamic Institute, Johannesburg (1421/2000), p. 104.

65 Abū al-Fiḍā' ʿImād ad-Dīn Ismāʿīl ibn ʿUmar ibn Kathīr al-Qurashī al-Dimashqī, *Musnad al-Fārūq*, Faiyum, Dār al-Falāḥ (1430/2009), 582.

There is not a leader alive in the world today, locally, nationally, or internationally, who would show a fraction of the concern that Sayyidunā ʿUmar ﷺ had for his people. He was the Amīr al-Muʾminīn of a caliphate that spanned across three continents, and he still patrolled the streets at night in search of individuals to help. He did so without even introducing himself, lest he felt pride. His concern extended to every man, woman, and child, young or old, free or enslaved. Yet, despite all of this, despite the depth of his concern for others and the height of his generosity, he continued to pray to Allah ﷻ for a gentler heart and a more generous nature, praying,

.اللَّهُمَّ إِنِّي ضَعِيفٌ فَقَوِّنِي وَإِنِّي شَدِيدٌ فَلَيِّنِي وَإِنِّي بَخِيلٌ فَسَخِّنِي

O Allah, I am weak so make me strong, I am harsh so make me gentle, and I am miserly so make me generous.[66]

How could he not be this way, when following in the footsteps of giants? He had the titanic example of the Prophet ﷺ and Sayyidunā Abū Bakr ﷺ to follow, with their merciful hearts, adamantine wills, and magnanimous spirits. Sayyidunā ʿUmar ibn al-Khaṭṭāb ﷺ himself narrates,

أَمَرَنَا رَسُولُ اللَّهِ ﷺ يَوْمًا أَنْ نَتَصَدَّقَ فَوَافَقَ ذَلِكَ مَالاً عِنْدِي فَقُلْتُ الْيَوْمَ أَسْبِقُ أَبَا بَكْرٍ إِنْ سَبَقْتُهُ يَوْمًا فَجِئْتُ بِنِصْفِ مَالِي فَقَالَ رَسُولُ اللَّهِ ﷺ مَا أَبْقَيْتَ لأَهْلِكَ؟ قُلْتُ مِثْلَهُ . قَالَ وَأَتَى أَبُو بَكْرٍ – رضى الله عنه – بِكُلِّ مَا عِنْدَهُ فَقَالَ لَهُ رَسُولُ اللَّهِ ﷺ مَا أَبْقَيْتَ لأَهْلِكَ؟ قَالَ أَبْقَيْتُ .لَهُمُ اللَّهَ وَرَسُولَهُ . قُلْتُ لاَ أُسَابِقُكَ إِلَى شَىْءٍ أَبَدًا

Allah's Messenger once ordered us to give ṣadaqah at a time when I had some wealth in my possession. I said to myself, "If ever there were to be a day on which I surpass Sayyidunā Abū Bakr in anything, then this is that day." I then presented myself before the Prophet with half of my wealth. Allah's Messenger asked, "What did you leave for your family?" I replied, "The same amount." Sayyidunā Abū Bakr brought with him all that he

66 *Muṣannaf Ibn Abī Shaybah* 5179.

owned. Allah's Messenger asked, "What did you leave for your family?" He replied, "I left them Allah and His Messenger." I said, "I will never surpass you in anything!"[67]

This was the example he sought to emulate, and he strived tirelessly to achieve it, constantly pushing himself to greater heights of caring and greater depths of concern. Not only did he seek to meet this example himself, but advised and encouraged others to do so, especially those he placed in positions of leadership.

عَنْ أَبِي عُثْمَانَ، أَنَّ عُمَرَ رَضِيَ اللَّهُ عَنْهُ اسْتَعْمَلَ رَجُلاً، فَقَالَ الْعَامِلُ: إِنَّ لِي كَذَا وَكَذَا مِنَ الْوَلَدِ، مَا قَبَّلْتُ وَاحِدًا مِنْهُمْ، فَزَعَمَ عُمَرُ، أَوْ قَالَ عُمَرُ: إِنَّ اللَّهَ عَزَّ وَجَلَّ لاَ يَرْحَمُ مِنْ عِبَادِهِ إِلاَّ أَبَرَّهُمْ.

Abū ʿUthmān ﷺ reported that Sayyidunā ʿUmar ﷺ once appointed a man as governor. The appointee said, "I have such-and-such a number of children and I have never kissed any of them." Sayyidunā ʿUmar said, "Allah the Mighty and Majestic will not show mercy to His slaves except for the kindest of them."[68]

The above statement echoes the famous saying of the Prophet of Allah ﷺ,

مَنْ لاَ يَرْحَمُ لاَ يُرْحَمُ

He who does not show mercy, will not be shown mercy.[69]

Only those who have it in them to exercise mercy to those who are in subordinate positions to them, such as one's children, employees, servants, staff, etc., are worthy of receiving mercy themselves. A heartless person cannot

67 *Sunan Abī Dāwūd*, 1678.

68 *Al-Adab al-Mufrad*, 99.

69 *Al-Adab al-Mufrad*, 95.

call for Divine Mercy, and an unkind man cannot expect His Kindness. A leader must reflect the Divine Attributes of Allah ﷻ in their leadership, and Allah's ﷻ Divine Mercy is invoked at the beginning of 113 out of 114 *sūrahs* in the Qur'an, as both the 'All-Merciful' and the 'Very-Merciful', denoting His Mercy being extended generally upon all of creation, and specifically to every individual. From those chosen to be leaders, Allah ﷻ expects an aspiration to reflect these same qualities. Ibn Sābiṭ ؓ narrates that Sayyidunā 'Umar ibn al-Khaṭṭāb ؓ said,

لَيْسَ شَيْءٌ أَحَبَّ إِلَى اللَّهِ عَزَّ وَجَلَّ، وَلَا أَعَمَّ نَفْعًا مِنْ حِلْمِ إِمَامٍ وَرِفْقِهِ، وَلَيْسَ شَيْءٌ أَبْغَضَ إِلَى اللَّهِ وَلَا أَعَمَّ ضَرَرًا مِنْ جَهْلِ إِمَامٍ وَخُرْقِهِ.

> There is nothing more beloved to Allah nor more beneficial to the people, than a leader's gentleness and clemency; there is nothing more hated by Allah, nor more harmful to the people, than a leader's foolishness and harshness.[70]

Further to this, Sayyidunā 'Umar ibn al-Khaṭṭāb ؓ also advocated for thankfulness towards fellow human beings as a means of invoking Mercy and Grace upon them, stating,

لَوْ يَعْلَمُ أَحَدُكُمْ مَا لَهُ فِي قَوْلِهِ لِأَخِيهِ: جَزَاكَ اللَّهُ خَيْرًا، لَأَكْثَرَ مِنْهَا بَعْضُكُمْ لِبَعْضٍ.

> If one of you knew what he gets for saying to his brother, "May Allah reward you with good", you would say it abundantly to one another.[71]

Sayyidunā 'Umar's ؓ advice is of extreme benefit. Creating a culture of thankfulness and care for one another within the community simultaneously creates an environment of perpetual Divine Mercy, with each individual

---

70   Wakīʿ ibn al-Jarrāḥ, *Kitāb al-Zuhd*, 419.
71   *Muṣannaf Ibn Abī Shaybah*, 3664.

continuously praying for the other. Such prayers are always answered, just as Sayyidunā Abū Bakr al-Ṣiddīq ﷺ explained,

إِنَّ دَعْوَةَ الأَخِ فِي اللهِ تُسْتَجَابُ.

The supplication of a brother in Allah is answered.[72]

Fairness

عَنِ الْمِسْوَرِ بْنِ مَخْرَمَةَ، وَإِنَّ إِحْدَى أَصَابِعِي فِي جُرْحِهِ، هَذِهِ أَوْ هَذِهِ، وَهُوَ يَقُولُ:

يَا مَعْشَرَ قُرَيْشٍ، إِنِّي لَا أَخَافُ النَّاسَ عَلَيْكُمْ، إِنَّمَا أَخَافُكُمْ عَلَى النَّاسِ، إِنِّي قَدْ تَرَكْتُ فِيكُمْ ثِنْتَيْنِ لَنْ تَبْرَحُوا بِخَيْرٍ مَا لَزِمْتُمُوهُمَا: الْعَدْلُ فِي الْحُكْمِ، وَالْعَدْلُ فِي الْقَسْمِ.

Sayyidunā ʿUmar ibn al-Khaṭṭāb ﷺ said,

O kinsfolk of the Quraysh! I do not fear that you will be overpowered by the people, but rather that you will overpower them. Indeed, I have left you two things that will guarantee you a good state, should you hold fast to them: justice in governance and justice in the distribution of the spoils of war.[73]

Sayyidunā ʿUmar ibn al-Khaṭṭāb ﷺ was al-Fārūq, and as such he always differentiated truth from falsehood and took the side of truth. Amongst the wisdom he left behind for the Ummah of the Prophet ﷺ was to impress upon us all the necessity of fairness in Islam. The danger he saw for the Muslims was not that the Muslims would become oppressed, but that they would carry out oppression themselves, and thus he insisted that we practice justice in governance and distribution, as justice and fairness in these matters go hand in hand. Saʿīd ibn Musayyib ﷺ narrated an interesting exchange, stating,

72 *Al-Adab al-Mufrad*, 624.

73 *Muṣannaf Ibn Abī Shaybah*, 32636.

أَنَّ عُمَرَ بْنَ الْخَطَّابِ اخْتَصَمَ إِلَيْهِ مُسْلِمٌ وَيَهُودِيٌّ فَرَأَى عُمَرُ أَنَّ الْحَقَّ لِلْيَهُودِيِّ فَقَضَى لَهُ.

Sayyidunā ʿUmar ibn al-Khaṭṭāb was once presented with a dispute between a Muslim and a Jew. Sayyidunā ʿUmar saw that the truth lay with the Jew and so he ruled in his favour.[74]

The race or religion of the people involved was not important, nor did it matter whether someone was a blood relative, a friend, or an enemy. Sayyidunā ʿUmar ibn al-Khaṭṭāb ﷺ always ruled in favour of the truth and the above incident is a clear example of this. As Muslims, each of us should also make our decisions based on what is right and true, no matter how great or small our decisions are. The truth is the truth, and a Muslim will always remain on the side of truth.

During a conversation between Sayyidunā ʿUmar ibn al-Khaṭṭāb ﷺ and Kaʿb ﷺ, the following exchange took place,

قَالَ مَا أَخْوَفُ شَيْءٍ تَخَوَّفُهُ عَلَى أُمَّةِ مُحَمَّدٍ صَلَّى اللَّهُ عَلَيْهِ وَسَلَّمَ قَالَ أَئِمَّةً مُضِلِّينَ قَالَ عُمَرُ صَدَقْتَ قَدْ أَسَرَّ ذَلِكَ إِلَيَّ وَأَعْلَمَنِيهِ رَسُولُ اللَّهِ صَلَّى اللَّهُ عَلَيْهِ وَسَلَّمَ.

ʿUmar said, "What do you most fear for the Ummah of Muhammad?"
Kaʿb said, "Misleading leaders."

ʿUmar said, "You have spoken the truth. The Messenger of Allah told me this in private and informed me of it."[75]

The average Muslim must side with truth and speak only the truth, but a Muslim leader is required to be doubly truthful. Part of being fair and just as a leader of people is to be open and honest about decisions and the reasons behind them. To mislead people is to be unjust to them, and a Muslim must never be unjust.

---

74 *Muwaṭṭa' Imām Mālik*, 1403.

75 *Musnad Imām Aḥmad*, 293.

Teaching Until the End

عَنْ مَعْدَانَ بْنِ أَبِي طَلْحَةَ الْيَعْمَرِيِّ: أَنَّ عُمَرَ بْنَ الْخَطَّابِ رَضِيَ اللَّهُ عَنْهُ قَامَ عَلَى الْمِنْبَرِ يَوْمَ الْجُمُعَةِ فَحَمِدَ اللَّهَ وَأَثْنَى عَلَيْهِ ثُمَّ ذَكَرَ رَسُولَ اللَّهِ صَلَّى اللَّهُ عَلَيْهِ وَسَلَّمَ وَذَكَرَ أَبَا بَكْرٍ رَضِيَ اللَّهُ عَنْهُ ثُمَّ قَالَ:

رَأَيْتُ رُؤْيَا لَا أُرَاهَا إِلَّا لِحُضُورِ أَجَلِي رَأَيْتُ كَأَنَّ دِيكًا نَقَرَنِي نَقْرَتَيْنِ قَالَ وَذَكَرَ لِي أَنَّهُ دِيكٌ أَحْمَرُ فَقَصَصْتُهَا عَلَى أَسْمَاءَ بِنْتِ عُمَيْسٍ امْرَأَةِ أَبِي بَكْرٍ رَضِيَ اللَّهُ عَنْهُمَا فَقَالَتْ يَقْتُلُكَ رَجُلٌ مِنْ الْعَجَمِ.

Sayyidunā ʿUmar ibn al-Khaṭṭāb stood on the pulpit on Friday, praised Allah, remembered the Prophet of Allah and Abū Bakr, and then said:

"I saw a dream that I can only interpret as meaning that my death draws near; I saw a rooster pecking me twice, and I was told that it was a red rooster. I relayed this dream to Asmā' bint ʿUmays, the wife of Abū Bakr, and she said, 'You will be killed by a Persian man.'"

قَالَ: وَإِنَّ النَّاسَ يَأْمُرُونَنِي أَنْ أَسْتَخْلِفَ، وَإِنَّ اللَّهَ لَمْ يَكُنْ لِيُضَيِّعَ دِينَهُ وَخِلَافَتَهُ الَّتِي بَعَثَ بِهَا نَبِيَّهُ صَلَّى اللَّهُ عَلَيْهِ وَسَلَّمَ، وَإِنْ يَعْجَلْ بِي أَمْرٌ فَإِنَّ الشُّورَى فِي هَؤُلَاءِ السِّتَّةِ الَّذِينَ مَاتَ نَبِيُّ اللَّهِ صَلَّى اللَّهُ عَلَيْهِ وَسَلَّمَ وَهُوَ عَنْهُمْ رَاضٍ. فَمَنْ بَايَعْتُمْ مِنْهُمْ فَاسْمَعُوا لَهُ وَأَطِيعُوا، وَإِنِّي أَعْلَمُ أَنَّ أُنَاسًا سَيَطْعَنُونَ فِي هَذَا الْأَمْرِ، أَنَا قَاتَلْتُهُمْ بِيَدِي هَذِهِ عَلَى الْإِسْلَامِ، أُولَئِكَ أَعْدَاءُ اللَّهِ الْكُفَّارُ الضُّلَّالُ.

He continued, "The people are asking me to appoint a successor, but Allah will not cause His religion and His caliphate, with which He sent His Prophet to be lost. If death comes to me soon, then the caliphate is to be decided by these six men with whom the Messenger of Allah was pleased when he died. Whichever of them you swear allegiance to, then heed him and obey. I know that some will object to this matter. I have fought them with my own hands in the defence of Islam. They are the enemies of Allah and misguided disbelievers (kuffār).

وَايْمُ اللَّهِ، مَا أَتْرُكُ فِيمَا عَهِدَ إِلَيَّ رَبِّي فَاسْتَخْلَفَنِي شَيْئًا أَهَمَّ إِلَيَّ مِنْ الْكَلَالَةِ. وَايْمُ اللَّهِ، مَا أَغْلَظَ لِي نَبِيُّ اللَّهِ صَلَّى اللَّهُ عَلَيْهِ وَسَلَّمَ فِي شَيْءٍ مُنْذُ صَحِبْتُهُ أَشَدَّ مَا أَغْلَظَ لِي فِي شَأْنِ الْكَلَالَةِ، حَتَّى طَعَنَ بِإِصْبَعِهِ فِي صَدْرِي، وَقَالَ: تَكْفِيكَ آيَةُ الصَّيْفِ الَّتِي نَزَلَتْ فِي آخِرِ سُورَةِ النِّسَاءِ. وَإِنِّي إِنْ أَعِشْ فَسَأَقْضِي فِيهَا بِقَضَاءٍ يَعْلَمُهُ مَنْ يَقْرَأُ وَمَنْ لَا يَقْرَأُ.

"By Allah, I leave behind nothing that my Lord instructed me to do, and I came to the position of Caliph on that basis, that is more important to me than the kalālah.[76] By Allah, the Prophet of Allah never emphasised any issue to me since I accompanied him more than the issue of kalālah, to the point that he poked me in the chest with his finger and said, 'Is not the Āyah al-Sayf which appears at the end of Sūrah al-Nisā' sufficient for you?' If I live, I will issue a decree that will be so clear that those who read the Qur'an and those who do not read it will be able to make decisions concerning it."

وَإِنِّي أُشْهِدُ اللَّهَ عَلَى أُمَرَاءِ الْأَمْصَارِ، إِنِّي إِنَّمَا بَعَثْتُهُمْ لِيُعَلِّمُوا النَّاسَ دِينَهُمْ وَيُبَيِّنُوا لَهُمْ سُنَّةَ نَبِيِّهِمْ صَلَّى اللَّهُ عَلَيْهِ وَسَلَّمَ وَيَرْفَعُوا إِلَيَّ مَا عُمِّيَ عَلَيْهِمْ.

"I call upon Allah to bear witness over the governors of all the regions, for I only sent them to be just, to teach the people their religion and the Sunnah of the Prophet, and to refer to me concerning any difficult matter."

ثُمَّ إِنَّكُمْ أَيُّهَا النَّاسُ تَأْكُلُونَ مِنْ شَجَرَتَيْنِ لَا أُرَاهُمَا إِلَّا خَبِيثَتَيْنِ، هَذَا الثُّومُ وَالْبَصَلُ. وَايْمُ اللَّهِ، لَقَدْ كُنْتُ أَرَى نَبِيَّ اللَّهِ صَلَّى اللَّهُ عَلَيْهِ وَسَلَّمَ يَجِدُ رِيحَهُمَا مِنَ الرَّجُلِ فَيَأْمُرُ بِهِ، فَيُؤْخَذُ بِيَدِهِ فَيُخْرَجُ بِهِ مِنَ الْمَسْجِدِ حَتَّى يُؤْتَى بِهِ الْبَقِيعَ، فَمَنْ أَكَلَهُمَا لَا بُدَّ فَلْيُمِتْهُمَا طَبْخًا.

"O people, you eat two plants which I find to be nothing but repugnant: the onion and the garlic. I remember that if the Messenger of Allah noticed their smell coming from a man in the masjid, he would issue orders that he

76 Kalālah is a term in Islamic inheritance meaning a person who has no direct ascendants or descendants at the time of death.

be taken out from the mosque to al-Baqīʿ. Whoever must eat them, let him cook them until [the smell] dies."

.قَالَ فَخَطَبَ النَّاسَ يَوْمَ الْجُمُعَةِ وَأُصِيبَ يَوْمَ الْأَرْبِعَاءِ

The narrator, Maʿdān ibn Abī Ṭalḥah, said, "He addressed the people on Friday and was attacked on Wednesday."[77]

Allah ﷻ sometimes warns those who are close to Him of their coming deaths so they may settle their affairs, increase their worship, and seek His forgiveness. This was one such occasion. Less than five days before his murder, Sayyidunā ʿUmar ibn al-Khaṭṭāb رضي الله عنه saw it in a dream and knew that his time in this world was drawing to an end and he would soon rejoin his most beloved companions in the grave. The content of the speech is indeed interesting. Sayyidunā ʿUmar رضي الله عنه began by preparing the Muslims for his coming death by providing a list of six men who would succeed him, namely: Sayyidunā ʿUthmān ibn ʿAffān, Sayyidunā ʿAlī ibn Abī Ṭālib ibn ʿAbd al-Muṭṭalib, Sayyidunā ʿAbd al-Raḥmān ibn ʿAwf, Sayyidunā Saʿd ibn Abī Waqqāṣ, Sayyidunā al-Zubayr ibn al-ʿAwwām, and Sayyidunā Ṭalḥah ibn ʿUbayd Allāh al-Taymī رضي الله عنهم. These men were from amongst the earliest Ṣaḥābah and were six of the 'Ten Promised Paradise' (*al-ʿAsharah al-Mubashsharah*). Empires always fall from within, and he feared that the Muslims would fall into civil strife, so he instructed the Muslims to remain united under a single banner. His son, ʿAbdullāh ibn ʿUmar رضي الله عنه narrated that he asked Sayyidunā ʿUmar ibn al-Khaṭṭāb رضي الله عنه about the appointing of a successor, to which he replied,

إِنْ أَتْرُكْ فَقَدْ تَرَكَ مَنْ هُوَ خَيْرٌ مِنِّي رَسُولُ اللَّهِ صَلَّى اللَّهُ عَلَيْهِ وَسَلَّمَ وَإِنْ أَسْتَخْلِفْ فَقَدْ اسْتَخْلَفَ مَنْ هُوَ خَيْرٌ مِنِّي أَبُو بَكْرٍ رَضِيَ اللَّهُ عَنْهُ.

77 *Musnad Imām Aḥmad*, 89.

If I do not [appoint a successor], one who is better than me did not either, namely the Messenger of Allah; if I do, one who is better than me did it too, namely Abū Bakr .[78]

He then instructed the governors of the Ummah to be just and teach the people the Qur'an and Sunnah, highlighting throughout his sermon the need for strict adherence to the Sunnah, giving the example of the Prophet's ﷺ dislike for the smells of garlic or onions coming from the mouths of the believers in the masjid.

These were the matters of most importance to him.

On Wednesday morning, the 20th of Dhū al-Ḥijjah, 23H, ʿAmr ibn Maymūn رضي الله عنه attended the masjid for Fajr prayer, which was always led by the Amīr al-Mu'minīn ʿUmar ibn al-Khaṭṭāb رضي الله عنه. In a long narration, ʿAmr ibn Maymūn رضي الله عنه narrated the following events,

قَالَ إِنِّي لَقَائِمٌ مَا بَيْنِي وَبَيْنَهُ إِلاَّ عَبْدُ اللَّهِ بْنُ عَبَّاسٍ غَدَاةَ أُصِيبَ، وَكَانَ إِذَا مَرَّ بَيْنَ الصَّفَّيْنِ قَالَ اسْتَوُوا. حَتَّى إِذَا لَمْ يَرَ فِيهِنَّ خَلَلاً تَقَدَّمَ فَكَبَّرَ، وَرُبَّمَا قَرَأَ سُورَةَ يُوسُفَ، أَوِ النَّحْلَ، أَوْ نَحْوَ ذَلِكَ، فِي الرَّكْعَةِ الأُولَى حَتَّى يَجْتَمِعَ النَّاسُ، فَمَا هُوَ إِلاَّ أَنْ كَبَّرَ فَسَمِعْتُهُ يَقُولُ قَتَلَنِي — أَوْ أَكَلَنِي —الْكَلْبُ.

On the day Sayyidunā ʿUmar ibn al-Khaṭṭāb was stabbed, I was standing with no one between us except Sayyidunā ʿAbdullāh ibn ʿAbbās. Whenever Sayyidunā ʿUmar passed between the two rows, he would say, "Straighten your lines" until he saw no defects in the lines, and then he would go forth and start the prayer with takbīr. He would recite Sūrah Yūsuf, al-Naḥl, or similar in the first rakʿah to give people time to join the prayer. As soon as he said the takbīr I heard him say, "The dog has killed (or bitten) me!"[79]

---

78 *Musnad Imām Aḥmad*, 299; *Ṣaḥīḥ al-Bukhārī*, 7218; *Ṣaḥīḥ Muslim*, 1823.

79 *Ṣaḥīḥ al-Bukhārī*, 3700.

The dog in question was Abū Lu'lu'ah Pērōz, a Sassanian Persian slave of the Magian faith who had been working as a blacksmith in Medina to earn himself enough to buy his freedom from al-Mughīrah ibn Shuʿbah ﷺ. His true motivations for the murder of the Second Caliph are to this day unclear, but what is clear is that he had planned the murder of Sayyidunā ʿUmar ibn al-Khaṭṭāb ﷺ well in advance, forging a double-edged knife to commit the atrocity, and waiting amongst the ranks of worshippers at the masjid before the dawn prayer to assassinate Sayyidunā ʿUmar ibn al-Khaṭṭāb ﷺ, as it was widely known that he would lead the Fajr prayers there. He had waited until the *ṣalāh* had started to ensure that his cowardly act would not be stopped by anyone among the ranks of the Muslims and that Sayyidunā ʿUmar ibn al-Khaṭṭāb ﷺ would have his back to him and would therefore be unable to defend himself. ʿAmr ibn Maymūn ﷺ continues,

حِينَ طَعَنَهُ، فَطَارَ الْعِلْجُ بِسِكِّينٍ ذَاتِ طَرَفَيْنِ لاَ يَمُرُّ عَلَى أَحَدٍ يَمِينًا وَلاَ شِمَالاً إِلاَّ طَعَنَهُ حَتَّى طَعَنَ ثَلاَثَةَ عَشَرَ رَجُلاً، مَاتَ مِنْهُمْ سَبْعَةٌ، فَلَمَّا رَأَى ذَلِكَ رَجُلٌ مِنَ الْمُسْلِمِينَ، طَرَحَ عَلَيْهِ بُرْنُسًا، فَلَمَّا ظَنَّ الْعِلْجُ أَنَّهُ مَأْخُوذٌ نَحَرَ نَفْسَهُ.

Having stabbed him, the infidel used a double-edged knife and did not pass a man to his left or right, except that he stabbed him as well, until he had stabbed thirteen men, seven of whom died. Witnessing the events, one of the Muslims threw a burnoose over him. Realising that he had been captured, the infidel killed himself.[80]

The assassination thus cost the lives of eight people due to the ranks of the Muslims in prayer lines being so closely linked that there was no escape for him without going through the unarmed crowd. Having been captured, unmanned by the thought of facing judgement for his crimes, the cowardly disbeliever Abū Lu'lu'ah took the weakling's path and stabbed himself. The word "نَحَرَ" is used here, implying that he stabbed himself by driving the

80 Ibid.

knife upward into his jugular vein, as this word is often used for the sacrificing of camels that are usually slaughtered in this manner.

ʿAmr ibn Maymūn ﵁ narrates,

وَتَنَاوَلَ عُمَرُ يَدَ عَبْدِ الرَّحْمَنِ بْنِ عَوْفٍ فَقَدَّمَهُ، فَمَنْ يَلِي عُمَرَ فَقَدْ رَأَى الَّذِي أَرَى، وَأَمَّا نَوَاحِي الْمَسْجِدِ فَإِنَّهُمْ لاَ يَدْرُونَ غَيْرَ أَنَّهُمْ قَدْ فَقَدُوا صَوْتَ عُمَرَ وَهُمْ يَقُولُونَ سُبْحَانَ اللَّهِ سُبْحَانَ اللَّهِ. فَصَلَّى بِهِمْ عَبْدُ الرَّحْمَنِ صَلاَةً خَفِيفَةً.

Sayyidunā ʿUmar held the hand of ʿAbd al-Raḥmān ibn ʿAwf and forwarded him to lead the prayer. Those who were standing by Sayyidunā ʿUmar's side saw what I saw, but the people elsewhere in the masjid did not see anything. However, having lost the voice of Sayyidunā ʿUmar, they began to say, "Subḥān Allāh! Subḥān Allāh!" ʿAbd al-Raḥmān ibn ʿAwf led the people in a short prayer.[81]

This was Sayyidunā ʿUmar ibn al-Khaṭṭāb ﵁. Mortally wounded with his life blood flowing out from a gaping wound, he appointed an *imam* to lead the prayer and ensured that the *ṣalāh* was completed. Many of the people in the masjid did not even fully know what had taken place at this stage, but this was Sayyidunā ʿUmar ﵁ and thus *ṣalāh* came first.

ʿAmr ibn Maymūn ﵁ narrates,

فَلَمَّا انْصَرَفُوا. قَالَ يَا ابْنَ عَبَّاسٍ، انْظُرْ مَنْ قَتَلَنِي. فَجَالَ سَاعَةً، ثُمَّ جَاءَ، فَقَالَ غُلاَمُ الْمُغِيرَةِ. قَالَ الصَّنَعُ قَالَ نَعَمْ. قَالَ قَاتَلَهُ اللَّهُ لَقَدْ أَمَرْتُ بِهِ مَعْرُوفًا، الْحَمْدُ لِلَّهِ الَّذِي لَمْ يَجْعَلْ مَنِيَّتِي بِيَدِ رَجُلٍ يَدَّعِي الإِسْلاَمَ، قَدْ كُنْتَ أَنْتَ وَأَبُوكَ تُحِبَّانِ أَنْ تَكْثُرَ الْعُلُوجُ بِالْمَدِينَةِ وَكَانَ الْعَبَّاسُ أَكْثَرَهُمْ رَقِيقًا. فَقَالَ إِنْ شِئْتَ فَعَلْتُ. أَىْ إِنْ شِئْتَ قَتَلْنَا. قَالَ كَذَبْتَ، بَعْدَ مَا تَكَلَّمُوا بِلِسَانِكُمْ، وَصَلَّوْا قِبْلَتَكُمْ وَحَجُّوا حَجَّكُمْ.

81 Ibid.

When they finished the prayer, Sayyidunā ʿUmar said, "O Ibn ʿAbbās, go and see who has slain me."

Ibn ʿAbbās left for a short time and then returned and said, "The slave of al-Mughīrah."

On that, Sayyidunā ʿUmar asked, "The craftsman?"

Ibn ʿAbbās said, "Yes."

Sayyidunā ʿUmar said, "May Allah curse him. I treated him justly. All praise is for Allah Who did not cause me to die at the hand of a man who claims Islam. Indeed your father and you used to love to have more infidels in Medina."

al-ʿAbbās had the greatest number of slaves. Ibn ʿAbbās said to Sayyidunā ʿUmar, "If it is your will, we will act." He meant, "If you wish it, we will kill them."

Sayyidunā ʿUmar said, "You are mistaken, [you cannot] after they have spoken your language, prayed towards your qiblah, and performed your Hajj."

Sayyidunā ʿUmar ﵁ treated all people well, Muslim or non-Muslim, man or woman, young or old, the free and the slave. He had treated his murderer well in his life, and even as his life slowly flowed away from him, he did not seek revenge but instead instructed mercy and kindness.

About the "short time" mentioned above, Ibn ʿAbbās ﵁ narrates that,

لَمَّا طُعِنَ عُمَرُ رَضِيَ اللَّهُ عَنْهُ كُنْتُ فِيمَنْ حَمَلَهُ حَتَّى أَدْخَلْنَاهُ الدَّارَ، فَقَالَ لِي: يَا ابْنَ أَخِي، اذْهَبْ فَانْظُرْ مَنْ أَصَابَنِي، وَمَنْ أَصَابَ مَعِي، فَذَهَبْتُ فَجِئْتُ لِأُخْبِرُهُ، فَإِذَا الْبَيْتُ مَلآنُ، فَكَرِهْتُ أَنْ أَتَخَطَّى رِقَابَهُمْ، وَكُنْتُ حَدِيثَ السِّنِّ، فَجَلَسْتُ، وَكَانَ يَأْمُرُ إِذَا أَرْسَلَ أَحَدًا بِالْحَاجَةِ أَنْ يُخْبِرَهُ بِهَا، وَإِذَا هُوَ مُسَجًّى، وَجَاءَ كَعْبٌ فَقَالَ: وَاللَّهِ لَئِنْ دَعَا أَمِيرُ الْمُؤْمِنِينَ

لَيُبْقِيَنَّهُ اللَّهُ وَلَيَرْفَعَنَّهُ لِهَذِهِ الأُمَّةِ حَتَّى يَفْعَلَ فِيهَا كَذَا وَكَذَا، حَتَّى ذَكَرَ الْمُنَافِقِينَ فَسَمَّى وَكَنَّى، قُلْتُ: أُبَلِّغُهُ مَا تَقُولُ؟ قَالَ: مَا قُلْتُ إِلاَّ وَأَنَا أُرِيدُ أَنْ تُبَلِّغَهُ، فَتَشَجَّعْتُ فَقُمْتُ، فَتَخَطَّيْتُ رِقَابَهُمْ حَتَّى جَلَسْتُ عِنْدَ رَأْسِهِ، قُلْتُ: إِنَّكَ أَرْسَلْتَنِي بِكَذَا، وَأَصَابَ مَعَكَ كَذَا، ثَلاَثَةَ عَشَرَ، وَأَصَابَ كُلَيْبًا الْجَزَّارَ وَهُوَ يَتَوَضَّأُ عِنْدَ الْمِهْرَاسِ، وَإِنَّ كَعْبًا يَحْلِفُ بِاللَّهِ بِكَذَا، فَقَالَ: ادْعُوا كَعْبًا، فَدُعِيَ، فَقَالَ: مَا تَقُولُ؟ قَالَ: أَقُولُ كَذَا وَكَذَا، قَالَ: لاَ وَاللَّهِ لاَ أَدْعُو، وَلَكِنْ شَقِيٌّ عُمَرُ إِنْ لَمْ يَغْفِرِ اللَّهُ لَهُ.

When Sayyidunā ʿUmar was attacked, I was one of those who carried him to his house. He said to me, "O nephew, go and see who wounded me and who was wounded with me."

I went, and when I returned to tell him I found the room was full and I disliked stepping over others for I was young, and thus I sat down. Sayyidunā ʿUmar's rule when he sent someone for a task was that it was to be kept confidential. Sayyidunā ʿUmar had a cover over him. Kaʿb came and said, "By Allah, if the Amīr al-Mu'minīn makes supplication, Allah will allow him to remain alive and restore him to the Ummah until he does such-and-such and such-and-such", until he (Sayyidunā Kaʿb) mentioned the hypocrites by their names and kunyas.

I said, "Shall I convey your words to him?"

Kaʿb said, "I only said it because I intended you to do so."

I steeled myself, stood, and stepped over the people until I sat by Sayyidunā ʿUmar's head. I said, "You sent me to find out such-and-such; thirteen people were wounded with you, and Kulayb ibn al-Jazzār was wounded while he was doing ablution (wuḍū') from the cistern. Kaʿb swore such-and-such by Allah."

He said, "Summon Kaʿb."

He was called and Sayyidunā ʿUmar asked, "What did you say?"

He replied, “I said such-and-such.”

Sayyidunā ʿUmar said, “No, by Allah, I will not make that supplication, but ʿUmar will be wretched if Allah does not forgive him.”[82]

Sayyidunā ʿUmar ﷺ was well-prepared to meet death and yearned to meet his beloved friends once more. Despite the words of Kaʿb ﷺ, he would not make any supplication to avoid facing death, but instead sought only Allah's ﷻ forgiveness.

ʿAmr ibn Maymūn ﷺ then states,

فَاحْتُمِلَ إِلَى بَيْتِهِ فَانْطَلَقْنَا مَعَهُ، وَكَأَنَّ النَّاسَ لَمْ تُصِبْهُمْ مُصِيبَةٌ قَبْلَ يَوْمَئِذٍ، فَقَائِلٌ يَقُولُ لاَ بَأْسَ. وَقَائِلٌ يَقُولُ أَخَافُ عَلَيْهِ، فَأُتِيَ بِنَبِيذٍ فَشَرِبَهُ فَخَرَجَ مِنْ جَوْفِهِ، ثُمَّ أُتِيَ بِلَبَنٍ فَشَرِبَهُ فَخَرَجَ مِنْ جُرْحِهِ، فَعَلِمُوا أَنَّهُ مَيِّتٌ، فَدَخَلْنَا عَلَيْهِ، وَجَاءَ النَّاسُ يُثْنُونَ عَلَيْهِ، وَجَاءَ رَجُلٌ شَابٌّ، فَقَالَ أَبْشِرْ يَا أَمِيرَ الْمُؤْمِنِينَ بِبُشْرَى اللَّهِ لَكَ مِنْ صُحْبَةِ رَسُولِ اللَّهِ ﷺ وَقَدَمٍ فِي الإِسْلاَمِ مَا قَدْ عَلِمْتَ، ثُمَّ وَلِيتَ فَعَدَلْتَ، ثُمَّ شَهَادَةٌ. قَالَ وَدِدْتُ أَنَّ ذَلِكَ كَفَافٌ لاَ عَلَيَّ وَلاَ لِي. فَلَمَّا أَدْبَرَ، إِذَا إِزَارُهُ يَمَسُّ الأَرْضَ. قَالَ رُدُّوا عَلَيَّ الْغُلاَمَ قَالَ ابْنَ أَخِي ارْفَعْ ثَوْبَكَ، فَإِنَّهُ أَبْقَى لِثَوْبِكَ وَأَتْقَى لِرَبِّكَ، يَا عَبْدَ اللَّهِ بْنَ عُمَرَ انْظُرْ مَا عَلَيَّ مِنَ الدَّيْنِ. فَحَسَبُوهُ فَوَجَدُوهُ سِتَّةً وَثَمَانِينَ أَلْفًا أَوْ نَحْوَهُ، قَالَ إِنْ وَفَى لَهُ مَالُ آلِ عُمَرَ، فَأَدِّهِ مِنْ أَمْوَالِهِمْ، وَإِلاَّ فَسَلْ فِي بَنِي عَدِيِّ بْنِ كَعْبٍ، فَإِنْ لَمْ تَفِ أَمْوَالُهُمْ فَسَلْ فِي قُرَيْشٍ، وَلاَ تَعْدُهُمْ إِلَى غَيْرِهِمْ، فَأَدِّ عَنِّي هَذَا الْمَالَ.

Then Sayyidunā ʿUmar was carried to his house and we went with him. It was as if the people had never suffered a calamity before this day. One would say, “Worry not!” and another would say, “I fear for him!”

An infusion of dates was brought to him. He drank it, but it poured forth from [the wound in] his stomach. Then milk was brought to him. He drank it, and it also poured out of his wound. The people thus knew

---

82 *Al-Adab al-Mufrad*, 1143.

that he would die. We went to him, and the people came too, praising him. A youth came and said, "O Amīr al-Mu'minīn, receive glad tidings from Allah due to your close companionship with Allah's Messenger, your superiority in Islam which you well know, then you became the ruler and you ruled justly, and now you have been martyred."

Sayyidunā ʿUmar said, "I hope that these privileges will counterbalance me so that I neither lose nor gain anything."

When the young man turned to leave, his clothes were nearly touching the ground. Sayyidunā ʿUmar said, "Call the boy back to me." Then Sayyidunā ʿUmar said, "O nephew, lift your clothes, for this will keep your clothes clean and keep you in taqwā of your Lord." [Sayyidunā ʿUmar continued:] "O ʿAbdullāh ibn ʿUmar! See how much debt I owe."

So it was calculated and it amounted to eighty-six thousand or similar. Sayyidunā ʿUmar said, "If the property of ʿUmar's family covers it, then pay the debt thereof; if not, then request it from Banī ʿAdiyy ibn Kaʿb; if that too is insufficient, ask for it from the Quraysh tribe, and do not ask for it from anyone else. Pay this debt on my behalf."[83]

Just like his blessed companions before him, he would take on debts to help others, and just like them he would leave the world behind with little to his name, despite the impact he had on the world. He ensured that his debts would be paid off as one of his last acts.

Regarding the incident where he was given *nabīdh* (a date infusion) and milk to drink, Salīm ﵁ narrates a more detailed account from ʿAbdullāh ibn ʿUmar ﵄, who states,

قَالَ عُمَرُ أَرْسِلُوا إِلَيَّ طَبِيبًا يَنْظُرُ إِلَى جُرْحِي هَذَا قَالَ فَأَرْسَلُوا إِلَى طَبِيبٍ مِنْ الْعَرَبِ فَسَقَى

83 *Ṣaḥīḥ al-Bukhārī*, 3700.

عُمَرَ نَبِيذًا فَشُبِّهَ النَّبِيذُ بِالدَّمِ حِينَ خَرَجَ مِنْ الطَّعْنَةِ الَّتِي تَحْتَ السُّرَّةِ قَالَ فَدَعَوْتُ طَبِيبًا آخَرَ مِنْ الْأَنْصَارِ مِنْ بَنِي مُعَاوِيَةَ فَسَقَاهُ لَبَنًا فَخَرَجَ اللَّبَنُ مِنْ الطَّعْنَةِ صَلْدًا أَبْيَضَ فَقَالَ لَهُ الطَّبِيبُ يَا أَمِيرَ الْمُؤْمِنِينَ اعْهَدْ فَقَالَ عُمَرُ صَدَقَنِي أَخُو بَنِي مُعَاوِيَةَ وَلَوْ قُلْتَ غَيْرَ ذَلِكَ كَذَّبْتُكَ قَالَ فَبَكَى عَلَيْهِ الْقَوْمُ حِينَ سَمِعُوا ذَلِكَ فَقَالَ لَا تَبْكُوا عَلَيْنَا مَنْ كَانَ بَاكِيًا فَلْيَخْرُجْ أَلَمْ تَسْمَعُوا مَا قَالَ رَسُولُ اللَّهِ صَلَّى اللَّهُ عَلَيْهِ وَسَلَّمَ قَالَ يُعَذَّبُ الْمَيِّتُ بِبُكَاءِ أَهْلِهِ عَلَيْهِ.

فَمِنْ أَجْلِ ذَلِكَ كَانَ عَبْدُ اللَّهِ لَا يُقِرُّ أَنْ يُبْكَى عِنْدَهُ عَلَى هَالِكٍ مِنْ وَلَدِهِ وَلَا غَيْرِهِمْ.

Sayyidunā ʿUmar said, "Send for a doctor to examine this wound of mine."

So they sent for a doctor from amongst the Arabs, who gave Sayyidunā ʿUmar some nabīdh. The nabīdh was mixed with blood when it came out of the wound beneath his navel. I called for a second doctor from amongst the Anṣār, from the tribe of Banū Muʿāwiyah. He gave him milk and it came out of the wound solid and white. The doctor said to him, "O Amīr al-Mu'minīn, give your final instructions."

Sayyidunā ʿUmar said, "The brother from Banū Muʿāwiyah has spoken the truth. If you had said anything else, I would not have believed you."

The people wept for him when they heard this, but he said, "Do not weep for us; whoever wishes to weep, let him leave. Did you not hear what the Messenger of Allah said? He said, 'The deceased is tormented by his family's weeping for him.'"

[Sālim ﵁ said:] Because of this, ʿAbdullāh did not approve of weeping if a son of his or anyone else died.[84]

Despite his closeness to the Prophet of Allah ﷺ, his position in Islam, and his martyrdom, Sayyidunā ʿUmar ﵁ still did not think highly of himself and remained humble even in death. He gave sincere advice to those who came

84 *Musnad Imām Aḥmad*, 294, *Ṣaḥīḥ al-Bukhārī*, 1292; *Ṣaḥīḥ Muslim*, 927.

to visit him, and it is a testament to how he lived his life that the advice he gave did not change even in the moments of his death. He lived in constant knowledge that any moment could be his last, and thus his words did not change when the finality of his worldly life became clear to all. In another narration, Ḥumayd ibn ʿAbd al-Raḥmān al-Ḥimyarī ﵁ narrated that Ibn ʿAbbās ﵁ said in Basra,

أَنَا أَوَّلُ مَنْ أَتَى عُمَرَ رَضِيَ اللَّهُ عَنْهُ حِينَ طُعِنَ فَقَالَ احْفَظْ عَنِّي ثَلَاثًا فَإِنِّي أَخَافُ أَنْ لَا يُدْرِكَنِي النَّاسُ أَمَّا أَنَا فَلَمْ أَقْضِ فِي الْكَلَالَةِ قَضَاءً وَلَمْ أَسْتَخْلِفْ عَلَى النَّاسِ خَلِيفَةً وَكُلُّ مَمْلُوكٍ لَهُ عَتِيقٌ فَقَالَ لَهُ النَّاسُ اسْتَخْلِفْ فَقَالَ أَيَّ ذَلِكَ أَفْعَلُ فَقَدْ فَعَلَهُ مَنْ هُوَ خَيْرٌ مِنِّي إِنْ أَدَعْ إِلَى النَّاسِ أَمْرَهُمْ فَقَدْ تَرَكَهُ نَبِيُّ اللَّهِ عَلَيْهِ الصَّلَاةُ وَالسَّلَامُ وَإِنْ أَسْتَخْلِفْ فَقَدْ اسْتَخْلَفَ مَنْ هُوَ خَيْرٌ مِنِّي أَبُو بَكْرٍ رَضِيَ اللَّهُ عَنْهُ فَقُلْتُ لَهُ أَبْشِرْ بِالْجَنَّةِ صَاحَبْتَ رَسُولَ اللَّهِ صَلَّى اللَّهُ عَلَيْهِ وَسَلَّمَ فَأَطَلْتَ صُحْبَتَهُ وَوُلِّيتَ أَمْرَ الْمُؤْمِنِينَ فَقَوِيتَ وَأَدَّيْتَ الْأَمَانَةَ فَقَالَ أَمَّا تَبْشِيرُكَ إِيَّايَ بِالْجَنَّةِ فَوَاللَّهِ لَوْ أَنَّ لِي قَالَ عَفَّانُ فَلَا وَاللَّهِ الَّذِي لَا إِلَهَ إِلَّا هُوَ لَوْ أَنَّ لِي الدُّنْيَا بِمَا فِيهَا لَافْتَدَيْتُ بِهِ مِنْ هَوْلِ مَا أَمَامِي قَبْلَ أَنْ أَعْلَمَ الْخَبَرَ وَأَمَّا قَوْلُكَ فِي أَمْرِ الْمُؤْمِنِينَ فَوَاللَّهِ لَوَدِدْتُ أَنَّ ذَلِكَ كَفَافًا لَا لِي وَلَا عَلَيَّ وَأَمَّا مَا ذَكَرْتَ مِنْ صُحْبَةِ نَبِيِّ اللَّهِ صَلَّى اللَّهُ عَلَيْهِ وَسَلَّمَ فَذَلِكَ.

I was the first to visit Sayyidunā ʿUmar when he was stabbed. He said, "Learn from me three things, for I fear that the people will not visit me [before my death]. As for me, I did not pass any judgement regarding kalālah, I did not appoint any successor to be in charge of the people after me, and every slave of mine will be free."

The people said to him, "Appoint a successor."

He said, "Whatever I do, it was done by someone better than me. If I leave the people to decide their affairs, Allah's Messenger did that; if I appoint someone, then one who is better than me did that, namely Sayyidunā Abū Bakr."

I said to him, "Receive the glad tidings of Paradise; you accompanied the Messenger of Allah and your companionship with him was long;

you were appointed in charge of the believers and you both showed strength and fulfilled the trust."

He said, "As for your glad tidings to me of Paradise (here, another narrator, 'Affān ﵁ reports that he said, 'No by Allah, besides Whom there is no god'), if I had the entire world and all it contains, I would give it in ransom from the terror of what lies before me, before even knowing the outcome. As for what you say about my being in charge of the believers' affairs, by Allah, I wish that I could get out of it without gaining or losing anything. As for what you said about me accompanying Allah's Messenger, that is true."[85]

Returning to the narration of 'Amr ibn Maymūn ﵁, he continues that Sayyidunā 'Umar ﵁ then said to 'Abdullāh ﵁,

انْطَلِقْ إِلَى عَائِشَةَ أُمِّ الْمُؤْمِنِينَ فَقُلْ يَقْرَأُ عَلَيْكِ عُمَرُ السَّلاَمَ. وَلاَ تَقُلْ أَمِيرُ الْمُؤْمِنِينَ. فَإِنِّي لَسْتُ الْيَوْمَ لِلْمُؤْمِنِينَ أَمِيرًا، وَقُلْ يَسْتَأْذِنُ عُمَرُ بْنُ الْخَطَّابِ أَنْ يُدْفَنَ مَعَ صَاحِبَيْهِ. فَسَلَّمَ وَاسْتَأْذَنَ، ثُمَّ دَخَلَ عَلَيْهَا، فَوَجَدَهَا قَاعِدَةً تَبْكِي فَقَالَ يَقْرَأُ عَلَيْكِ عُمَرُ بْنُ الْخَطَّابِ السَّلاَمَ وَيَسْتَأْذِنُ أَنْ يُدْفَنَ مَعَ صَاحِبَيْهِ. فَقَالَتْ كُنْتُ أُرِيدُهُ لِنَفْسِي، وَلأُوثِرَنَّ بِهِ الْيَوْمَ عَلَى نَفْسِي.

فَلَمَّا أَقْبَلَ قِيلَ هَذَا عَبْدُ اللَّهِ بْنُ عُمَرَ قَدْ جَاءَ. قَالَ ارْفَعُونِي، فَأَسْنَدَهُ رَجُلٌ إِلَيْهِ، فَقَالَ مَا لَدَيْكَ قَالَ الَّذِي تُحِبُّ يَا أَمِيرَ الْمُؤْمِنِينَ أَذِنَتْ. قَالَ الْحَمْدُ لِلَّهِ، مَا كَانَ مِنْ شَيْءٍ أَهَمُّ إِلَيَّ مِنْ ذَلِكَ، فَإِذَا أَنَا قَضَيْتُ فَاحْمِلُونِي ثُمَّ سَلِّمْ فَقُلْ يَسْتَأْذِنُ عُمَرُ بْنُ الْخَطَّابِ، فَإِنْ أَذِنَتْ لِي فَأَدْخِلُونِي، وَإِنْ رَدَّتْنِي رُدُّونِي إِلَى مَقَابِرِ الْمُسْلِمِينَ.

Go to Umm al-Mu'minīn Sayyidah 'Ā'ishah and say, "'Umar sends his salām", but do not say Amīr al-Mu'minīn, for today I am not the commander of the believers. Say, "'Umar ibn al-Khaṭṭāb seeks permission to be buried with his two companions."

85 *Musnad Imām Aḥmad*, 322.

Sayyidunā ʿAbdullāh [went and] greeted Umm al-Muʾminīn Sayyidah ʿĀʾishah and asked for permission to enter. On entering, he found her sitting and weeping. He said to her, "ʿUmar ibn al-Khaṭṭāb sends his salutations and asks permission to be buried with his two companions."

She replied, "I had intended this place for myself, but today I prefer ʿUmar over myself."

When he returned it was said [to Sayyidunā ʿUmar], "Sayyidunā ʿAbdullāh ibn ʿUmar has arrived."

Sayyidunā ʿUmar said, "Lift me up."

Somebody supported him and Sayyidunā ʿUmar asked his son, "What news?"

He replied, "O Amīr al-Muʾminīn, it is as you wish. She has given permission."

Sayyidunā ʿUmar said, "All praise is for Allah, there was nothing more important to me than this. When I die, take me, and greet Sayyidah ʿĀʾishah and say, 'ʿUmar ibn al-Khaṭṭāb asks for your permission. If she grants it, bury me there; if she refuses, take me to the graveyard of the Muslims.'"[86]

He wanted nothing more than to be buried by his two most beloved friends and companions: the Beloved of Allah and the Muslims ﷺ and his greatest companion, Sayyidunā Abū Bakr al-Ṣiddīq رضي الله عنه. Even as the ruler of the Muslim world, he did not wish to use his position to influence the decision of Umm al-Muʾminīn Sayyidah ʿĀʾishah رضي الله عنها, as she had just as much right as him to be buried beside her blessed husband ﷺ and her esteemed father رضي الله عنه. The love that the Ṣaḥābah had for one another is clear to see, for in this greatest of honours Umm al-Muʾminīn Sayyidah ʿĀʾishah رضي الله عنها preferred Sayyidunā

86 *Ṣaḥīḥ al-Bukhārī*, 3700.

ʿUmar ibn al-Khaṭṭāb ﷺ over herself and granted the permission. Despite this, Sayyidunā ʿUmar ﷺ asked that the permission be asked for a second time after his death so that she would have the chance to rethink the matter.

ʿAmr ibn Maymūn ﷺ continues,

وَجَاءَتْ أُمُّ الْمُؤْمِنِينَ حَفْصَةُ وَالنِّسَاءُ تَسِيرُ مَعَهَا، فَلَمَّا رَأَيْنَاهَا قُمْنَا، فَوَلَجَتْ عَلَيْهِ فَبَكَتْ عِنْدَهُ سَاعَةً، وَاسْتَأْذَنَ الرِّجَالُ، فَوَلَجَتْ دَاخِلاً لَهُمْ، فَسَمِعْنَا بُكَاءَهَا مِنَ الدَّاخِلِ. فَقَالُوا أَوْصِ يَا أَمِيرَ الْمُؤْمِنِينَ اسْتَخْلِفْ.

قَالَ مَا أَجِدُ أَحَقَّ بِهَذَا الأَمْرِ مِنْ هَؤُلاَءِ النَّفَرِ أَوِ الرَّهْطِ الَّذِينَ تُوُفِّيَ رَسُولُ اللَّهِ ﷺ وَهْوَ عَنْهُمْ رَاضٍ. فَسَمَّى عَلِيًّا وَعُثْمَانَ وَالزُّبَيْرَ وَطَلْحَةَ وَسَعْدًا وَعَبْدَ الرَّحْمَنِ وَقَالَ يَشْهَدُكُمْ عَبْدُ اللَّهِ بْنُ عُمَرَ وَلَيْسَ لَهُ مِنَ الأَمْرِ شَىْءٌ – كَهَيْئَةِ التَّعْزِيَةِ لَهُ – فَإِنْ أَصَابَتِ الإِمْرَةُ سَعْدًا فَهْوَ ذَاكَ، وَإِلاَّ فَلْيَسْتَعِنْ بِهِ أَيُّكُمْ مَا أُمِّرَ، فَإِنِّي لَمْ أَعْزِلْهُ عَنْ عَجْزٍ وَلاَ خِيَانَةٍ.

وَقَالَ أُوصِي الْخَلِيفَةَ مِنْ بَعْدِي بِالْمُهَاجِرِينَ الأَوَّلِينَ أَنْ يَعْرِفَ لَهُمْ حَقَّهُمْ، وَيَحْفَظَ لَهُمْ حُرْمَتَهُمْ، وَأُوصِيهِ بِالأَنْصَارِ خَيْرًا، الَّذِينَ تَبَوَّءُوا الدَّارَ وَالإِيمَانَ مِنْ قَبْلِهِمْ، أَنْ يُقْبَلَ مِنْ مُحْسِنِهِمْ، وَأَنْ يُعْفَى عَنْ مُسِيئِهِمْ، وَأُوصِيهِ بِأَهْلِ الأَمْصَارِ خَيْرًا فَإِنَّهُمْ رِدْءُ الإِسْلاَمِ، وَجُبَاةُ الْمَالِ، وَغَيْظُ الْعَدُوِّ، وَأَنْ لاَ يُؤْخَذَ مِنْهُمْ إِلاَّ فَضْلُهُمْ عَنْ رِضَاهُمْ، وَأُوصِيهِ بِالأَعْرَابِ خَيْرًا، فَإِنَّهُمْ أَصْلُ الْعَرَبِ وَمَادَّةُ الإِسْلاَمِ أَنْ يُؤْخَذَ مِنْ حَوَاشِي أَمْوَالِهِمْ وَتُرَدَّ عَلَى فُقَرَائِهِمْ، وَأُوصِيهِ بِذِمَّةِ اللَّهِ وَذِمَّةِ رَسُولِهِ ﷺ أَنْ يُوفَى لَهُمْ بِعَهْدِهِمْ، وَأَنْ يُقَاتَلَ مِنْ وَرَائِهِمْ، وَلاَ يُكَلَّفُوا إِلاَّ طَاقَتَهُمْ.

Then came Umm al-Mu'minīn Sayyidah Ḥafṣah accompanied by many other women. When we saw her, we went away. She went in [to see her father Sayyidunā ʿUmar] and wept for some time. When the men asked for permission to enter, she went into another room, and we heard her weeping inside. The people said [to Sayyidunā ʿUmar], "O Amīr al-Mu'minīn, appoint a successor."

Sayyidunā ʿUmar said, "I do not find anyone more suitable for the job than the following persons or group with whom Allah's Messenger had been pleased before he died." Sayyidunā ʿUmar then mentioned Sayyidunā ʿAlī, Sayyidunā ʿUthmān, Sayyidunā al-Zubayr, Ṭalḥah, Saʿd and ʿAbd al-Rahmān (ibn ʿAwf) and then said, "'Abdullāh ibn ʿUmar will be a witness for you, but he will have no share in rule, and his being the witness will compensate him for not sharing the right of ruling. If Sayyidunā Saʿd becomes the ruler, it will be good; otherwise, whoever becomes the ruler should seek his help as I have not dismissed him due to inability or dishonesty."

Sayyidunā ʿUmar added, "I recommend that my successor takes care of the early Emigrants (Muhājirīn), knows their rights, and protects their honour and sacred things; that he be kind to the Helpers (Anṣār) who lived in Medina before the Muhājirīn and faith had entered their hearts before them; that he accept the good of their righteous ones and excuse their wrong-doers; that he does good to all the townsfolk, as they are the protectors of Islam, the givers of wealth, and the sources of anger for the enemy, and that nothing be taken from them except with their consent and from their surplus; that he does good to the Arab Bedouins, as they are the origins of the Arabs and the material of Islam, and that he takes from what is inferior amongst their properties and distribute it to the poor amongst them; and with regards to the protectees of Allah and His Prophet (ahl al-dhimmah) that he fulfils their contracts, fights for them, and does not overburden them with what is beyond their ability."[87]

The advice that he provided for his successor in his final moments deserves to be looked into further, as it also shows what the chief concerns of Sayyidunā ʿUmar ؓ were for his people. The fundamental message of all the above advice was one of kindness towards others. As we have seen, this was a central theme throughout his life and his legendary gigantic frame held within

---

87 Ibid.

it a great deal of softness and kindness for those in his care, and therefore his final advice to his successor was continuous advice to be kind to his subjects.

He specified the most deserving groups of people first (the early *Muhājirīn* and *Anṣār*), which shows that giving preference to those that have been given preference by Allah ﷻ is a noble and good thing, and thus we too should give preference to the pious amongst us, as well as our scholars and our teachers.

Following the most deserving of kindness, he then advised general kindness towards all the people under Muslim rule, namely: the towns-folk, the Bedouins, and the *ahl al-dhimmah* (non-Muslim subjects of the Muslim state).

ʿAmr ibn Maymūn's ﵁ narration continues,

فَلَمَّا قُبِضَ خَرَجْنَا بِهِ فَانْطَلَقْنَا نَمْشِي فَسَلَّمَ عَبْدُ اللهِ بْنُ عُمَرَ قَالَ يَسْتَأْذِنُ عُمَرُ بْنُ الْخَطَّابِ. قَالَتْ أَدْخِلُوهُ. فَأُدْخِلَ، فَوُضِعَ هُنَالِكَ مَعَ صَاحِبَيْهِ.

So when Sayyidunā ʿUmar passed away, we carried him out and set off walking. ʿAbdullāh ibn ʿUmar greeted Umm al-Mu'minīn Sayyidah ʿĀ'ishah with salām and said, "ʿUmar ibn al-Khaṭṭāb seeks permission."

Umm al-Mu'minīn Sayyidah ʿĀ'ishah said, "Bring him inside."

He was brought in and buried beside his two companions.[88]

And so it was that Sayyidunā ʿUmar ibn al-Khaṭṭāb ﵁, the Commander of the Faithful and the father-in-law of the Prophet ﷺ passed away and joined his two dearest companions in this life and the next. He had lived his life in their close company, he was buried in their close company, and *in shā' Allāh*,

88 Ibid

he will be raised in their close company and live by their sides forever in the gardens of the loftiest levels of Paradise. *Āmīn*.

ʿAbdullāh ibn ʿAbbās ﵄ narrated the following event just after Sayyidunā ʿUmar ibn al-Khaṭṭāb ﵁ passed away,

إِنِّي لَوَاقِفٌ فِي قَوْمٍ، فَدَعَوُا اللَّهَ لِعُمَرَ بْنِ الْخَطَّابِ وَقَدْ وُضِعَ عَلَى سَرِيرِهِ، إِذَا رَجُلٌ مِنْ خَلْفِي قَدْ وَضَعَ مِرْفَقَهُ عَلَى مَنْكِبِي، يَقُولُ: رَحِمَكَ اللَّهُ، إِنْ كُنْتُ لأَرْجُو أَنْ يَجْعَلَكَ اللَّهُ مَعَ صَاحِبَيْكَ، لأَنِّي كَثِيرًا مِمَّا كُنْتُ أَسْمَعُ رَسُولَ اللَّهِ ﷺ يَقُولُ كُنْتُ وَأَبُو بَكْرٍ وَعُمَرُ، وَفَعَلْتُ وَأَبُو بَكْرٍ وَعُمَرُ، وَانْطَلَقْتُ وَأَبُو بَكْرٍ وَعُمَرُ. فَإِنْ كُنْتُ لأَرْجُو أَنْ يَجْعَلَكَ اللَّهُ مَعَهُمَا. فَالْتَفَتُّ فَإِذَا هُوَ عَلِيُّ بْنُ أَبِي طَالِبٍ.

As I stood amongst the people who were praying to Allah for Sayyidunā ʿUmar ibn al-Khaṭṭāb, who lay on his bed, a man behind me rested his arm on my shoulder and eulogised [to the body of Sayyidunā ʿUmar ibn al-Khaṭṭāb], "May Allah bestow on you His Mercy. Ever did I hope that Allah would keep you with your two companions, for I often heard Allah's Messenger saying, 'I, Abū Bakr, and ʿUmar were here', 'I, Abū Bakr, and ʿUmar did this', and, 'I, Abū Bakr, and ʿUmar set out' ... I hoped that Allah would keep you with them both."

I turned back to see that the speaker was Sayyidunā ʿAlī ibn Abī Ṭālib.[89]

ʿAbdullāh ibn ʿUmar ﵄ stated,

أَنَّ عُمَرَ بْنَ الْخَطَّابِ، غُسِّلَ وَكُفِّنَ وَصُلِّيَ عَلَيْهِ وَكَانَ شَهِيدًا يَرْحَمُهُ اللَّهُ.

Sayyidunā ʿUmar ibn al-Khaṭṭāb was washed and shrouded and prayed over, yet he was a martyr. May Allah have mercy on him.[90]

---

89 *Ṣaḥīḥ al-Bukhārī*, 3677.

90 *Muwaṭṭa' Imām Mālik*, 997.

In another narration, ʿAbdullāh ibn ʿUmar ﷺ stated,

صُلِّيَ عَلَى عُمَرَ بْنِ الْخَطَّابِ فِي الْمَسْجِدِ.

The prayer over ʿUmar ibn al-Khaṭṭāb was done in the masjid.[91]

ʿAmr ibn Maymūn's ﷺ narration concludes with the following words,

فَلَمَّا فُرِغَ مِنْ دَفْنِهِ اجْتَمَعَ هَؤُلاَءِ الرَّهْطُ، فَقَالَ عَبْدُ الرَّحْمَنِ اجْعَلُوا أَمْرَكُمْ إِلَى ثَلاَثَةٍ مِنْكُمْ. فَقَالَ الزُّبَيْرُ قَدْ جَعَلْتُ أَمْرِي إِلَى عَلِيٍّ. فَقَالَ طَلْحَةُ قَدْ جَعَلْتُ أَمْرِي إِلَى عُثْمَانَ. وَقَالَ سَعْدٌ قَدْ جَعَلْتُ أَمْرِي إِلَى عَبْدِ الرَّحْمَنِ بْنِ عَوْفٍ.

فَقَالَ عَبْدُ الرَّحْمَنِ أَيُّكُمَا تَبَرَّأَ مِنْ هَذَا الأَمْرِ فَنَجْعَلُهُ إِلَيْهِ، وَاللَّهُ عَلَيْهِ وَالإِسْلاَمُ لَيَنْظُرَنَّ أَفْضَلَهُمْ فِي نَفْسِهِ. فَأُسْكِتَ الشَّيْخَانِ، فَقَالَ عَبْدُ الرَّحْمَنِ أَفَتَجْعَلُونَهُ إِلَيَّ، وَاللَّهُ عَلَيَّ أَنْ لاَ آلُوَ عَنْ أَفْضَلِكُمْ. قَالاَ نَعَمْ. فَأَخَذَ بِيَدِ أَحَدِهِمَا فَقَالَ لَكَ قَرَابَةٌ مِنْ رَسُولِ اللَّهِ ﷺ وَالْقَدَمُ فِي الإِسْلاَمِ مَا قَدْ عَلِمْتَ، فَاللَّهُ عَلَيْكَ لَئِنْ أَمَّرْتُكَ لَتَعْدِلَنَّ، وَلَئِنْ أَمَّرْتُ عُثْمَانَ لَتَسْمَعَنَّ وَلَتُطِيعَنَّ. ثُمَّ خَلاَ بِالآخَرِ فَقَالَ لَهُ مِثْلَ ذَلِكَ، فَلَمَّا أَخَذَ الْمِيثَاقَ قَالَ ارْفَعْ يَدَكَ يَا عُثْمَانُ. فَبَايَعَهُ، فَبَايَعَ لَهُ عَلِيٌّ، وَوَلَجَ أَهْلُ الدَّارِ فَبَايَعُوهُ.

When he was buried, the group [that had been selected by Sayyidunā ʿUmar] held a meeting. ʿAbd al-Raḥmān said, "Reduce the candidates for leadership to three of you."

al-Zubayr said, "I give up my right to Sayyidunā ʿAlī."

Ṭalḥah said, "I give up my right to Sayyidunā ʿUthmān."

Saʿd said, "I give up my right to Sayyidunā ʿAbd al-Raḥmān ibn ʿAwf."

91 *Muwaṭṭa' Imām Mālik*, 545.

ʿAbd al-Raḥmān then said [to Sayyidunā ʿUthmān and Sayyidunā ʿAlī], "Now, which of you is willing to give up his right of leadership so he may choose the better of the [remaining] two with Allah and Islam as his witnesses." Both of the sheikhs remained silent. ʿAbd al-Raḥmān then said, "Will you both leave this matter to me? I take Allah as my Witness that I will choose the better of you?"

They both said, "Yes."

ʿAbd al-Raḥmān took the hand of one (Sayyidunā ʿAlī) and said, "You are related to the Messenger of Allah and one of the earliest Muslims, as you well know. I ask you by Allah to promise that if I select you as a ruler, you will do justice, and if I select Sayyidunā ʿUthmān as a ruler you will listen to him and obey him." He then took the other (Sayyidunā ʿUthmān) aside and repeated the same.

Having secured this covenant, he said, "O ʿUthmān, raise your hand."

And so he gave him (Sayyidunā ʿUthmān) his pledge of allegiance, and then Sayyidunā ʿAlī gave him his pledge of allegiance, and then all of the people gave him their pledges of allegiance.[92]

Thus, Sayyidunā ʿUthmān ibn ʿAffān ﷺ became the Third Caliph of Islam. He was chosen from amongst six of the greatest Companions of the Prophet ﷺ in a solemn and sincere meeting wherein the betterment of the world was placed at the forefront of their decision-making. It was a meeting devoid of pomp and politics, and, unlike the gatherings of monarchs, dictators, and democratically elected presidents of today, there were no ulterior motives of internal scheming; six great men sat down in a room together and chose the best of them to rule.

---

92 *Ṣaḥīḥ al-Bukhārī*, 3700.

3

Al-Ghanī: "Dhū al-Nūrayn" ʿUthmān ibn ʿAffān

From the dawn of time until the Final Resurrection, no man will ever share in the grace with which he was honoured. There will only ever be one "Man of the Two Lights", for no other soul in all past and future history shall ever be blessed with the matrimony of two daughters of any Prophet, let alone the daughters of the greatest Prophet of them all ﷺ. He was a man of such good looks that he was forced to veil his face, lest he becomes a means of trial and tribulation; he was a man so immense in generosity that he equipped whole hosts for the defence and honour of Islam; and he was a man of such spiritual excellence that he was of the Ten who were promised Paradise. His quality was recognised by all his peers:

عَنِ ابْنِ عُمَرَ – رضى الله عنهما – قَالَ كُنَّا فِي زَمَنِ النَّبِيِّ ﷺ لاَ نَعْدِلُ بِأَبِي بَكْرٍ أَحَدًا ثُمَّ عُمَرَ ثُمَّ عُثْمَانَ، ثُمَّ نَتْرُكُ أَصْحَابَ النَّبِيِّ ﷺ لاَ نُفَاضِلُ بَيْنَهُمْ.

Ibn ʿUmar said, "During the lifetime of the Prophet
we considered Abū Bakr as peerless, then ʿUmar, and then

'Uthmān in superiority, after whom we did not differentiate between the Ṣaḥābah of the Prophet .[1]

Sayyidunā 'Uthmān ibn 'Affān ﷺ was the man charged with taking up the reins of the caliphate after Sayyidunā 'Umar's ﷺ golden reign, becoming the third Rightly-Guided Caliph of Islam. During an age of miraculous conquest, he was the commander-in-chief of the armies of Islam as they met with success upon success across the East and West of the known world.

Through it all, his humility and humbleness remained par excellence. His relationship with the Qur'an was such that he was its final gatherer, his name forever attached to its script, to be rewarded for its recital forevermore. His devotion to its recital was such that he wore out the pages of several tomes. He spent nights pouring over its words, and when he left this world, he left it reciting, his blood unjustly shed, bearing testimony to a life dyed in Godly colour:

صِبْغَةَ ٱللَّهِ ۖ وَمَنْ أَحْسَنُ مِنَ ٱللَّهِ صِبْغَةً ۖ وَنَحْنُ لَهُۥ عَـٰبِدُونَ

[We dye ourselves in] the colour of Allah. And who is better at colouring than Allah? It is Him we worship.[2]

His Name and Lineage

His full name was Abū 'Abdullāh 'Uthmān ibn 'Affān ibn Abī al-'Āṣ ibn Umayyah ibn 'Abd Shams ibn 'Abd Manāf ibn Quṣayy ibn Kilāb. His lineage joined with that of the Beloved Prophet ﷺ at 'Abd Manāf. His maternal grandmother was the full sister of the Prophet's ﷺ father 'Abdullāh ibn 'Abd al-Muṭṭalib, and may even have been his twin, so his mother Arwā bint Kurayz was a first cousin to the Beloved Prophet ﷺ.

---

1 *Ṣaḥīḥ al-Bukhārī*, 3697.

2 *al-Baqarah*, 2:138.

Before Islam

Sayyidunā ʿUthmān ﵁ was known for his modesty, generosity, and eloquence even during the Period of Ignorance (*Jāhiliyyah*). He was greatly loved and respected by all, averse as he was to all immorality. He states in his own words,

وَايْمُ اللهِ مَا زَنَيْتُ فِي جَاهِلِيَّةٍ وَلَا إِسْلَامٍ وَمَا ازْدَدْتُ لِلْإِسْلَامِ إِلَّا حَيَاءً

By Allah, I never fornicated during the Jāhiliyyah nor during Islam. And Islam has only increased my modesty.[3]

As for the love of his people for him, it is said that mothers would sing to their children as they put them to bed:

أَحِبُّكَ وَالرَّحْمَنِ حُبَّ قُرَيْشٍ لِعُثْمَانِ

My love for you, I swear by al-Raḥmān,

Is like Quraysh's love for their ʿUthmān.[4]

Accepting Islam

ʿUthmān ﵁ was the fourth man to Become Muslim after Abū Bakr ﵁, Ali ibn Talib ﵁ and Zaid ibn Harithah ﵁. It was Abū Bakr ﵁ who invited him to Islam, and he responded to the call immediately without any hesitation. He was thirty-four years old at that time.

---

3 Abū Nuʿaym al-Aṣbahānī, *Ḥilyah al-Awliyā' wa Ṭabaqāt al-Aṣfiyā'*, Dār al-Fikr, Beirut (1416/1996), Vol. 1 p. 60.

4 ʿAlī al-Ṣallābī, *ʿUthmān ibn ʿAffān: Dhū al-Nūrayn*, Dār al-Salām, Riyadh (2007), p. 18.

Modesty and Humility

عَنْ عَبْدِ اللَّهِ الرُّومِيِّ، قَالَ: بَلَغَنِي أَنَّ عُثْمَانَ رَضِيَ اللَّهُ عَنْهُ قَالَ:

لَوْ أَنِّي بَيْنَ الْجَنَّةِ وَالنَّارِ لَا أَدْرِي إِلَى أَيِّهِمَا يُؤْمَرُ بِي لَاخْتَرْتُ أَنْ أَكُونَ رَمَادًا قَبْلَ أَنْ أَعْلَمَ إِلَى أَيِّهِمَا أَصِيرُ.

Sayyidunā ʿUthmān ibn ʿAffān ﷺ said:

If I were between Heaven and Hell, not knowing which I was being ordered to, I would choose to be ashes before I learned which I would be sent to.[5]

Of the many high and noble qualities that Sayyidunā ʿUthmān ibn ʿAffān ﷺ was known for, modesty and humility are amongst the most prominent. He was a man of great spiritual stature, one of the Ten Promised Paradise, about whom the Prophet ﷺ said,

لِكُلِّ نَبِيٍّ رَفِيقٌ فِي الْجَنَّةِ، وَرَفِيقِي فِيهَا عُثْمَانُ بْنُ عَفَّانَ.

Every Prophet has a companion in Paradise, and my companion is ʿUthmān ibn ʿAffān.[6]

Despite this, Sayyidunā ʿUthmān ibn ʿAffān ﷺ, inherently modest and deeply humble, worried about the outcome of his judgement on the Day of Requital, just as his dear friends had worried before him. Such was the depth of his modesty and humility that the Prophet ﷺ described him thus,

وَأَصْدَقُهَا حَيَاءً عُثْمَانُ

... And the most sincere (of this Ummah) in modesty is ʿUthmān.[7]

---

5 Aḥmad ibn Ḥanbal, *Kitāb al-Zuhd*, 686.

6 Aḥmad ibn Ḥanbal, *Faḍā'il al-Ṣaḥābah*, 757.

7 Aḥmad ibn Ḥanbal, *Faḍā'il al-Ṣaḥābah*, 803.

Sayyidunā ʿUthmān's ﷺ modesty was indeed unmatched, even amongst the Ṣaḥābah. Despite his great wealth, he never flaunted it and lived his entire life in simplicity. He abhorred flamboyance, showing-off, and boastfulness, and chose asceticism over ease, despite having access to the trappings of wealth throughout his lifetime.

He was extremely shy, and never sought fame, nor did he wish for others to follow him. He was chosen as the Third Caliph for his ability to lead the Muslims and not for desire to attain the leadership position. Regarding his shyness, al-Ḥasan ﷺ states,

إِنْ كَانَ لَيَكُونُ فِي الْبَيْتِ وَالْبَابُ عَلَيْهِ مُغْلَقٌ فَمَا يَضَعُ عَنْهُ الثَّوْبَ لِيُفِيضَ عَلَيْهِ الْمَاءَ يَمْنَعُهُ الْحَيَاءُ أَنْ يُقِيمَ صُلْبَهُ.

> If he was in his home with the door closed, he would not remove his garment to pour water on himself, and shyness prevented him from standing up straight.[8]

He was the epitome of shyness. Even in a room in his own house, behind closed doors with no one else around, he would not fully undress, nor would he stand up straight. Sayyidunā ʿUthmān ﷺ understood that no one is ever truly alone or unwatched, and thus his behaviour reflected this, even when there was no other person present to witness his actions.

It is recorded that when he first stood on the pulpit to address the Muslims as the Commander of the Faithful, he became momentarily tongue-tied, due to a lifetime of abstention from front-facing leadership roles within the Ṣaḥābah. He then stated,

أَنْتُمْ إِلَى إِمَامٍ فَعَّالٍ أَحْوَجُ مِنْكُمْ إِلَى إِمَامٍ قَوَّالٍ.

---

8 *Musnad Imām Aḥmad*, 543.

You are more in need of an effective leader than you are of an eloquent leader.[9]

Despite his extreme modesty and shyness, Sayyidunā ʿUthmān ﷺ was an entirely honest and upright man, and thus, even in this situation, where his modesty and humility were on full display, he admitted to himself and the Ummah that his leadership was indeed needed at the time and that skilful administration and masterful statecraft were far more useful qualities in a leader than eloquence in speech and extroverted confidence on the pulpit.

Regarding his asceticism, it would not be too much to say that it stood out even amongst his esteemed peers, as he was one of the few Muslims who embraced Islam at the very beginning and managed to not only keep hold of his wealth beyond *hijrah* but continue to increase it. Yet we read of countless occasions which show that his access to comforts, as both one of the wealthiest traders in Arabia and the Caliph of the Rāshidūn Empire, did not distract him from his goals of worshipping Allah ﷻ and caring for the Ummah. He managed this by forgoing comfort for the sake of hardship, and wealth for the sake of simplicity. Maymūn ibn Mihrān ﷺ narrates,

أَخْبَرَنِي الْهَمْدَانِيُّ أَنَّهُ رَأَى عُثْمَانَ بْنَ عَفَّانَ رَحْمَةُ اللَّهِ عَلَيْهِ عَلَى بَغْلَةٍ وَخَلْفَهُ عَلَيْهَا غُلَامُهُ نَائِلٌ وَهُوَ خَلِيفَةٌ.

Al-Hamdānī told me that he saw Sayyidunā ʿUthmān ibn ʿAffān upon a mule and his servant, Nā'il, was sitting behind him, while he was the Caliph.[10]

Sayyidunā ʿUthmān ibn ʿAffān ﷺ had in his possession hundreds, if not thousands of camels, as can be seen from the narrations describing him as

9 Abū al-Faḍl Aḥmad ibn Muḥammad ibn Aḥmad al-Maydānī, *Majmaʿ al-Amthāl*, Vol. 2, p.453.

10 Aḥmad ibn Ḥanbal, *Kitāb al-Zuhd*, 672.

equipping a third of the Muslim army personally; yet for himself he preferred a mule, likely because he saw his beloved Prophet ﷺ do the same. The fact that he was sharing his mule with his servant shows just how careful Sayyidunā ʿUthmān ibn ʿAffān ؓ was about avoiding lavish living. As the Caliph of an empire that spanned from Persia to North Africa, one would have expected Sayyidunā ʿUthmān ؓ to have a retinue of guards to protect him and ensure his safety, especially following the assassination of his predecessor, but this was not so. al-Hamdānī ؓ narrates,

$$\text{رَأَيْتُ عُثْمَانَ نَائِمًا فِي الْمَسْجِدِ فِي مِلْحَفَةٍ لَيْسَ حَوْلَهُ أَحَدٌ وَهُوَ أَمِيرُ الْمُؤْمِنِينَ}$$

I saw Sayyidunā ʿUthmān sleeping in the masjid in a blanket with no one around him, and he was the Commander of the Faithful [at the time].¹¹

Sayyidunā ʿUthmān ibn ʿAffān ؓ had such trust in Allah ﷻ that despite the fate of his beloved companion, Sayyidunā ʿUmar ibn al-Khaṭṭāb ؓ, he wrapped himself in a simple blanket and slept on the masjid floor alone, free of worry or fear. When one has complete trust in Allah ﷻ, as we will see later, one is capable of great deeds of bravery and courage. Sayyidunā ʿUthmān ibn ʿAffān's ؓ courage was thus legendary.

Sayyidunā ʿUthmān ibn ʿAffān ؓ did not expect others to live up to the high standards of modesty and humility that he had set for himself. He would maintain the highest levels of strictness in terms of his own asceticism, but would spend lavishly on the people and ensure they were comfortable and well-fed. Shuraḥbīl ibn Muslim ؓ stated about Sayyidunā ʿUthmān ibn ʿAffān ؓ,

$$\text{كَانَ يُطْعِمُ النَّاسَ طَعَامَ الْإِمَارَةِ وَيَدْخُلُ إِلَى بَيْتِهِ فَأَكَلَ الْخَلَّ وَالزَّيْتَ}$$

---

11 Aḥmad ibn Ḥanbal, *Kitāb al-Zuhd*, 674.

He used to feed the people the food of the emirate, and then enter his house and consume vinegar and oil.[12]

The same leniency on others also extended to his household, as Zubayr ibn 'Abdullāh narrates from his grandfather, who stated about Sayyidunā 'Uthmān ibn 'Affān ☙,

مَا كَانَ يُوقِظُ أَحَدًا مِنْ أَهْلِهِ مِنَ اللَّيْلِ إِلَّا أَنْ يَجِدَهُ يَقْظَانَ فَيَدْعُوهُ فَيُنَاوِلُهُ وُضُوءَهُ وَكَانَ يَصُومُ الدَّهْرَ

He would not wake any of his family at night; if he found him awake, he would call him and help him with his wuḍū'. He was forever fasting.[13]

This was Sayyidunā 'Uthmān ibn 'Affān ☙, conscientiously striving to better himself spiritually whilst being so merciful to his subordinates that he remained careful not to wake them at night for supererogatory prayers, lest it be too difficult for them.

His continuous practice of fasting daily and standing in prayer nightly was well-known to those close to him, and numerous narrations point to this, such as the narration by Sayyidah Zuhaymah ☙ who states,

كَانَ عُثْمَانُ رَضِيَ اللَّهُ عَنْهُ يَصُومُ النَّهَارَ وَيَقُومُ اللَّيْلَ إِلَّا هَجْعَةً مِنْ أَوَّلِهِ

Sayyidunā 'Uthmān, may Allah be pleased with him, would fast during the day and stand awake [in prayer] at night, except for a period of sleep at the beginning of it.[14]

---

12 Aḥmad ibn Ḥanbal, *Kitāb al-Zuhd*, 684.
13 Aḥmad ibn Ḥanbal, *Kitāb al-Zuhd*, 670.
14 Aḥmad ibn Ḥanbal, *Kitāb al-Zuhd*, 688.

Despite his leniency on others regarding their adherence to the concept of asceticism, he had a deep dislike for people choosing to live extravagantly, and of intentional pomposity, flamboyance, and profligacy.

On one occasion, when Sayyidunā ʿUmar ibn al-Khaṭṭāb and Sayyidunā ʿUthmān ibn ʿAffān ﷺ were invited to a Muslim's house for a meal, Ḥumayd ibn Nuʿaym ﷺ narrates that,

أَنَّ عُمَرَ وَعُثْمَانَ رَضِيَ اللَّهُ عَنْهُمَا دُعِيَا إِلَى طَعَامٍ فَلَمَّا خَرَجَا قَالَ عُثْمَانُ لِعُمَرَ: قَدْ شَهِدْنَا طَعَامًا لَوَدِدْنَا أَنْ لَمْ نَشْهَدْهُ. قَالَ: لِمَ. قَالَ إِنِّي أَخَافُ أَنْ يَكُونَ صَنَعَ مِيَاهَاةً.

Sayyidunā ʿUmar and Sayyidunā ʿUthmān were invited to a meal and, when they left, Sayyidunā ʿUthmān said to Sayyidunā ʿUmar, "We have witnessed a meal that we wish we had not witnessed."

Sayyidunā ʿUmar said, "Why?"

Sayyidunā ʿUthmān said, "I fear that he was showing off."[15]

Sayyidunā ʿUthmān ibn ʿAffān's ﷺ dislike for showing off was so great that even a hint of pretentiousness was distasteful to him. Being completely free from this vice himself, he could not abide by it in others, for Sayyidunā ʿUthmān ﷺ was such a man who would sell the entire world, if he possessed it, for the sake of the Hereafter.

Selling the World to Earn the Hereafter

عَنْ عَطَاءِ بْنِ فَرُّوخَ، مَوْلَى الْقُرَشِيِّينَ أَنَّ عُثْمَانَ رَضِيَ اللَّهُ عَنْهُ اشْتَرَى مِنْ رَجُلٍ أَرْضًا فَأَبْطَأَ عَلَيْهِ فَلَقِيَهُ فَقَالَ لَهُ مَا مَنَعَكَ مِنْ قَبْضِ مَالِكَ قَالَ إِنَّكَ غَبَنْتَنِي فَمَا أَلْقَى مِنَ النَّاسِ أَحَدًا إِلَّا وَهُوَ يَلُومُنِي قَالَ أَوَ ذَلِكَ يَمْنَعُكَ قَالَ نَعَمْ قَالَ فَاخْتَرْ بَيْنَ أَرْضِكَ وَمَالِكَ ثُمَّ قَالَ قَالَ

15 Aḥmad ibn Ḥanbal, *Kitāb al-Zuhd*, 669.

رَسُولُ اللَّهِ صَلَّى اللَّهُ عَلَيْهِ وَسَلَّمَ أَدْخَلَ اللَّهُ عَزَّ وَجَلَّ الْجَنَّةَ رَجُلًا كَانَ سَهْلًا مُشْتَرِيًا وَبَائِعًا وَقَاضِيًا وَمُقْتَضِيًا.

ʿAṭā ibn Farrūkh, a mawlā of the Quraysh, narrated that Sayyidunā ʿUthmān bought some land from a man and the man did not seek payment for it. Then, when he met him, he said to him, "What prevented you from coming and taking your money?"

He replied, "You were unfair to me. I have not met anyone since except that he reproaches me."

Sayyidunā ʿUthmān said, "Is this the reason?"

He said, "Yes."

Sayyidunā ʿUthmān said, "Then choose between your land and your money." He then added, "The Messenger of Allah said, 'Allah admitted to Paradise a man who was easy-going in buying and selling when paying off a debt, and when asking for a debt owed to him.'"[16]

This was how Sayyidunā ʿUthmān al-Ghanī ﷺ did business. He was considerate of the other party, ensuring that the trade was fair and that all involved were happy with the outcome. Were it not the case, as can be seen here, he was easy-going and left the matter to his opposite to decide on whether the trade was acceptable to him or not. Every saying of the Prophet ﷺ he knew of, he acted upon.

His way of doing business was shaped by the Sunnah of the Prophet ﷺ, as Saʿīd ibn al-Musayyib ﷺ narrates,

سَمِعْتُ عُثْمَانَ رَضِيَ اللَّهُ عَنْهُ يَخْطُبُ عَلَى الْمِنْبَرِ وَهُوَ يَقُولُ:

16 *Musnad Imām Aḥmad*, 410.

كُنْتُ أَبْتَاعُ التَّمْرَ مِنْ بَطْنٍ مِنْ الْيَهُودِ يُقَالُ لَهُمْ بَنُو قَيْنُقَاعَ فَأَبِيعُهُ بِرِبْحٍ فَبَلَغَ ذَلِكَ رَسُولَ اللَّهِ صَلَّى اللَّهُ عَلَيْهِ وَسَلَّمَ فَقَالَ:

يَا عُثْمَانُ إِذَا اشْتَرَيْتَ فَاكْتَلْ وَإِذَا بِعْتَ فَكِلْ.

I heard Sayyidunā ʿUthmān delivering a sermon (khuṭbah) from the minbar. He said:

"I used to buy dates from one of the Jewish clans who were known as the Banū Qaynuqāʿ and sell them for a profit. News of this reached Allah's Messenger, who said, 'O ʿUthmān, when you buy, take only what is due, and when you sell, give their dues with nothing less.'"[17]

It can be seen clearly in how he did business that the words of the Prophet ﷺ were constantly at the forefront of his thoughts, as can be seen in every aspect of his life.

Despite his business manners being extremely fair to all involved, or perhaps it is better to say because of them, he was blessed with an ever-increasing fortune of worldly wealth, which he continuously exhausted for the sake of his fellow Muslims. Wealth traded for the sake of Allah ﷻ is always a profitable transaction, and Sayyidunā ʿUthmān رضي الله عنه understood this deeply and lived by this practice.

A clear example of this can be seen in the narration of al-Aḥnaf رضي الله عنه, who narrates,

انْطَلَقْنَا حُجَّاجًا فَمَرَرْنَا بِالْمَدِينَةِ فَبَيْنَمَا نَحْنُ فِي مَنْزِلِنَا إِذْ جَاءَنَا آتٍ فَقَالَ النَّاسُ مِنْ فَزَعٍ فِي الْمَسْجِدِ فَانْطَلَقْتُ أَنَا وَصَاحِبِي فَإِذَا النَّاسُ مُجْتَمِعُونَ عَلَى نَفَرٍ فِي الْمَسْجِدِ قَالَ فَتَخَلَّلْتُهُمْ حَتَّى قُمْتُ عَلَيْهِمْ فَإِذَا عَلِيُّ بْنُ أَبِي طَالِبٍ وَالزُّبَيْرُ وَطَلْحَةُ وَسَعْدُ بْنُ أَبِي وَقَّاصٍ قَالَ فَلَمْ يَكُنْ ذَلِكَ بِأَسْرَعَ مِنْ أَنْ جَاءَ عُثْمَانُ يَمْشِي فَقَالَ أَهَاهُنَا عَلِيٌّ قَالُوا نَعَمْ قَالَ أَهَاهُنَا الزُّبَيْرُ قَالُوا نَعَمْ قَالَ

17 *Musnad Imām Aḥmad*, 445.

أَهَاهُنَا طَلْحَةُ قَالُوا نَعَمْ قَالَ أَهَاهُنَا سَعْدٌ قَالُوا نَعَمْ قَالَ أَنْشُدُكُمْ بِاللَّهِ الَّذِي لَا إِلَهَ إِلَّا هُوَ أَتَعْلَمُونَ أَنَّ رَسُولَ اللَّهِ صَلَّى اللَّهُ عَلَيْهِ وَسَلَّمَ قَالَ مَنْ يَبْتَاعُ مِرْبَدَ بَنِي فُلَانٍ غَفَرَ اللَّهُ لَهُ فَابْتَعْتُهُ فَأَتَيْتُ رَسُولَ اللَّهِ صَلَّى اللَّهُ عَلَيْهِ وَسَلَّمَ فَقُلْتُ إِنِّي قَدْ ابْتَعْتُهُ فَقَالَ اجْعَلْهُ فِي مَسْجِدِنَا وَأَجْرُهُ لَكَ قَالُوا نَعَمْ قَالَ أَنْشُدُكُمْ بِاللَّهِ الَّذِي لَا إِلَهَ إِلَّا هُوَ أَتَعْلَمُونَ أَنَّ رَسُولَ اللَّهِ صَلَّى اللَّهُ عَلَيْهِ وَسَلَّمَ قَالَ مَنْ يَبْتَاعُ بِئْرَ رُومَةَ فَابْتَعْتُهَا بِكَذَا وَكَذَا فَأَتَيْتُ رَسُولَ اللَّهِ صَلَّى اللَّهُ عَلَيْهِ وَسَلَّمَ فَقُلْتُ إِنِّي قَدْ ابْتَعْتُهَا يَعْنِي بِئْرَ رُومَةَ فَقَالَ اجْعَلْهَا سِقَايَةً لِلْمُسْلِمِينَ وَأَجْرُهَا لَكَ قَالُوا نَعَمْ قَالَ أَنْشُدُكُمْ بِاللَّهِ الَّذِي لَا إِلَهَ إِلَّا هُوَ أَتَعْلَمُونَ أَنَّ رَسُولَ اللَّهِ صَلَّى اللَّهُ عَلَيْهِ وَسَلَّمَ نَظَرَ فِي وُجُوهِ الْقَوْمِ يَوْمَ جَيْشِ الْعُسْرَةِ فَقَالَ مَنْ يُجَهِّزُ هَؤُلَاءِ غَفَرَ اللَّهُ لَهُ فَجَهَّزْتُهُمْ حَتَّى مَا يَفْقِدُونَ خِطَامًا وَلَا عِقَالًا قَالُوا اللَّهُمَّ نَعَمْ قَالَ اللَّهُمَّ اشْهَدْ اللَّهُمَّ اشْهَدْ اللَّهُمَّ اشْهَدْ ثُمَّ انْصَرَفَ.

We set out for Ḥajj and passed by Medina. Whilst we were in our camp, someone came by and said, "There is a commotion in the masjid."

My companion and I set out, and we found the people gathered around a group in the masjid. I pushed through them until I got to them, and found Sayyidunā ʿAlī ibn Abī Ṭālib, Sayyidunā al-Zubayr, Sayyidunā Ṭalḥah, and Sayyidunā Saʿd ibn Abī Waqqāṣ. Soon after Sayyidunā ʿUthmān came walking and asked, "Is Sayyidunā ʿAlī here?"

They said, "Yes."

He said, "Is Sayyidunā al-Zubayr here?"

They said, "Yes."

He said, "Is Sayyidunā Ṭalḥah here?"

They said, "Yes."

He said, "Is Sayyidunā Saʿd here?"

They said, "Yes."

He said, "I adjure you by Allah, beside Whom there is no other deity, do you know that the Messenger of Allah said, 'Whoever buys the date-drying place of Banū So-and-so, Allah will forgive him', and that I bought it and went to the Messenger of Allah and said, 'I have bought it', to which he said, 'Add it to our masjid and the reward for it will be yours'?"

They said, "Yes."

He said, "I adjure you by Allah, beside Whom there is no other deity, do you know that the Messenger of Allah once said, 'Who will buy the well of Rūmah?' and that I bought it for such and such, then went to the Messenger of Allah and said, 'I have bought it, as in the well of Rūmah', to which he replied, 'Make it a water source for the Muslims and the reward for it will be yours'?"

They said, "Yes."

He said, "I adjure you by Allah, beside Whom there is no other deity, do you know that the Messenger of Allah looked at the faces of the people on the day of the Army of Hardship[18] and said, 'Whoever equips these men, Allah will forgive him', so I equipped them until they were not even without reins or ropes?"

They said, "By Allah, yes."

He said, "O Allah, bear witness! O Allah, bear witness! O Allah, bear witness!" Then he left.[19]

No opportunity to help his brothers and sisters came to him except that he took it immediately. Whenever the Prophet ﷺ requested someone to spend wealth in the path of Allah ﷻ, it was well-known to all that Sayyidunā ʿUthmān ibn ʿAffān ؓ would arrive soon after having carried out the task.

18 This refers to the Tabūk Campaign.

19 *Musnad Imām Aḥmad*, 511.

He put the needs of the Muslims above his own and we see in the above example how cost, the extent of the ask, and any worldly benefit were of no concern to him. He extended the masjid, slaked the thirsts of the people, and equipped an army at a moment's notice.

Likewise, it is in our own best interests to do the same with our own wealth, to spend lavishly on our brothers and sisters who are in need of our aid, and to spare no expense in financing the institutions of the Muslims. Oftentimes we hear ourselves complaining of the state of the Muslims, of a lack of standards in education or a lack of professionalism in other fields, but rarely do we ask ourselves what we have done to facilitate change. If the issue is financial, then donate; if the issue is educational, then learn; and if the issue is professional, then become the change you seek to make.

Regarding business etiquette and methods of creating wealth, Sayyidunā ʿUthmān ﷺ warned people against doing things that could lead, or even force, oneself or others into sin. Abū Suhayl ibn Mālik narrates from his father that he heard Sayyidunā ʿUthmān ibn ʿAffān ﷺ say in a sermon,

لاَ تُكَلِّفُوا الأَمَةَ غَيْرَ ذَاتِ الصَّنْعَةِ الْكَسْبَ فَإِنَّكُمْ مَتَى كَلَّفْتُمُوهَا ذَلِكَ كَسَبَتْ بِفَرْجِهَا وَلاَ تُكَلِّفُوا الصَّغِيرَ الْكَسْبَ فَإِنَّهُ إِذَا لَمْ يَجِدْ سَرَقَ وَعِفُّوا إِذْ أَعَفَّكُمُ اللَّهُ وَعَلَيْكُمْ مِنَ الْمَطَاعِمِ بِمَا طَابَ مِنْهَا.

Do not oblige the slave-girl to earn, unless she has a skill. When you oblige her to do so, she will earn by prostitution; do not oblige the child to earn, for if he does not find it, he will steal. Have integrity as Allah has integrity with you, and you must feed them good food.[20]

Herein is a lesson in how to treat our subordinates – treat them well, with integrity and afford them respect, and do not oblige them to carry out tasks

20 *Muwaṭṭa' Imām Mālik*, 1808.

they are unable to complete. Doing so forces them into sin, which you will be liable for.

What benefit is there in overworking the people we are charged to look after? Is it merely to gather more wealth? For what purpose are we doing this? There is no benefit in gathering wealth to oneself and withholding it from those in need, not in this world and not in the Hereafter. Imam Mālik ﵀ states in his *Muwaṭṭa'* that Sayyidunā ʿUthmān ibn ʿAffān ﵁ forbade "*al-ḥukrah*", meaning hoarding.[21] Indeed, outside of one's basic necessities, there is little need for anything else. All excess will be questioned about on the Day of Requital. In a Hadith transmitted by Sayyidunā ʿUthmān ibn ʿAffān ﵁ himself, the Prophet ﷺ is reported to have said,

كُلُّ شَيْءٍ سِوَى ظِلِّ بَيْتٍ وَجِلْفِ الْخُبْزِ وَثَوْبٍ يُوَارِي عَوْرَتَهُ وَالْمَاءِ فَمَا فَضَلَ عَنْ هَذَا فَلَيْسَ لِابْنِ آدَمَ فِيهِ حَقٌّ.

Everything but the shade of a house, a sack of bread, a garment to cover his ʿawrah, and water; anything more than this the son of Adam has no right to.[22]

Again, Sayyidunā ʿUthmān ibn ʿAffān ﵁ acted upon this advice to the letter, living a pure and simple life in spite of his wealth. This was his way: he spent the first third of his life being prepared for the companionship of the Prophet ﷺ, then second-third training in his noble company, and the final-third in acting upon what he had learned. He would do so to the very letter and was renowned for both his knowledge of the Sunnah and his meticulousness in acting upon it.

---

21 *Muwaṭṭa' Imām Mālik*, 1350.

22 *Musnad Imām Aḥmad*, 440.

Love and Knowledge of the Sunnah

عَنْ سَعِيدَ بْنَ الْمُسَيَّبِ، يَقُولُ: رَأَيْتُ عُثْمَانَ قَاعِدًا فِي الْمَقَاعِدِ، فَدَعَا بِطَعَامٍ مِمَّا مَسَّتْهُ النَّارُ، فَأَكَلَهُ ثُمَّ قَامَ إِلَى الصَّلَاةِ فَصَلَّى، ثُمَّ قَالَ عُثْمَانُ: قَعَدْتُ مَقْعَدَ رَسُولِ اللَّهِ صَلَّى اللَّهُ عَلَيْهِ وَسَلَّمَ وَأَكَلْتُ طَعَامَ رَسُولِ اللَّهِ وَصَلَّيْتُ صَلَاةَ رَسُولِ اللَّهِ صَلَّى اللَّهُ عَلَيْهِ وَسَلَّمَ.

Sayyidunā Saʿīd ibn al-Musayyib said, "I saw Sayyidunā ʿUthmān sitting in al-Maqāʿid. He called for food that had been touched by fire and ate it, then he stood to pray and prayed.

Then Sayyidunā ʿUthmān said, 'I sat where Allah's Messenger sat, ate the food that Allah's Messenger ate, and offered the prayer that Allah's Messenger offered.'"[23]

This was always his way. His love for Prophet ﷺ and the Prophet's ﷺ ways ran deeply. It was in his blood. Time and again we read how he emulated the Prophet's ﷺ actions to the letter and then pointed this out to others so they might also do exactly as he had done.

Another example of this can be found in the narration from Ḥumrān ibn Abān ؓ, who states with regards to Sayyidunā ʿUthmān ibn ʿAffān ؓ,

أَنَّهُ دَعَا بِمَاءٍ فَتَوَضَّأَ وَمَضْمَضَ وَاسْتَنْشَقَ ثُمَّ غَسَلَ وَجْهَهُ ثَلَاثًا وَذِرَاعَيْهِ ثَلَاثًا ثَلَاثًا وَمَسَحَ بِرَأْسِهِ وَظَهْرِ قَدَمَيْهِ ثُمَّ ضَحِكَ فَقَالَ لِأَصْحَابِهِ أَلَا تَسْأَلُونِي عَمَّا أَضْحَكَنِي فَقَالُوا مِمَّ ضَحِكْتَ يَا أَمِيرَ الْمُؤْمِنِينَ قَالَ رَأَيْتُ رَسُولَ اللَّهِ صَلَّى اللَّهُ عَلَيْهِ وَسَلَّمَ دَعَا بِمَاءٍ قَرِيبًا مِنْ هَذِهِ الْبُقْعَةِ فَتَوَضَّأَ كَمَا تَوَضَّأْتُ ثُمَّ ضَحِكَ فَقَالَ أَلَا تَسْأَلُونِي مَا أَضْحَكَنِي فَقَالُوا مَا أَضْحَكَكَ يَا رَسُولَ اللَّهِ فَقَالَ إِنَّ الْعَبْدَ إِذَا دَعَا بِوَضُوءٍ فَغَسَلَ وَجْهَهُ حَطَّ اللَّهُ عَنْهُ كُلَّ خَطِيئَةٍ أَصَابَهَا بِوَجْهِهِ فَإِذَا غَسَلَ ذِرَاعَيْهِ كَانَ كَذَلِكَ وَإِنْ مَسَحَ بِرَأْسِهِ كَانَ كَذَلِكَ وَإِذَا طَهَّرَ قَدَمَيْهِ كَانَ كَذَلِكَ.

---

23 *Musnad Imām Aḥmad*, 505.

He called for water and did wuḍū'. He rinsed his mouth and nose, then he washed his face three times, his arms three times each, and wiped his head and the tops of his feet. He smiled and said to his companions, "Are you not going to ask me what made me smile?"

They said, "What made you smile, O Amīr al-Mu'minīn?"

He said, "I saw the Messenger of Allah call for water near this spot, then he did wuḍū' as I have done it, then he smiled and said, 'Are you not going to ask me what made me smile?' They said, 'What made you smile, O Messenger of Allah?' He said, 'If a person calls for water for wuḍū' and then washes his face, Allah will remove from him every sin that he committed with his face; when he washes his arms, the same applies; when he wipes his head, the same applies; when he purifies his feet, the same applies.'"[24]

In another narration, Ḥumrān ﷺ states,

رَأَيْتُ عُثْمَانَ – رضى الله عنه – تَوَضَّأَ، فَأَفْرَغَ عَلَى يَدَيْهِ ثَلاَثًا، ثُمَّ تَمَضْمَضَ وَاسْتَنْثَرَ، ثُمَّ غَسَلَ وَجْهَهُ ثَلاَثًا، ثُمَّ غَسَلَ يَدَهُ الْيُمْنَى إِلَى الْمَرْفِقِ ثَلاَثًا، ثُمَّ غَسَلَ يَدَهُ الْيُسْرَى إِلَى الْمَرْفِقِ ثَلاَثًا، ثُمَّ مَسَحَ بِرَأْسِهِ، ثُمَّ غَسَلَ رِجْلَهُ الْيُمْنَى ثَلاَثًا، ثُمَّ الْيُسْرَى ثَلاَثًا، ثُمَّ قَالَ رَأَيْتُ رَسُولَ اللَّهِ ﷺ تَوَضَّأَ نَحْوَ وُضُوئِي هَذَا، ثُمَّ قَالَ مَنْ تَوَضَّأَ وُضُوئِي هَذَا، ثُمَّ يُصَلِّي رَكْعَتَيْنِ، لاَ يُحَدِّثُ نَفْسَهُ فِيهِمَا بِشَيْءٍ، إِلاَّ غُفِرَ لَهُ مَا تَقَدَّمَ مِنْ ذَنْبِهِ.

I saw Sayyidunā 'Uthmān doing wuḍū'. He washed his hands thrice, rinsed his mouth, then cleaned his nose, and washed his face thrice. He then washed his right forearm up to the elbow thrice, then the left forearm up to the elbow thrice; then he wiped his head with water and washed his right foot thrice and then his left foot thrice. He then said, "I saw Allah's Messenger performing wuḍū' the way I have done wuḍū'" and then said, 'Whoever performs wuḍū' like my present wuḍū' and then offers two

24 *Musnad Imām Aḥmad*, 406.

rakʿah in which he does not think of worldly things, all his previous sins will be forgiven."[25]

Sayyidunā ʿUthmān ibn ʿAffān ؓ knew that success lay in following the Commands of Allah ﷻ as demonstrated through the Sunnah of the Prophet ﷺ. He was given glad tidings of Paradise in this very world; moreover, he was given the status of being the Prophet's ﷺ companion in Paradise. It is unfortunate that we, the so-called followers of the Prophet ﷺ, are far away from him despite having access to all the information his Ṣaḥābah collected about him. How can we believe that we will find success through any other path or find benefit in any other way? The people who truly knew him and followed his way completely without question have indeed succeeded in this life and the next. They were promised Paradise. Allah ﷻ has highlighted His happiness with them in the Qur'an, and books are being written about their successes even now. Sayyidunā ʿUthmān ؓ tackled every issue he faced throughout his life by referring back to what Allah ﷻ says in the Qur'an or what the Prophet ﷺ taught him.

Abān ibn ʿUthmān ؓ narrates from Sayyidunā ʿUthmān ibn ʿAffān ؓ that once he saw a funeral procession and stood up for it. He then said,

رَأَيْتُ رَسُولَ اللَّهِ صَلَّى اللَّهُ عَلَيْهِ وَسَلَّمَ رَأَى جَنَازَةً فَقَامَ لَهَا.

I saw the Messenger of Allah witness a funeral and stand up for it.[26]

Yaʿlā ibn Umayyah ؓ narrated another incident when he was performing *ṭawāf* with Sayyidunā ʿUthmān ibn ʿAffān ؓ,

طُفْتُ مَعَ عُثْمَانَ فَاسْتَلَمْنَا الرُّكْنَ قَالَ يَعْلَى فَكُنْتُ مِمَّا يَلِي الْبَيْتَ فَلَمَّا بَلَغْنَا الرُّكْنَ الْغَرْبِيَّ الَّذِي يَلِي الْأَسْوَدَ جَرَرْتُ بِيَدِهِ لِيَسْتَلِمَ فَقُلْتُ أَلَا تَسْتَلِمُ قَالَ فَقَالَ أَلَمْ تَطُفْ مَعَ

---

25 *Ṣaḥīḥ al-Bukhārī*, 1934.
26 *Musnad Imām Aḥmad*, 426.

رَسُولِ اللَّهِ صَلَّى اللَّهُ عَلَيْهِ وَسَلَّمَ فَقُلْتُ بَلَى قَالَ أَرَأَيْتَهُ يَسْتَلِمُ هَذَيْنِ الرُّكْنَيْنِ الْغَرْبِيَّيْنِ قُلْتُ لَا قَالَ أَفَلَيْسَ لَكَ فِيهِ أُسْوَةٌ حَسَنَةٌ قُلْتُ بَلَى قَالَ فَانْفُذْ عَنْكَ.

I circumambulated with Sayyidunā ʿUthmān and he touched the corner. I was next to the House and when I reached the western corner, which is next to the Black Stone. I took his hand to touch the corner and he said, "What is the matter?"

I said, "Are you not going to touch it?"

He said, "Did you not circumambulate with the Messenger of Allah?"

I said, "Of course."

He said, "Did you see him touch these two western corners?"

I said, "No."

He said, "Do you not have a good example in him?"

I said, "Of course."

He said, "Then do not bother with this."[27]

Sayyidunā ʿUthmān ibn ʿAffān ؓ only saw benefit in following the Sunnah of the Prophet ﷺ; anything that was not according to the Sunnah would thus be dismissed by him as waste of time. From the aforementioned narration, we can also see his method of teaching others. He did not rebuke anyone, nor shut them down. He would show them practically how to do something, ask questions, and then present the Hadith he was acting upon, to ensure that people would remember the lesson. Even his method of teaching was an example of following the Sunnah. On this occasion during *ṭawāf*, we can see how he appeals to Yaʿlā ibn Umayyah's ؓ own experience of

27 *Musnad Imām Aḥmad*, 512.

circumambulating with the Prophet ﷺ, highlighting the learner's prior experience and knowledge. In this way, the lesson takes the form of a reminder and is thus less confrontational, which also makes it more palatable and beneficial for the learner.

His love for the Sunnah was so great that he would act on it at every opportunity and would also create the opportunity to act upon it, as was the case with the example of making *wuḍū'* mentioned above. Ḥumrān ؓ states,

$$\text{كَانَ عُثْمَانُ رَضِيَ اللَّهُ عَنْهُ يَغْتَسِلُ كُلَّ يَوْمٍ مَرَّةً مِنْ مُنْذُ أَسْلَمَ.}$$

Sayyidunā 'Uthmān bathed every day since accepting Islam.[28]

Regarding the depth of his knowledge of the Law, Sayyidunā Ibn Shihāb ؓ says,

$$\text{لَوْ هَلَكَ عُثْمَانُ بْنُ عَفَّانَ وَزَيْدُ بْنُ ثَابِتٍ فِي بَعْضِ الزَّمَانِ لَهَلَكَ عِلْمُ الْفَرَائِضِ إِلَى يَوْمِ الْقِيَامَةِ، وَلَقَدْ جَاءَ عَلَى النَّاسِ زَمَانٌ وَمَا يَعْلَمُهَا غَيْرُهُمَا.}$$

If Sayyidunā 'Uthmān ibn 'Affān and Sayyidunā Zayd ibn Thābit perished at a particular time, the knowledge of inheritance would have perished with them until the Day of Resurrection, for a time came upon the people when no one knew it except them.[29]

His love and understanding for the Law and the Sunnah were complete. He was known even amongst the Ṣaḥābah for his knowledge in *fiqh* (jurisprudence) and his capabilities as judge. He had a thirst for knowledge which could not be slaked, and the gathering of knowledge made him a successful diplomat and head of state.

---

28 *Musnad Imām Aḥmad*, 484.
29 Aḥmad ibn Ḥanbal, *Faḍā'il al-Ṣaḥābah*, 745.

Abstention from Evil

عَنْ عَبْدِ الرَّحْمَنِ بْنِ الْحَارِثِ، قَالَ: سَمِعْتُ عُثْمَانَ رضى الله عنه، يَقُولُ:

اجْتَنِبُوا الْخَمْرَ فَإِنَّهَا أُمُّ الْخَبَائِثِ إِنَّهُ كَانَ رَجُلٌ مِمَّنْ خَلاَ قَبْلَكُمْ تَعَبَّدَ فَعَلِقَتْهُ امْرَأَةٌ غَوِيَّةٌ فَأَرْسَلَتْ إِلَيْهِ جَارِيَتَهَا فَقَالَتْ لَهُ إِنَّا نَدْعُوكَ لِلشَّهَادَةِ فَانْطَلَقَ مَعَ جَارِيَتِهَا فَطَفِقَتْ كُلَّمَا دَخَلَ بَابًا أَغْلَقَتْهُ دُونَهُ حَتَّى أَفْضَى إِلَى امْرَأَةٍ وَضِيئَةٍ عِنْدَهَا غُلاَمٌ وَبَاطِيَةُ خَمْرٍ فَقَالَتْ إِنِّي وَاللَّهِ مَا دَعَوْتُكَ لِلشَّهَادَةِ وَلَكِنْ دَعَوْتُكَ لِتَقَعَ عَلَىَّ أَوْ تَشْرَبَ مِنْ هَذِهِ الْخَمْرَةِ كَأْسًا أَوْ تَقْتُلَ هَذَا الْغُلاَمَ. قَالَ فَاسْقِينِي مِنْ هَذَا الْخَمْرِ كَأْسًا. فَسَقَتْهُ كَأْسًا. قَالَ زِيدُونِي. فَلَمْ يَرِمْ حَتَّى وَقَعَ عَلَيْهَا وَقَتَلَ النَّفْسَ. فَاجْتَنِبُوا الْخَمْرَ فَإِنَّهَا وَاللَّهِ لاَ يَجْتَمِعُ الإِيمَانُ وَإِدْمَانُ الْخَمْرِ إِلاَّ لَيُوشِكُ أَنْ يُخْرِجَ أَحَدُهُمَا صَاحِبَهُ.

ʿAbd al-Raḥmān ibn al-Ḥārith narrated that he heard Sayyidunā ʿUthmān ﷺ say:

"Avoid alcohol for it is the mother of all evils. There was a man from those who preceded you who was a devoted worshipper. An immoral woman fell in love with him and sent her slave girl to him, saying, 'We call you to bear witness.'

So he set out with her slave girl; each time he entered a door, she locked it behind him, until he came upon a beautiful woman who had with her a boy and a vessel of wine. She said, 'By Allah, I did not call you to bear witness, rather I called you to sleep with me, drink a cup of this wine, or kill this boy.'

He said, 'Then pour me a cup of wine.'

So she poured him a cup. He said, 'Give me more.'

He did not stop until he had slept with her and killed the boy. So avoid alcohol for, by Allah, faith and alcoholism cannot coexist until one expels the other."[30]

Any conversation on the subject of abstinence from sin often begins with the matron of the whorehouse of sin and the root of evil deeds: alcohol, and by extension, all intoxicants. The above saying of Sayyidunā 'Uthmān ibn 'Affān ؓ perfectly demonstrates the dangers that alcohol presents. The man he spoke of was in a situation where the multiple locked doors presented two predicaments. He was unable to leave of his own accord, and there was no other apparent witness to his deeds except the woman who desired him. Given the option of the three sins, he chose what he believed to be the least of the three, but as we know, this was not the case. Drinking the wine made him want to drink more and drinking more led to intoxication and addiction. Before he knew it, he had murdered a child and engaged in fornication. In this way, the woman got exactly what she had wanted: the man was now forever bound to her, lest she revealed the secret of what he had done to the rest of the world.

All sins have an addictive quality to them. The more one engages in them, the more they become normalised and part of one's life, until a time comes when one feels unable to go without sinning. Alcohol is the worst of them, because it leads to all the others. Sayyidunā 'Uthmān ibn 'Affān's ؓ warning against alcohol thus protects wide swathes of society from falling into a myriad of unknown sins.

It is also true that the sins one commits have an effect on one's appearance at a spiritual level. Ḥammād ibn Zayd ؓ reports that Sayyidunā 'Uthmān ibn 'Affān ؓ said,

مَا مِنْ عَامِلٍ يَعْمَلُ عَمَلًا إِلَّا كَسَاهُ اللَّهُ رِدَاءَ عَمَلِهِ.

---

30   *Sunan al-Nasā'ī*, 5666.

There is no action one carries out except that Allah garbs him in the garment of his actions.[31]

One's actions thus either anoint or sully him. The people of Allah ﷻ, who do good works and are God-fearing, have a light upon their faces that inclines hearts towards them and creates feelings of love and respect in others. The people of sin are often shunned by the good-hearted and only ever attract like-minded people toward them: a thief attracts a thief, an addict attracts an addict, and a fornicator attracts a fornicator.

Sayyidunā ʿUthmān ibn ʿAffān ؓ was known for his complete abstention from all evil deeds. Any man who followed the Sunnah of the Prophet ﷺ as closely and completely as he did could not fall into the traps of sin, although it is also true that it was in his *fiṭrah* (nature) to avoid sin, and he did so even prior to the Age of Islam.

Some sins are such that they remain hidden within the hearts of the sinners, not unlike the many locked doors that hide the worshipper's sins in the opening quotation of this section, and therefore are allowed to proliferate and fester. These sins are often not physically acted out but are instead crimes of character and can lead to great harm if allowed to metastasise.

The diseases of spitefulness, jealousy, and hatred are such sins. They can harm the target if acted upon in some way, and will no doubt ravage the heart of a pious Muslim like wildfires spreading through dry woodlands. Bearing such feelings within oneself is a sure way to self-harm spiritually, mentally, and physically. Sayyidunā ʿUthmān ibn ʿAffān ؓ states,

إنَّ لكل شيء آفةً، ولكل نعمة عاهة، وإن آفة هذا الدِّين وعاهة هذه النعمة عَيَّابُونَ طَعَّانُون، يُرُونَكم ما تحبون، ويُسِرُّون ما تكرهون. طَغَام مثلُ النعام يتبعون أول ناعق.

31 Aḥmad ibn Ḥanbal, *Kitāb al-Zuhd*, 667.

Everything has an undermining quality, and every grace has a weakness. The underminer of this faith and the weakness of this grace are those who dishonour others and harbour hatred; they reveal what you like and conceal what you dislike. They are ignoramuses who, like ostriches, follow the first to crow.[32]

Such people, who hold disdain for others in their hearts, burn themselves by holding onto the coals of hatred but can inflict great harm upon the Ummah as well if they allow this hatred to manifest into action. They show others what they want to see and hear but hide their true feelings and thoughts from them. The closing simile puts the final nail in the coffin for such folk, as Sayyidunā ʿUthmān ibn ʿAffān ﷺ compares them to a crowd of ostriches that chase after whoever is the first to make a sound and have no intellect or high moral standards of their own by which to judge their leaders.

They hold tight to their jealousy of good people and leaders strong in faith and burn within when they see them succeeding or content. Sayyidunā ʿUthmān ibn ʿAffān ﷺ advised the following with regard to such people,

يَكْفِيكَ مِنَ الْحَاسِدِ أَنَّهُ يَغْتَمُّ وَقْتَ سُرُورِكَ.

It is enough for a jealous person to be saddened by your time of happiness.[33]

As such, one should not allow jealous people to succeed by becoming upset or hurt by their jealousy or unkind words; the greatest retribution against such people and the best response is to continue being happy and content with your life, and let the ignoble ones burn with jealousy.

It is important for us to not hold any disdain in our hearts for such people, or for anyone who has wronged us. Though admittedly this is easier in

32 Abū al-Faḍl Aḥmad ibn Muḥammad al-Maydānī, *Majmaʿ al-Amthāl*, Vol. 2, p. 453.

33 Ibid.

some situations than others, it should nevertheless be our goal to not allow hatred to become ascendant within ourselves. As Sayyidunā ʿUthmān ﷺ said,

أَسْتَغْفِرُ اللَّهَ إِنْ كُنْتُ ظَلَمْتُ، وَقَدَ عَفَوْتُ إِنْ كُنْتُ ظُلِمْتُ.

I seek Allah's forgiveness if I have wronged someone, and I have forgiven whoever has wronged me.[34]

Attaining forgiveness from our own sins is possible only when we are forgiving in nature ourselves. How can it be that we hold no mercy within us for others but then seek mercy from the Creator? Indeed, He is the All-Merciful and the Very-Merciful, of this there is no doubt. The Prophet ﷺ said it beautifully when he explained,

ارْحَمُوا تُرْحَمُوا وَاغْفِرُوا يَغْفِرْ اللَّهُ لَكُمْ.

Be merciful, and you will receive mercy; Forgive, and Allah will forgive you.[35]

The Qur'an and ʿUthmān

عَنْ سُفْيَانَ بْنِ عُيَيْنَةَ، قَالَ: قَالَ عُثْمَانُ رَحِمَهُ اللهُ:

وَمَا أُحِبُّ أَنْ يَأْتِيَ عَلَيَّ يَوْمٌ وَلَا لَيْلَةٌ إِلَّا أَنْظُرُ فِي اللهِ

يَعْنِي الْقِرَاءَةَ فِي الْمُصْحَفِ.

---

34 Khalīfah ibn Khayyāṭ, *Tārīkh Khalīfah ibn Khayyāṭ*, 171.

35 *Al-Adab al-Mufrad*, 380.

Sufyān ibn ʿUyaynah narrated that Sayyidunā ʿUthmān ibn ʿAffān said,

"I dislike letting a day or night pass without looking at Allah."

Meaning, reciting whilst looking into the muṣḥaf.[36]

The relationship between Sayyidunā ʿUthmān ibn ʿAffān and the Holy Qur'an is known to all. He spent his days reciting it by looking into his *muṣḥaf* (written copy of the Qur'an) and spent his nights reciting it in a long *rakʿah* of prayer. The Qur'an that we read today is written in the ʿUthmānī orthographical script and it was collated by Sayyidunā ʿUthmān in the form and order that we still know it to be, and it will remain so until the end of days, *in shā' Allāh*. He employed Zayd ibn Thābit, ʿAbdullāh ibn al-Zubayr, Saʿd ibn al-ʿĀṣ, and ʿAbd al-Rahmān ibn al-Ḥārith ibn Hāshim to compile the standardised, complete version of the Qur'an, which was then copied and sent throughout the Caliphate to be copied further and memorised. In so doing, the Qur'an was preserved in written form as well as preserved orally. It is perhaps the single greatest service to Islam that Sayyidunā ʿUthmān ibn ʿAffān carried out, and as a result of his foresight and vision, he continues to reap the reward of this monumental achievement.

As stated in the previous sections, Sayyidunā ʿUthmān ibn ʿAffān acted on everything the Prophet taught him. It therefore comes as no surprise that the following Hadith of the Prophet was narrated by Sayyidunā ʿUthmān ibn ʿAffān himself,

أَفْضَلُكُمْ مَنْ تَعَلَّمَ الْقُرْآنَ وَ عَلَّمَهُ.

The best of you is the one who learns the Qur'an and teaches it.[37]

---

36 Aḥmad ibn Ḥanbal, *Kitāb al-Zuhd*, 681.

37 *Musnad Imām Aḥmad*, 405.

What greater learner and what greater teacher can there be over the one who arranged for its collation into a single, standardised *muṣḥaf* and then propagated the Qur'an through which hundreds of millions have memorised the entire text. On a personal level, Sayyidunā ʿUthmān ؓ learned the Qur'an, recited it daily, and studied its meanings deeply. He was known to be one of the most knowledgeable from the Ṣaḥābah on the subject of the Qur'an and knew many of its gems and benefits. For example, about teaching the Qur'an, Abū al-Khayr ؓ narrated that Sayyidunā ʿUthmān ibn ʿAffān ؓ said,

مَنْ قَرَأَ آخِرَ آلِ عِمْرَانَ فِي لَيْلَةٍ، كُتِبَ لَهُ قِيَامُ لَيْلَةٍ.

> Whoever recites the last verses of Sūrah Āl-ʿImrān at night, the standing of the whole night in prayer will be written for him.[38]

Such great benefit from a tiny act! Sayyidunā ʿUthmān ibn ʿAffān's ؓ giant intellect was always focused on the Qur'an and the teachings of his most beloved friend ﷺ. Despite knowing these great benefits that make living a life well-spent easy and accessible to all Muslims, he continued to strive to learn more about the Qur'an and immerse himself in its endless depths. al-Ḥasan ؓ narrates that the Commander of the Faithful, Sayyidunā ʿUthmān ibn ʿAffān ؓ, said,

لَوْ أَنَّ قُلُوبَنَا طَهَرَتْ مَا شَبِعَنَا مِنْ كَلَامِ رَبِّنَا. وَإِنِّي لَأَكْرَهُ أَنْ يَأْتِيَ عَلَيَّ يَوْمٌ لَا أَنْظُرُ فِيهِ الْمُصْحَفِ.

وَمَا مَاتَ عُثْمَانُ حَتَّى خَرَقَ مُصْحَفَهُ مِنْ كَثْرَةِ مَا كَانَ يُدِيمُ النَّظَرَ فِيهَا.

> "Were our hearts clean, their desire for the Word of our Lord would never be satisfied; indeed, I hate that a day passes without me looking into the muṣḥaf."

---

38 Abū Muḥammad al-Dārimī, *Sunan al-Dārimī*, 3439.

al-Ḥasan added, "And Sayyidunā ʿUthmān did not die until his Qur'an had become torn due to his constantly looking into it."[39]

Sayyidunā ʿUthmān ibn ʿAffān's ﵁ heart was never satiated, regardless of how much time he spent reading the Qur'an. He would recite it constantly, looking into the *muṣḥaf*. Every moment spent looking at its pages only increased his love for the Words of Allah ﷻ. He had a complete certainty of belief in the wisdom contained therein and ruled according to it. He famously said,

.ما يَزَعُ اللهُ بِالسُّلْطَانِ أَكْثَرَ مِمَّا يَزَعُ بِالْقُرْآنِ

Allah does not inspire with the Sultan more than he inspires with the Qur'an.[40]

He placed the Qur'an far above himself or any other ruler, and thus gave the Words of Allah ﷻ the position they deserved. He gave himself entirely to the rulings of the Qur'an, choosing to rule by them and be ruled by them. Saʿd ibn Ibrāhīm ﵀ narrates from his father who says that he heard Sayyidunā ʿUthmān ﵁ say,

.إِنْ وَجَدْتُمْ فِي الْحَقِّ أَنْ تَضَعُوا رِجْلِي فِي قَيْدٍ فَضَعُوهُمَا

If you find it in the Truth (the Qur'an) that you should put my legs in fetters, then fetter them.[41]

These words were spoken during the siege of his house that would ultimately end with his murder. Such was his belief in the infallibility of the Words of Allah ﷻ that he was willing to give himself completely to their judgement.

---

39 Abū Bakr Aḥmad ibn al-Ḥusayn al-Bayhaqī, *Shuʿab al-Īmān*, 2030.

40 Abū al-Faḍl Aḥmad ibn Muḥammad ibn Aḥmad al-Maydānī, *Majmaʿ al-Amthāl*, Vol. 2, p. 453.

41 Khalīfah ibn Khayyāṭ, *Tārīkh Khalīfah ibn Khayyāṭ*, 171.

This is what true Islamic leadership looks like. Complete adherence to the Qur'an and the Sunnah, and absolute conviction in the truth and guidance that lies within them. Much of the problems in modern society in general, and modern Islamic leadership specifically, can be traced back to one fatal flaw: an unwillingness to give precedence to the Qur'an and Sunnah in the way that they deserve.

Perhaps, then, it is fitting to finish this section and pave the way for a discussion on the most heart-breaking chapter in the history of the Rāshidūn Caliphate, with a quote from the wife of Sayyidunā 'Uthmān ibn 'Affān ﷺ, who said to his murderers when they killed him,

لَقَدْ قَتَلْتُمُوهُ وَإِنَّهُ لَيُحْيِي اللَّيْلَ كُلَّهُ بِالْقُرْآنِ فِي رَكْعَةٍ

You killed him, and he used to enliven the entire night by reciting the Qur'an in a rak'ah.[42]

Patience and Courage in the Face of Death

حَدَّثَنَا وَكِيعٌ عَنْ إِسْمَاعِيلَ بْنِ أَبِي خَالِدٍ قَالَ: قَالَ قَيْسٌ فَحَدَّثَنِي أَبُو سَهْلَةَ أَنَّ عُثْمَانَ رَضِيَ اللَّهُ عَنْهُ قَالَ يَوْمَ الدَّارِ حِينَ حُصِرَ:

إِنَّ رَسُولَ اللَّهِ صَلَّى اللَّهُ عَلَيْهِ وَسَلَّمَ عَهِدَ إِلَيَّ عَهْدًا فَأَنَا صَابِرٌ عَلَيْهِ.

قَالَ قَيْسٌ: فَكَانُوا يَرَوْنَهُ ذَلِكَ الْيَوْمَ.

Abū Sahlah narrated that Sayyidunā 'Uthmān ﷺ said whilst besieged on the Day of the House:

42 Aḥmad ibn Ḥanbal, *Kitāb al-Zuhd*, 673.

"Allah's Messenger advised me and I swore to comply with it, and so I shall bear it with patience."

Qays said, "People believed that it was that day."[43]

Indeed, Sayyidunā ʿUthmān ibn ʿAffān ﷺ did face death with absolute patience and courage, showing kindness and mercy to even those who would ultimately murder him. We have already discussed how closely to the Qur'an and Sunnah Sayyidunā ʿUthmān ﷺ stuck; how diligently he acted upon Divine guidance; and how complete his belief in Allah ﷻ and His Messenger ﷺ was. Here is the ultimate example of all those qualities. Even on the day of his murder, he remained fixed and resolute on the advice of the Prophet ﷺ and the promise Sayyidunā ʿUthmān ﷺ had made to him.

There are many Hadiths where the Messenger of Allah ﷺ prophesised the events that would unfold on this terrible day and pointed to the innocence and righteousness of Sayyidunā ʿUthmān ibn ʿAffān ﷺ. Murrah al-Bahzī ﷺ narrates,

قَالَ رَسُولُ اللَّهِ صَلَّى اللهُ عَلَيْهِ وَسَلَّمَ: تَهِيجُ عَلَى الْأَرْضِ فِتَنٌ كَصَيَاصِي الْبَقَرِ

فَمَرَّ رَجُلٌ مُتَقَنِّعٌ، فَقَالَ رَسُولُ اللَّهِ صَلَّى اللهُ عَلَيْهِ وَسَلَّمَ: هَذَا وَأَصْحَابُهُ يَوْمَئِذٍ عَلَى الْحَقِّ

فَقُمْتُ إِلَيْهِ فَكَشَفْتُ قِنَاعَهُ وَأَقْبَلْتُ بِوَجْهِهِ إِلَى رَسُولِ اللَّهِ صَلَّى اللهُ عَلَيْهِ وَسَلَّمَ فَقُلْتُ: يَا رَسُولَ اللَّهِ، هُوَ هَذَا؟

قَالَ: هُوَ هَذَا

قَالَ: فَإِذَا بِعُثْمَانَ بْنِ عَفَّانَ.

43 *Musnad Imām Aḥmad*, 407.

The Messenger of Allah said, "Strife will rage upon the earth like the hunters of cattle." A man passed by with his face covered and the Messenger of Allah said, "On that day, he and his companions will be upon the truth."

I stood and went to him, uncovered his head, and presented his face to the Messenger of Allah. I said, "O Messenger of Allah, is he the one?"

He said, "He is this one."

Behold! It was Sayyidunā ʿUthmān ibn ʿAffān.[44]

In another narration, Abū Mūsā ﵁ narrates,

النَّبِيَّ ﷺ دَخَلَ حَائِطًا وَأَمَرَنِي بِحِفْظِ باب الْحَائِطِ، فَجَاءَ رَجُلٌ يَسْتَأْذِنُ، فَقَالَ: ائْذَنْ لَهُ وَبَشِّرْهُ بِالْجَنَّةِ. فَإِذَا أَبُو بَكْرٍ، ثُمَّ جَاءَ آخَرُ يَسْتَأْذِنُ فَقَالَ: ائْذَنْ لَهُ وَبَشِّرْهُ بِالْجَنَّةِ. فَإِذَا عُمَرُ، ثُمَّ جَاءَ آخَرُ يَسْتَأْذِنُ، فَسَكَتَ هُنَيْهَةً ثُمَّ قَالَ: ائْذَنْ لَهُ وَبَشِّرْهُ بِالْجَنَّةِ عَلَى بَلْوَى سَتُصِيبُهُ. فَإِذَا عُثْمَانُ بْنُ عَفَّانَ.

The Prophet entered a garden and ordered me to guard its gate. A man came and asked permission to enter. The Prophet said, "Permit him and give him the glad tidings of Paradise."

Behold! It was Sayyidunā Abū Bakr.

Another man then came and asked permission to enter. The Prophet said, "Permit him and give him the glad tidings of Paradise."

Behold! It was Sayyidunā ʿUmar.

Then another man came, asking permission to enter. The Prophet remained silent for a short while and then said, "Permit him, and give him the glad tidings of Paradise despite the calamity which will befall him."

44 Aḥmad ibn Ḥanbal, *Faḍā'il al-Ṣaḥābah*, 720.

Behold! It was Sayyidunā ʿUthmān ibn ʿAffān.[45]

There are many similar Hadiths to this that demonstrate that both the Prophet ﷺ and, as a result, Sayyidunā ʿUthmān ibn ʿAffān ؓ knew about the events that would lead to the latter's death. This information makes Sayyidunā ʿUthmān ibn ʿAffān's ؓ resoluteness and bravery during this time even more awe-inspiring.

The events that transpired on that day of turmoil and strife were preceded by years of propaganda, espionage, and slander against Sayyidunā ʿUthmān ؓ from various emerging sects, hypocrites, and outright disbelievers. Chief amongst these hypocrites was ʿAbdullāh ibn Sabāʾ al-Ḥimyarī, a man of Yemenite Jewish origin and an apparent convert to Islam who seemingly greatly revered Sayyidunā ʿAlī ؓ. It is likely that this was part of his plot to create divisions between the Muslims.

Near the end of this campaign to remove Sayyidunā ʿUthmān ؓ from the position of Caliph, a delegation from Egypt of some 700 people arrived in Medina, complaining of their governor's tyranny. Sayyidunā ʿUthmān ؓ advised them to choose their own leader and he would have the governor replaced. They chose ʿAbdullāh ibn Abī Bakr ؓ, and Sayyidunā ʿUthmān ibn ʿAffān ؓ agreed. As they returned home, on the third day of their journey an African slave caught up to them carrying a message seemingly from Sayyidunā ʿUthmān ؓ to the governor. He was searched and they found a sealed message ordering the death of ʿAbdullāh ibn Abī Bakr ؓ and some companions of his. The Egyptians returned to Medina and besieged the house of Sayyidunā ʿUthmān ؓ, who admitted that the slave, the horse, and the seal were indeed his, while stating he had not written the message and had no knowledge of it. It would transpire that the message was written by Marwān ibn al-Ḥakam. For the next 22 days Sayyidunā ʿUthmān ؓ

45 *Saḥīḥ al-Bukhārī*, 3695.

remained besieged and imprisoned in his home, refusing to give up Marwān ibn al-Ḥakam to the Egyptians to face mob justice and extrajudicial killing.[46]

They sought the death of Marwān ibn al-Ḥakam and the abdication of the Caliphate, threatening death to Sayyidunā ʿUthmān ﷺ should he not acquiesce. To these people, Sayyidunā ʿUthmān ﷺ remained kind and merciful, sincerely advising them to turn away from the dark path they had set out upon, lest they face a terrible fate. al-Ḥasan ﷺ narrates,

قَالَ عُثْمَانُ: لَا تَقْتُلُونِي، فَوَاللهِ، لَئِنْ قَتَلْتُمُونِي، لَا تُقَاتِلُونَ عَدُوًّا جَمِيعًا أَبَدًا، وَلَا تَقْتَسِمُونَ فَيْئًا جَمِيعًا أَبَدًا، وَلَا تُصَلُّونَ جَمِيعًا أَبَدًا.

قَالَ الْحَسَنُ: فَوَاللهِ، إِنْ صَلَّى اللهُ الْقَوْمَ جَمِيعًا، إِنَّ قُلُوبَهُمْ لَمُخْتَلِفَةٌ.

Sayyidunā ʿUthmān said, "Do not kill me, for by Allah if you kill me you will never fight an enemy united, never unite in dispersing the shadows, and never unite in prayer."

al-Ḥasan said, "By Allah, if Allah were to make the people all pray together, their hearts would still be divided."[47]

It is a sad state of affairs that from the day that he was murdered until this very day, the Muslims have remained divided in rule, in war, and in prayer. We bicker and fight amongst ourselves over arbitrary matters whilst the enemies of Islam oppress our brothers and sisters and we are unable, or unwilling, to lift a finger to help them. Is this not the terrible division that Sayyidunā ʿUthmān ﷺ foresaw and warned us about? How can it be that we are divided by imaginary lines in the sand drawn by enemies, and we remain bound by the rules that govern these so-called "national borders"? How can I stand metres from my sister and watch as her honour is taken from her, or

46 Gibril Fouad Haddad, *The Rightly Guided Caliphs: Abū Bakr, ʿUmar, ʿUthmān, ʿAlī*, Institute for Spiritual and Cultural Understanding, Michigan (1444/ 2023), p. 215.

47 Khalīfah ibn Khayyāṭ, *Tārīkh Khalīfah ibn Khayyāṭ*, p. 171.

watch my brother be murdered in front of me and do nothing? Indeed, it is a terrible situation and only the Help of Allah ﷻ and a return to the principles of Islam and brotherhood can free us from the imagined shackles that bind us to complacency, apraxia, and inaction.

Regarding the siege of Sayyidunā ʿUthmān's ؓ home, Abū Umāmah ibn Sahl ؓ narrates,

كُنَّا مَعَ عُثْمَانَ رَضِيَ اللَّهُ عَنْهُ وَهُوَ مَحْصُورٌ فِي الدَّارِ فَدَخَلَ مَدْخَلًا كَانَ إِذَا دَخَلَهُ يَسْمَعُ كَلَامَهُ مَنْ عَلَى الْبَلَاطِ قَالَ فَدَخَلَ ذَلِكَ الْمَدْخَلَ وَخَرَجَ إِلَيْنَا فَقَالَ إِنَّهُمْ يَتَوَعَّدُونِي بِالْقَتْلِ آنِفًا قَالَ قُلْنَا يَكْفِيكَهُمُ اللَّهُ يَا أَمِيرَ الْمُؤْمِنِينَ.

قَالَ وَبِمَ يَقْتُلُونَنِي إِنِّي سَمِعْتُ رَسُولَ اللَّهِ صَلَّى اللَّهُ عَلَيْهِ وَسَلَّمَ يَقُولُ لَا يَحِلُّ دَمُ امْرِئٍ مُسْلِمٍ إِلَّا بِإِحْدَى ثَلَاثٍ رَجُلٌ كَفَرَ بَعْدَ إِسْلَامِهِ أَوْ زَنَى بَعْدَ إِحْصَانِهِ أَوْ قَتَلَ نَفْسًا فَيُقْتَلُ بِهَا فَوَاللَّهِ مَا أَحْبَبْتُ أَنَّ لِي بِدِينِي بَدَلًا مُنْذُ هَدَانِي اللَّهُ وَلَا زَنَيْتُ فِي جَاهِلِيَّةٍ وَلَا فِي إِسْلَامٍ قَطُّ وَلَا قَتَلْتُ نَفْسًا فَبِمَ يَقْتُلُونَنِي.

We were with Sayyidunā ʿUthmān when he was besieged in the house. He went to the entrance, from which his words could be heard, asking who was in the courtyard. He then came out to us and said, "Just now, they threatened to kill me."

We said, "Allah will suffice you against them, O Commander of the Faithful."

He said, "Why would they kill me? I heard the Messenger of Allah say, 'The blood of a Muslim is not permissible except in three cases: the man who disbelieves after becoming Muslim, fornicates after marriage or murders someone and is executed in return.' By Allah, I have never wished to change my religion after Allah guided me, nor committed fornication in either Ignorance or Islam nor have I killed anyone. So why would they kill me?"[48]

Such was his adherence to the Qur'an and Sunnah that he could not fathom how or why someone would act in a manner that was not governed by them. Abū Salamah ibn ʿAbd al-Raḥmān ﷺ narrates,

أَشْرَفَ عُثْمَانُ رَضِيَ اللَّهُ عَنْهُ مِنَ الْقَصْرِ وَهُوَ مَحْصُورٌ فَقَالَ أَنْشُدُ بِاللَّهِ مَنْ شَهِدَ رَسُولَ اللَّهِ صَلَّى اللَّهُ عَلَيْهِ وَسَلَّمَ يَوْمَ حِرَاءٍ إِذْ اهْتَزَّ الْجَبَلُ فَرَكَلَهُ بِقَدَمِهِ ثُمَّ قَالَ اسْكُنْ حِرَاءُ لَيْسَ عَلَيْكَ إِلَّا نَبِيٌّ أَوْ صِدِّيقٌ أَوْ شَهِيدٌ وَأَنَا مَعَهُ فَانْتَشَدَ لَهُ رِجَالٌ قَالَ أَنْشُدُ بِاللَّهِ مَنْ شَهِدَ رَسُولَ اللَّهِ صَلَّى اللَّهُ عَلَيْهِ وَسَلَّمَ يَوْمَ بَيْعَةِ الرِّضْوَانِ إِذْ بَعَثَنِي إِلَى الْمُشْرِكِينَ إِلَى أَهْلِ مَكَّةَ قَالَ هَذِهِ يَدِي وَهَذِهِ يَدُ عُثْمَانَ رَضِيَ اللَّهُ عَنْهُ فَبَايَعَ لِي فَانْتَشَدَ لَهُ رِجَالٌ قَالَ أَنْشُدُ بِاللَّهِ مَنْ شَهِدَ رَسُولَ اللَّهِ صَلَّى اللَّهُ عَلَيْهِ وَسَلَّمَ قَالَ مَنْ يُوَسِّعُ لَنَا بِهَذَا الْبَيْتِ فِي الْمَسْجِدِ بِبَيْتٍ فِي الْجَنَّةِ فَابْتَعْتُهُ مِنْ مَالِي فَوَسَّعْتُ بِهِ الْمَسْجِدَ فَانْتَشَدَ لَهُ رِجَالٌ قَالَ وَأَنْشُدُ بِاللَّهِ مَنْ شَهِدَ رَسُولَ اللَّهِ صَلَّى اللَّهُ عَلَيْهِ وَسَلَّمَ يَوْمَ جَيْشِ الْعُسْرَةِ قَالَ مَنْ يُنْفِقُ الْيَوْمَ نَفَقَةً مُتَقَبَّلَةً فَجَهَّزْتُ نِصْفَ الْجَيْشِ مِنْ مَالِي قَالَ فَانْتَشَدَ لَهُ رِجَالٌ وَأَنْشُدُ بِاللَّهِ مَنْ شَهِدَ رُومَةَ يُبَاعُ مَاؤُهَا ابْنَ السَّبِيلِ فَابْتَعْتُهَا مِنْ مَالِي فَأَبَحْتُهَا لِابْنِ السَّبِيلِ قَالَ فَانْتَشَدَ لَهُ رِجَالٌ.

Sayyidunā ʿUthmān looked out from the house when he was besieged and said, "I adjure by Allah anyone who was present with the Messenger of Allah on the day of Ḥirā',[49] when the mountain shook beneath his feet. He stamped his foot and said, 'Be still, Ḥirā', there is no one upon you but a Prophet, a Ṣiddīq, or a martyr', and I was with him."

Some of the men testified to what he said.

Then he said, "I adjure by Allah anyone who was present with the Messenger of Allah on the day of the Pledge of the Tree, when he had sent

48 *Musnad Imām Aḥmad*, 437.

49 It is possible that Mount Uḥud is meant here.

me to the polytheists, to the people of Mecca, and said, 'This is my hand and this is the hand of 'Uthmān', and he swore allegiance on my behalf."

Some of the men testified to what he said.

Then he said, "I adjure by Allah anyone who was present when the Messenger of Allah said, 'Who will expand the masjid by incorporating this house into it, in return for a house in Paradise?' and I bought it with my own wealth and expanded the masjid by incorporating it into it."

Some of the men testified to what he said.

Then he said, "I adjure by Allah anyone who saw the Messenger of Allah on the day of the Army of Hardship,[50] when he said, 'Who will spend today a spending that will be accepted by Allah?' and I equipped half of the army with my wealth."

Some of the men testified to what he said.

Then he said, "I adjure by Allah anyone who saw the water of the Well of Rūmah being sold to wayfarers, and then I bought it with my own wealth and gave it freely to wayfarers."

Some of the men testified to what he said.[51]

Here, Sayyidunā 'Uthmān ﵁ listed five occasions that each warrant some scrutiny. Some of them have been mentioned earlier in this chapter but the first two have not. The first occasion is quoted in *Ṣaḥīḥ al-Bukhārī*, wherein Anas ﵁ states,

صَعِدَ النَّبِيُّ ﷺ أُحُدًا، وَمَعَهُ أَبُو بَكْرٍ وَعُمَرُ وَعُثْمَانُ، فَرَجَفَ وَقَالَ:

50 The Campaign of Tabūk.

51 *Musnad Imām Aḥmad*, 420.

اسْكُنْ أُحُدُ – أَظُنُّهُ ضَرَبَهُ بِرِجْلِهِ – فَلَيْسَ عَلَيْكَ إِلاَّ نَبِيٌّ وَصِدِّيقٌ وَشَهِيدَانِ.

The Prophet ascended the mountain of Uḥud, and Abū Bakr, ʿUmar, and ʿUthmān were with him. The mountain trembled beneath them and the Prophet said, "O Uḥud, be still!" I think that the Prophet stamped on it with his foot, "For upon you there are none but a Prophet, a Ṣiddīq, and two martyrs."[52]

Again, both the status and the martyrdom of Sayyidunā ʿUthmān ibn ʿAffān ﵁ are clear from this narration, and indeed he was listed in the Sunnah as the fourth man in this group of veritable giants. On this occasion the mountain trembled beneath these men and became still on the order of the Prophet ﷺ.

Regarding the Pledge of the Tree, this was the occasion where the Muslims had travelled to Mecca for pilgrimage and had been stopped outside by the Quraysh. Sayyidunā ʿUthmān ibn ʿAffān ﵁ had been sent as a negotiator on behalf of the Muslims and had not returned for days. It was feared that he had been murdered and this was the catalyst for the famous Pledge of the Tree to take place. Each of the pilgrims took an oath of allegiance by holding onto the hand of the Prophet ﷺ. At the end, the following event took place, as narrated by ʿAbdullāh ibn ʿUmar ﵁,

فَقَالَ رَسُولُ اللَّهِ ﷺ بِيَدِهِ الْيُمْنَى هَذِهِ يَدُ عُثْمَانَ. وَضَرَبَ بِهَا عَلَى يَدِهِ فَقَالَ هَذِهِ لِعُثْمَانَ.

So the Messenger of Allah said of his right hand, "This is the hand of ʿUthmān", and he put it upon his other hand, and said, "This is for ʿUthmān."[53]

The Prophet ﷺ had clasped his hand to signify the inclusion of Sayyidunā ʿUthmān ﵁ in the Pledge. What greater honour could there have been on such an occasion? As Anas ﵁ stated,

---

52 *Sahīh al-Bukhārī*, 3699.

53 *Jāmiʿ al-Tirmidhī*, 3706.

.فَكَانَتْ يَدُ رَسُولِ اللَّهِ ﷺ لِعُثْمَانَ خَيْرًا مِنْ أَيْدِيهِمْ لأَنْفُسِهِمْ

The hand of the Messenger of Allah on behalf of Sayyidunā ʿUthmān was better than their own hands for themselves.[54]

Regarding the last three occasions mentioned by Sayyidunā ʿUthmān ﵁, these have already been covered earlier and there are likewise numerous narrations regarding the matters mentioned. For the sake of brevity, we will not re-tread these discussions again here.

As the siege on the house of Sayyidunā ʿUthmān ﵁ progressed, al-Mughīrah ibn Shuʿbah ﵁ narrates that he went to visit him and the following conversation took place,

قَالَ إِنَّكَ إِمَامُ الْعَامَّةِ وَقَدْ نَزَلَ بِكَ مَا تَرَى وَإِنِّي أَعْرِضُ عَلَيْكَ خِصَالًا ثَلَاثًا اخْتَرْ إِحْدَاهُنَّ إِمَّا أَنْ تَخْرُجَ فَتُقَاتِلَهُمْ فَإِنَّ مَعَكَ عَدَدًا وَقُوَّةً وَأَنْتَ عَلَى الْحَقِّ وَهُمْ عَلَى الْبَاطِلِ وَإِمَّا أَنْ نَخْرِقَ لَكَ بَابًا سِوَى الْبَابِ الَّذِي هُمْ عَلَيْهِ فَتَقْعُدَ عَلَى رَوَاحِلِكَ فَتَلْحَقَ بِمَكَّةَ فَإِنَّهُمْ لَنْ يَسْتَحِلُّوكَ وَأَنْتَ بِهَا وَإِمَّا أَنْ تَلْحَقَ بِالشَّامِ فَإِنَّهُمْ أَهْلُ الشَّامِ وَفِيهِمْ مُعَاوِيَةُ.

فَقَالَ عُثْمَانُ رَضِيَ اللَّهُ عَنْهُ أَمَّا أَنْ أَخْرُجَ فَأُقَاتِلَ فَلَنْ أَكُونَ أَوَّلَ مَنْ خَلَفَ رَسُولَ اللَّهِ صَلَّى اللَّهُ عَلَيْهِ وَسَلَّمَ فِي أُمَّتِهِ بِسَفْكِ الدِّمَاءِ وَأَمَّا أَنْ أَخْرُجَ إِلَى مَكَّةَ فَإِنَّهُمْ لَنْ يَسْتَحِلُّونِي بِهَا فَإِنِّي سَمِعْتُ رَسُولَ اللَّهِ صَلَّى اللَّهُ عَلَيْهِ وَسَلَّمَ يَقُولُ يُلْحِدُ رَجُلٌ مِنْ قُرَيْشٍ بِمَكَّةَ يَكُونُ عَلَيْهِ نِصْفُ عَذَابِ الْعَالَمِ فَلَنْ أَكُونَ أَنَا إِيَّاهُ وَأَمَّا أَنْ أَلْحَقَ بِالشَّامِ فَإِنَّهُمْ أَهْلُ الشَّامِ وَفِيهِمْ مُعَاوِيَةُ فَلَنْ أُفَارِقَ دَارَ هِجْرَتِي وَمُجَاوَرَةَ رَسُولِ اللَّهِ صَلَّى اللَّهُ عَلَيْهِ وَسَلَّمَ.

al-Mughīrah ibn Shuʿbah said, "You are the leader of the people and there has befallen upon you what you can see. I will suggest to you three options; choose one of them. Either go out and fight them, for you have both numbers and strength, and you are on the truth and they are on the falsehood; or we will make another door for you, other than the door they are

54 *Jāmiʿ al-Tirmidhī*, 3702.

guarding, then you can mount your steed and travel to Mecca for they will not try to kill you there; or you travel to al-Shām, for the people of al-Shām are good folk and among them is Sayyidunā Muʿāwiyah."

Sayyidunā ʿUthmān said, "As for going out and fighting, I will not be the first Caliph of Allah's Messenger to shed blood amongst his Ummah. As for leaving for Mecca because they will never try to kill me there, I heard Allah's Messenger say, 'A man of the Quraysh will do wrong in Mecca and upon him will be half the punishment of the world', and I will never be that man; as for going to al-Shām because they are the people of al-Shām and Sayyidunā Muʿāwiyah is among them, I shall never leave the land to which I migrated, where I am close to the Messenger of Allah."[55]

Given these three options, all of which were well within his power and the power of the Muslims to carry out, how many of us would have taken one of them and saved ourselves? Yet here we see from Sayyidunā ʿUthmān ibn ʿAffān ﷺ true examples of mercy, courage, and love.

The first option was to go out and fight. He had the numerical advantage, as well as the advantage of actual trained and blooded soldiers and strength of arms, but he refused to shed blood and remained soft-hearted and merciful towards his oppressors. Mercy can only be enacted when the giver has the strength to withhold it from the receiver; it can never be offered from a weak position. Sayyidunā ʿUthmān ﷺ could have ended the siege in an hour, but it would have cost many Muslim lives, and he refused to be the reason for such loss.

Many of the Ṣaḥābah came to him during that month, offering him support, manpower, and strength, urging him to dispel the besiegers by any means necessary and free himself from imprisonment. For example, Abū Hurayrah ﷺ narrates,

---

55 *Musnad Imām Aḥmad*, 481.

دَخَلْتُ عَلَى عُثْمَانَ رضي الله عنه يَوْمَ الدَّارِ فَقُلْتُ يَا أَمِيرَ الْمُؤْمِنِينَ طَابٌ أَمْ ضَرْبٌ فَقَالَ لِي يَا أَبَا هُرَيْرَةَ أَيَسُرُّكَ أَنْ تَقْتُلَ النَّاسَ جَمِيعًا وَإِيَّايَ مَعَهُمْ فَقُلْتُ لَا فَقَالَ وَاللَّهِ لَئِنْ قَتَلْتَ رَجُلًا وَاحِدًا لَكَأَنَّمَا قَتَلْتَ النَّاسَ جَمِيعًا فَرَجَعْتُ فَلَمْ أُقَاتِلْ.

I entered upon Sayyidunā 'Uthmān on the day of the siege of the house and said, "O Commander of the Faithful, I have come to give support or fight."

Sayyidunā 'Uthmān said to me, "O Abū Hurayrah, would it please you to 'kill all of humanity'[56] including me?"

I said, "No."

Sayyidunā 'Uthmān said, "By Allah, if you have killed one man it is as if you have killed all of humanity."

Thus, I returned, and I did not fight.[57]

Another such Ṣaḥābī was al-Ḥasan ibn 'Alī ☙. Imam Aḥmad ibn Ḥanbal ☙ writes,

فَلَمَّا دَخَلَ الْحَسَنُ عَلَيْهِ قَالَ: يَا أَمِيرَ الْمُؤْمِنِينَ، إِنَّا طَوْعُ يَدِكَ، فَمُرْنِي بِمَا شِئْتَ فَقَالَ لَهُ عُثْمَانُ: يَا ابْنَ أَخِي، ارْجِعْ فَاجْلِسْ فِي بَيْتِكَ حَتَّى يَأْتِيَ اللَّهُ بِأَمْرِهِ، فَلَا حَاجَةَ لِي فِي هِرَاقَةِ الدِّمَاءِ.

When al-Ḥasan came to him, he said, "O Commander of the Faithful, we are at your bidding. Command us with whatever you wish."

---

56 *Al-Mā'idah*, 32.
57 Abū 'Abdullāh Muḥammad ibn Sa'd ibn Manī' al-Baṣrī al-Hāshimī, *Kitāb al-Ṭabaqāt al-Kubrā*, 2871.

Sayyidunā ʿUthmān replied, "Dear nephew, return to your home and remain there until Allah concludes this matter. I do not need the shedding of blood."[58]

It was said that Zayd ibn Thābit ﷺ had marshalled a force of 300 Anṣār, including ʿAbdullāh ibn al-Zubayr, ʿAbdullāh ibn ʿUmar, Abū Hurayrah, al-Ḥasan, and al-Ḥusayn ﷺ. However, Sayyidunā ʿUthmān ﷺ forbade any use of force against the rebels.[59]

The second option was one of safety, for no Muslim would willingly shed blood in Mecca, yet here too Sayyidunā ʿUthmān ﷺ refused. His adherence to the Sunnah was such that the possibility that he would become the one prophesised in the Hadith of the Messenger of Allah ﷺ was enough to rule out the option – he would rather face his oppressors with courage and conviction than flee to Mecca and commit great injustice there should they follow him.

The third option also offered safety, and it would not leave him open to becoming the one mentioned in the Hadith. Yet here too Sayyidunā ʿUthmān ﷺ refused. He could not bear to be away from his Beloved Companion and Dear Friend ﷺ. In Medina he was close to him, while in al-Shām he would be far away. How could one who loves another so truly bear to be far away from even the grave of the beloved ﷺ? It was impossible for Sayyidunā ʿUthmān ﷺ, the man who had been promised to be the Prophet's ﷺ close companion in Paradise.

Sayyidunā ʿUthmān ibn ʿAffān ﷺ would thus face certain death with both courage and patience. Death for him was not a matter to fear. However, in his life he often thought about the grave, and this was the trial

---

58 Aḥmad ibn Ḥanbal, *Faḍāʾil al-Ṣaḥābah*, 753.

59 Gibril Fouad Haddad, *The Rightly Guided Caliphs: Abū Bakr, ʿUmar, ʿUthmān, ʿAlī*, p.216.

that worried him most, once again due to his complete submission to the Qur'an and Sunnah.

Hānī ﷺ, the freed slave of Sayyidunā ʿUthmān ﷺ, narrated,

كَانَ عُثْمَانُ رَضِيَ اللَّهُ عَنْهُ إِذَا وَقَفَ عَلَى قَبْرٍ بَكَى حَتَّى يَبُلَّ لِحْيَتَهُ فَقِيلَ لَهُ تَذْكُرُ الْجَنَّةَ وَالنَّارَ فَلَا تَبْكِي وَتَبْكِي مِنْ هَذَا فَقَالَ إِنَّ رَسُولَ اللَّهِ صَلَّى اللَّهُ عَلَيْهِ وَسَلَّمَ قَالَ الْقَبْرُ أَوَّلُ مَنَازِلِ الْآخِرَةِ فَإِنْ يَنْجُ مِنْهُ فَمَا بَعْدَهُ أَيْسَرُ مِنْهُ وَإِنْ لَمْ يَنْجُ مِنْهُ فَمَا بَعْدَهُ أَشَدُّ مِنْهُ قَالَ وَقَالَ رَسُولُ اللَّهِ صَلَّى اللَّهُ عَلَيْهِ وَسَلَّمَ وَاللَّهِ مَا رَأَيْتُ مَنْظَرًا قَطُّ إِلَّا وَالْقَبْرُ أَفْظَعُ مِنْهُ.

When Sayyidunā ʿUthmān would stand by a grave, he would weep until his beard became wet. It was said to him, "You remember Paradise and Hell and you do not weep, yet you weep for this?"

He said, "The Messenger of Allah said, 'The grave is the first stage of the Hereafter: if one is saved from it, then what comes after is easier; if one is not saved from it, then what comes after it is worse.' The Messenger of Allah also said, 'By Allah, I have never seen any frightening scene but that the grave is more frightening.'"[60]

Sayyidunā ʿUthmān ﷺ is also reported to have said,

خيرُ العباد مَنْ عَصَم واعتصم بكتاب الله تعالى، ونظر إلى قبر فبكى، وقَالَ: هو أولُ منازلِ الآخرة وآخر منازل الدنيا؛ فمن شُدِّد عليه فما بَعْده أشد، ومن هُوِّن عليه فما بعده أهون.

The best of servants is he who is steadfast and adheres to the Book of Allah Almighty, and looks to the grave and weeps, saying, "It is the first stage of the Hereafter and the last stage of the World. Whoever it is made difficult

60 *Musnad Imām Aḥmad*, 454.

for, what follows is more severe; and whoever it is made easy for, what follows is easier.[61]

For us lowly souls and simple folk it is even more important to follow this principle, adhere to the Qur'an and Sunnah, and understand the weight of the trials of the Grave. As Muslims, we should hold ourselves to account before we are held to account. A Muslim contemplates death often, but when it comes, he faces it bravely. Sayyidunā ʿUthmān ﷺ epitomised this mindset.

On the morning of the final day of Dhū al-Ḥijjah, on a Friday (*Jumuʿah*), Abū Saʿīd ﷺ, the freed slave of Sayyidunā ʿUthmān ibn ʿAffān ﷺ narrates,

أَنَّ عُثْمَانَ بْنَ عَفَّانَ، أَعْتَقَ عِشْرِينَ مَمْلُوكًا وَدَعَا بِسَرَاوِيلَ فَشَدَّهَا عَلَيْهِ وَلَمْ يَلْبَسْهَا فِي جَاهِلِيَّةٍ وَلَا إِسْلَامٍ وَقَالَ:

إِنِّي رَأَيْتُ رَسُولَ اللَّهِ صَلَّى اللَّهُ عَلَيْهِ وَسَلَّمَ الْبَارِحَةَ فِي الْمَنَامِ وَرَأَيْتُ أَبَا بَكْرٍ وَعُمَرَ رَضِيَ اللَّهُ عَنْهُمَا وَإِنَّهُمْ قَالُوا لِي اصْبِرْ فَإِنَّكَ تُفْطِرُ عِنْدَنَا الْقَابِلَةَ.

ثُمَّ دَعَا بِمُصْحَفٍ فَنَشَرَهُ بَيْنَ يَدَيْهِ فَقُتِلَ وَهُوَ بَيْنَ يَدَيْهِ.

Sayyidunā ʿUthmān ibn ʿAffān manumitted twenty slaves and called for some trousers and put them on; never had he worn them before, neither in the Age of Ignorance nor in Islam. He said, "Last night, I saw the Messenger of Allah in a dream, and I saw Sayyidunā Abū Bakr and Sayyidunā ʿUmar, and they all said to me, "Be patient, for you will break your fast with us tomorrow."

He called for the muṣḥaf and opened it in his hands. He was killed with it in front of him.[62]

---

61 Aḥmad ibn Muḥammad ibn Aḥmad al-Maydānī, *Majmaʿ al-Amthāl*, Vol. 2, p. 453.

62 *Musnad Imām Aḥmad*, 526.

This was the state in which he passed away. Having had the glad tidings of opening his fast on the morrow with his dearest friends, he freed 20 slaves and prepared himself for the meeting by donning fine clothes. In a fasted state, as he ever was, he sat down and opened the book that he had spent a lifetime reading, with the same love and awe with which he had always read it and began to recite without a hint of fear. He had sent away his guards and was alone in his house except for his family.

It was at this time that a group of the besiegers entered the house and fell upon Sayyidunā ʿUthmān ibn ʿAffān ﷺ. Khalīfah ibn Khayyāṭ ﷺ collected the following narrations:

عَن الْحَسَنِ، أَنَّ ابْنَ أَبِي بَكْرٍ أَخَذَ بِلِحْيَتِهِ، فَقَالَ عُثْمَان: لَقَدْ أَخَذْتَ مِنِّي مَأْخَذًا أَوْ قَعَدْتَ مِنِّي مَقْعَدًا مَا كَانَ أَبُوكَ لِيَقْعُدَهُ. فَخَرَجَ وَتَرَكَهُ.

عَن أَبِي سَعِيدٍ، قَالَ: دَخَلَ عَلَيْهِ رَجُلٌ مِنْ بَنِي سُدُوسٍ يُقَالُ لَهُ الْمَوْتُ الْأَسْوَدُ، فَخَنَقَهُ وَخَنَقَهُ قَبْلَ أَنْ يَضْرِبَ بِالسَّيْفِ، فَقَالَ: وَاللهِ مَا رَأَيْتُ شَيْئًا أَلْيَنَ مِنْ خِنَاقِهِ، لَقَدْ خَنَقْتُهُ حَتَّى رَأَيْتُ نَفْسَهُ مِثْلَ الْجَانِّ تَرَدَّدَ فِي جَسَدِهِ.

وَقَالَ فِي غَيْرِ حَدِيثِ أَبِي سَعِيدٍ: وَدَخَلَ التَّجِيبِيُّ، فَأَشْعَرَهُ مِشْقَصًا فَانْتَضَحَ الدَّمُ عَلَى قَوْلِهِ: فَسَيَكْفِيكَهُم الله.

al-Ḥasan narrates that Ibn Abī Bakr took hold of Sayyidunā ʿUthmān's beard, and Sayyidunā ʿUthmān said, "You have taken something from me, or you have taken a seat from me, that your father would never have." So he exited and left.

Abū Saʿīd narrates that a man from Banū Sudūs, called the Black Death, entered upon him and strangled him and strangled him, before striking him with his sword, and said, "By Allah, I have never seen anything easier than strangling him. I strangled him until I saw his soul flitting in his body like a Jinn."

Abū Saʿīd also narrates that al-Tujībī entered and sawed his hair. Blood spattered on His Words:

"But Allah will spare you their evil." [63]; [64]

During this assault, he was stabbed in the head with an arrow. His wife, Nā'ilah ﵂, and her servant tried to defend the Caliph, but the servant was murdered, and Sayyidah Nā'ilah ﵂ lost several fingers trying to stop the swords of the hypocrites from harming her beloved husband. It was only when she ran out of the house and cried for help that the cowardly murderers fled the scene,[65] leaving Sayyidunā ʿUthmān ibn ʿAffān ﵁, the third Caliph of Islam and fifth to accept the message of the Prophet ﷺ, soaked in blood and martyred, his Qur'an still open on the page he had been reading:

فَسَيَكْفِيكَهُمُ ٱللَّهُ ۚ وَهُوَ ٱلسَّمِيعُ ٱلْعَلِيمُ.

But Allah will spare you their evil. For He is the All-Hearing, All-Knowing.[66]

Such was the death of the beloved friend of the Prophet ﷺ and his companion in Paradise Sayyidunā ʿUthmān ibn ʿAffān ﵁ – murdered by multiple assailants in his own home while he recited the Qur'an.

As for ʿAbdullāh ibn Abī Bakr ﵄, he had entered the compound with the others, but was saved from the fate of being involved in the murder by the words of his father's dear friend, Sayyidunā ʿUthmān ﵁. As for the others, ʿAmrah bint Qays al-ʿAdawiyyah ﵂ narrates,

خَرَجْتُ مَعَ عَائِشَةَ رَحِمَهَا اللّٰهُ سَنَةَ قُتِلَ عُثْمَانُ إِلَى مَكَّةَ فَمَرَرْنَا بِالْمَدِينَةِ فَرَأَيْنَا الْمُصْحَفَ

63 *Al-Baqarah*, 137.

64 Khalīfah ibn Khayyāṭ, *Tārīkh Khalīfah ibn Khayyāṭ*, pp. 174-175.

65 Gibril Fouad Haddad, *The Rightly Guided Caliphs: Abū Bakr, ʿUmar, ʿUthmān, ʿAlī*, p.216.

66 *Al-Baqarah*, 137.

الَّذِي قُتِلَ وَهُوَ فِي حِجْرِهِ فَكَانَتْ أَوَّلُ قَطْرَةٍ قُطِرَتْ مِنْ دَمِهِ عَلَى هَذِهِ الْآيَةِ: {فَسَيَكْفِيكَهُمُ اللَّهُ وَهُوَ السَّمِيعُ الْعَلِيمُ} قَالَتْ عَمْرَةُ: فَمَا مَاتَ مِنْهُمْ رَجُلٌ سَوِيًّا.

I went out to Mecca with the Mother of the Believers, Sayyidah ʿĀ'ishah in the year Sayyidunā ʿUthmān was killed. We passed through Medina and saw the Qur'an that had been in his lap when he was killed and the first drop of blood he had bled had fallen on the verse:

"But Allah will spare you their evil. For He is the All-Hearing, All-Knowing."[67]

Not a man among them[68] died unharmed.[69]

Sayyidunā ʿUthmān ibn ʿAffān ﷺ was buried in his blood-soaked clothes and was not washed,[70] as was befitting the status of a martyr, and his funeral prayer was led by ʿAbdullāh ibn al-Zubayr ﷺ.[71]

Following his death, the Ṣaḥābah and the true Muslims were appalled by what had occurred in the house of Sayyidunā ʿUthmān ﷺ, and many of them cursed the killers. It is perhaps most interesting to see the reaction of his successor, Sayyidunā ʿAlī ﷺ. Muḥammad ibn al-Ḥanafiyyah ﷺ narrated,

بَلَغَ عَلِيًّا أَنَّ عَائِشَةَ تَلْعَنُ قَتَلَةَ عُثْمَانَ فِي الْمِرْبَدِ، قَالَ: فَرَفَعَ يَدَيْهِ حَتَّى بَلَغَ بِهِمَا وَجْهَهُ فَقَالَ: وَأَنَا أَلْعَنُ قَتَلَةَ عُثْمَانَ، لَعَنَهُمُ اللَّهُ فِي السَّهْلِ وَالْجَبَلِ، قَالَ مَرَّتَيْنِ أَوْ ثَلَاثًا

It reached Sayyidunā ʿAlī that the Mother of the Believers, Sayyidah ʿĀ'ishah, was cursing the killers of Sayyidunā ʿUthmān in al-Mirbad, so he raised his hands until they reached his face and said, "I curse the killers of

---

67 *Al-Baqarah*, 137.

68 His murderers.

69 Aḥmad ibn Ḥanbal, *Kitāb al-Zuhd*, 677.

70 *Musnad Imām Aḥmad*, 531.

71 *Musnad Imām Aḥmad*, 549.

Sayyidunā 'Uthmān, may Allah curse them in the plains and on the mountains." He said twice or thrice.[72]

Abd al-Raḥmān ibn Abī Laylā ؓ narrates,

اَرَأَيْتُ عَلِيًّا رَافِعًا حِضْنَيْهِ يَقُولُ: اللَّهُمَّ إِنِّي أَبْرَأُ إِلَيْكَ مِنْ دَمِ عُثْمَانَ!

I saw Sayyidunā 'Alī raising his arms and saying, "O Allah, I condemn the spilling of the blood of 'Uthmān!"[73]

Ḥassān ibn Yazīd ؓ narrates,

دَخَلْتُ الْمَسْجِدَ الْأَكْبَرَ، مَسْجِدَ الْكُوفَةِ، قَالَ: وَعَلِيُّ بْنُ أَبِي طَالِبٍ قَائِمٌ عَلَى الْمِنْبَرِ يَخْطُبُ النَّاسَ وَهُوَ يُنَادِي بِأَعْلَى صَوْتِهِ ثَلَاثَ مِرَارٍ: يَا أَيُّهَا النَّاسُ، يَا أَيُّهَا النَّاسُ، يَا أَيُّهَا النَّاسُ، إِنَّكُمْ تُكْثِرُونَ فِي عُثْمَانَ، فَإِنَّ مَثَلِي وَمَثَلَهُ كَمَا قَالَ اللَّهُ عَزَّ وَجَلَّ: ﴿وَنَزَعْنَا مَا فِي صُدُورِهِمْ مِنْ غِلٍّ إِخْوَانًا عَلَى سُرُرٍ مُتَقَابِلِينَ﴾.

I entered the largest masjid, the masjid of Kufa. Sayyidunā 'Alī ibn Abī Ṭālib was standing on the pulpit, addressing the people, and he called out at the top of his voice three times, "O people! O people! O people! You have overstepped in relation to Sayyidunā 'Uthmān, for the example of he and I are as Allah said:

'We will remove whatever bitterness they had in their hearts. In a friendly manner, they will be on thrones, facing one another.'[74]"[75]

---

72 Aḥmad ibn Ḥanbal, *Faḍā'il al-Ṣaḥābah*, 733.
73 Aḥmad ibn Ḥanbal, *Faḍā'il al-Ṣaḥābah*, 727.
74 *Al-Ḥijr*, 47.
75 Aḥmad ibn Ḥanbal, *Faḍā'il al-Ṣaḥābah*, 479.

Sayyidunā ʿAlī's ﷺ grief at the time of Sayyidunā ʿUthmān's ﷺ death was plain for all to see. He was deeply hurt and upset by the events that unfolded over that month, culminating in the cold-blooded murder of the Caliph. His sons, al-Ḥasan and al-Ḥusayn ﷺ, had been amongst those Ṣaḥābah who had stood watch outside the home of Sayyidunā ʿUthmān ibn ʿAffān ﷺ and had urged him to drive them away. Sayyidunā ʿUthmān ibn ʿAffān ﷺ had been a companion and close friend of his for over half a century, and they were both amongst the first people to accept Islam and thus their brotherhood had been the longest at that time.

How could one not grieve at such a time? A great and innocent man had been killed, a terrible wrong now threatened to plunge the Caliphate into darkness, and suddenly the Muslims were left leaderless. Muslim unity had been shattered, perhaps irreparably, and a great schism began to take shape. Years of turmoil and strife lay ahead, birthed by the black deed of the murderers of Sayyidunā ʿUthmān ﷺ and the machinations of the hypocrites and enemies of Islam. It was into such a world that the fourth Caliph of Islam took his rightful place amongst his most beloved companions. As the days of bloodied spears and shattered shields loomed over the Caliphate, there was still hope for the righteous and good even in this hour of wolves. For now, too was the time of al-Ḥaydar ﷺ.

The time of Sayyidunā ʿAlī ibn Abī Ṭālib ﷺ had come.

4

Al-Ḥaydar: "Abū Turāb" ʿAlī ibn Abī Ṭālib

From a desert whirlwind of disparate ever-warring tribes, the Beloved Prophet ﷺ had forged a single, united Ummah capable of toppling the great powers of antiquity, and of spreading Allah's ﷻ final message to humanity. Yet now the Ummah faced its first great and terrible schism, and the fate of Islam once more stood upon a precipice. The third Caliph had been murdered in the heart of Medina itself. The righteous cried out in fury for vengeance, and the wretched looked forward to the coming chaos with glee. Who could lead the ship of salvation now? Who could still the winds and calm the waves of the coming storm? Who else, but Islam's paradigmatic hero; who else but the wielder of Dhū al-Fiqār, the famous, twin-edged deadly sword forged of an ancient ore; who else but the man they called the Lion King, al-Ḥaydar?

The fourth of the Rightly Guided Caliphs was privileged with being the cousin, ward, and son-in-law to the Beloved Prophet ﷺ. Alongside his wife, the Prophet's ﷺ daughter, he stands as the ancestor to Islam's most honoured line, the line of the *Ahl al-Bayt*, the Prophetic Household.

His legendary courage and martial prowess were only matched by his profound knowledge and inward depth. He was the gateway to the city of esoteric knowledge and thus the founder of many of the Sufi paths; he was the iconic foundation upon which all future ideas of masculinity would be built. He was ʿAlī ibn Abī Ṭālib ibn ʿAbd al-Muṭṭalib ibn Hāshim ibn ʿAbd Manāf ibn Quṣayy ibn Kilāb ibn Murrah ibn Kaʿb ibn Lu'ayy ibn Ghālib ibn Fihr ibn Mālik ibn al-Naḍr ibn Kinānah ibn Khuzaymah ibn Mudrikah ibn Ilyās ibn Muḍar ibn Nizar ibn Maʿd ibn ʿAdnān.

Early Life and Acceptance of Islam

Ali ﷺ lived with the Prophet ﷺ since he was five. The Prophet's ﷺ kindness and affection towards him influenced him all his life as he grew up in his household. When the Prophet ﷺ received his mission through Jibreel ﷺ, he was only ten years old and immediately became a Muslim. He became aware of Islam when one day, coming back home, he saw the Prophet ﷺ and his noble wife Khadijah ﷺ praying. When asked about it, the Prophet ﷺ explained everything about Islam, but asked him to keep it secret for the moment. He thought about it that night and accepted Islam the next morning, declaring his faith to the Prophet ﷺ. When his father and the beloved uncle of the Prophet ﷺ Abu Talib came to know about his conversion, he approved his son's decision to become a Muslim, though he never became a Muslim himself.

A Life of Patience

حَدَّثَنَا أَبُو جَعْفَرٍ الرَّازِيُّ، عَنْ رَجُلٍ يُقَالُ لَهُ عُمَرُ، عَنْ مُحَمَّدِ بْنِ عَلِيٍّ قَالَ: قَالَ عَلِيٌّ رَضِيَ اللَّهُ عَنْهُ:

الصَّبْرُ مِنَ الْإِيمَانِ بِمَنْزِلَةِ الرَّأْسِ مِنَ الْجَسَدِ

Sayyidunā ʿAlī ibn Abī Ṭālib said:

Patience is to faith as the head is to the body.[1]

In the above quotation, Sayyidunā ʿAlī ﷺ explained the position of patience as the "head" of faith, as the head is the most honoured and noble part of the body; it holds a position of prominence and bears the most beautiful part of one's body in the form of the face. This is why nodding one's head is a sign of respect and bowing one's head is an act of worship. Having patience is a fundamental part of being a Muslim: without a head a body cannot function, and without patience a Muslim cannot truly act out his or her faith. Islam *requires* us to be patient, to dampen our desires and focus our hearts and minds on worship, awaiting the day when Allah ﷻ will reward the patient ones with Paradise and all the wonders that lie within.

Even in the case of seeking justice for the murder of Sayyidunā ʿUthmān ibn ʿAffān ﷺ, the Commander of the Faithful's view was that of patience. Though Ṭalḥah ﷺ, al-Zubayr ﷺ, the Mother of the Believers Sayyidah ʿĀ'ishah ﷺ, and Muʿāwiyah ﷺ all agreed that Sayyidunā ʿAlī ibn Abī Ṭālib ﷺ was the correct person to lead the Muslims as the Commander of the Faithful, they had disagreed with him with regard to bringing the murderers of Sayyidunā ʿUthmān ﷺ to justice. Sayyidunā ʿAlī's ﷺ view was to consolidate the unity of the Ummah first before seeking out the justice that Sayyidunā ʿUthmān ﷺ deserved. In this way, all parties agreed what needed to occur, but they differed in the order, with Sayyidunā ʿAlī ﷺ choosing patience and consolidation over righteous and swift justice. Neither party was more correct than the other; they simply had differing opinions.[2]

Sayyidunā ʿAlī ibn Abī Ṭālib ﷺ lived a life of complete simplicity, choosing poverty over pomp and need over greed. He cared little for the trappings and decorations of this world and understood the truth that many of us know but fool ourselves into thinking otherwise: that the world is transitory

1 Wakīʿ ibn al-Jarrāḥ, *Kitāb al-Zuhd*, 199.

2 Dr ʿAlī M. Ṣallābī, *ʿAlī ibn Abī Ṭālib*, Dār al-ʿĀlamiyyah, Riyadh (1431/2010), Vol. 2, pp. 35-37.

and impermanent; that our limited time here does not warrant all our attention, but only the small amount needed to get past it and that the life in the Hereafter is unending and the outcomes of the choices we make here will echo on in eternity for our reward or our ruin. Sayyidunā ʿAlī ؓ is reported to have said,

اَلدَّهْرُ يَوْمانِ: يَوْمٌ لَكَ، ويَومٌ عَلَيْكَ، فإن كانَ لَكَ فَلا تَبْطَرْ، وإن كانَ عَلَيْكَ فلاَ تَضْجَر.

Life is but two days: a day for you and against you. When it is in your favour, do not be ungrateful; when it is against you, do not be impatient.³

Sayyidunā ʿAlī ؓ thus always advised patience. When things are going well for you, gratitude is a must. One must never be slow to thank the Giver, for Allah's ﷻ favour can just as easily be taken away as granted. When matters become difficult and we feel we cannot cope, we must exercise patience and seek refuge in Allah ﷻ alone to grant us freedom from the hardships we face. This is true regardless of the situation we find ourselves in.

Sayyidunā ʿAlī ؓ also said,

العفافُ زينةُ الفقر، والشكر زينةُ الغنى.

Patience is the adornment of poverty, and gratitude is the adornment of wealth.⁴

When faced with the hardship of poverty, the one who is patient and trusts in Allah ﷻ is truly the most deserving of His favour. When granted ease through abundant wealth, showing one's gratitude to Allah ﷻ and helping those less fortunate is likewise deserving of His favour. Sayyidunā ʿAlī ؓ

---

3   Aḥmad ibn Muḥammad ibn Aḥmad al-Maydānī, *Majmaʿ al-Amthāl*, Vol. 2, p.454.
4   Aḥmad ibn Muḥammad ibn Aḥmad al-Maydānī, *Majmaʿ al-Amthāl*, Vol. 2, p.454.

was granted the ability to do both. Regarding this, Muḥammad ibn Ka'b al-Quraẓī ؓ narrates that Sayyidunā 'Alī ؓ said,

> لَقَدْ رَأَيْتُنِي مَعَ رَسُولِ اللَّهِ صَلَّى اللَّهُ عَلَيْهِ وَسَلَّمَ وَإِنِّي لَأَرْبِطُ الْحَجَرَ عَلَى بَطْنِي مِنَ الْجُوعِ وَإِنَّ صَدَقَتِي الْيَوْمَ لَأَرْبَعُونَ أَلْفًا.

You saw me with the Messenger of Allah with a stone tied to my stomach due to hunger, and today I am giving 40,000 in charity.[5]

Even in the most extreme situations, patience was always the advice of Sayyidunā 'Alī ؓ. al-Agharr ؓ narrates,

> نَظَرَ عَلِيُّ بْنُ أَبِي طَالِبٍ عَلَيْهِ السَّلَامُ إِلَى عَدِيِّ بْنِ حَاتِمٍ كَئِيبًا فَقَالَ يَا عَدِيُّ مَا لِيَ أَرَاكَ كَئِيبًا حَزِينًا
>
> قَالَ وَمَا يَمْنَعُنِي وَقَدْ قُتِلَ ابْنَايَ وَفُقِئَتْ عَيْنِي
>
> فَقَالَ يَا عَدِيُّ إِنَّهُ مَنْ رَضِيَ بِقَضَاءِ اللَّهِ جَرَى عَلَيْهِ وَكَانَ لَهُ أَجْرٌ وَمَنْ لَمْ يَرْضَ بِقَضَاءِ اللَّهِ جَرَى عَلَيْهِ وَحَبِطَ عَمَلُهُ.

Sayyidunā 'Alī ibn Abī Ṭālib once saw 'Adiyy ibn Ḥātim in dismay. Sayyidunā 'Alī said, "O 'Adiyy, why do I see you sad and distressed?"

'Adiyy said, "Why should I not be when my sons have been killed and my eye has been gouged?"

Sayyidunā 'Alī said, "O 'Adiyy, whoever is content with the Decree of Allah will be rewarded for it; whoever is displeased with the Decree of Allah will have his good deeds negated."[6]

---

5 Aḥmad ibn Ḥanbal, *Faḍā'il al-Ṣaḥābah*, 927.
6 Ibn Abī al-Dunyā, *al-Riḍā 'an Allāh bi Qaḍā'ihī*, 15.

The Ṣaḥābah were ever patient. Even in the field of war, where sons were slain and limbs were lost, their default position was one of patience. Sayyidunā ʿAlī's ﵁ advice to ʿAdiyy ibn Ḥātim ﵁ was a reminder to him, that even in the worst of times, when all may seem lost and terrible things have been done to us, we need to accept that all is from the Will and Decree of Allah ﷻ. These times are our greatest tests, and patience here will lead to great rewards. We need not look solely to the legends of the past to see examples of this. There are many of our brothers and sisters around the world who, perhaps this very day, are suffering great trials and hardships and facing the worst oppression. Yet, they respond only by saying "All praise is for Allah" and "Allah is enough for me and He is the best disposer of my affairs." For such people, their patience will be forever rewarded, and *in shā' Allāh* their pain and suffering will become like a distant memory or a passing cloud as they bathe in the Light of Allah ﷻ in the gardens of Paradise. Allah ﷻ states in the Qur'an:

وَلَمَّا رَءَا ٱلْمُؤْمِنُونَ ٱلْأَحْزَابَ قَالُوا۟ هَٰذَا مَا وَعَدَنَا ٱللَّهُ وَرَسُولُهُۥ وَصَدَقَ ٱللَّهُ وَرَسُولُهُۥ ۚ وَمَا زَادَهُمْ إِلَّآ إِيمَٰنًا وَتَسْلِيمًا

When the believers saw the enemy alliance, they said, "This is what Allah and His Messenger had promised us. The promise of Allah and His Messenger has come true." And this only increased them in faith and submission.[7]

Such people face hardship, and it only increases the strength of their faith. May Allah ﷻ accept them all into Paradise and accept the feeble and weak ones such as us with them too. *Āmīn*.

Contentedness in Simplicity

Sayyidunā ʿAlī ﵁ said:

---

7 *Al-Aḥzāb*, 22.

كُلُّ مُقْتَصَر عَلَيْهِ كافٍ.

Everything to which one limits himself suffices.[8]

Sayyidunā ʿAlī ﵁ would limit his access to the wealth of the world despite the abundance of it that would fill the coffers of the public treasury (*bayt al-māl*), and like his predecessors, would live a life of complete simplicity and hardship, choosing coarse cloths over fine silks and dry dates over delicacies. And therein lies the great secret to living a life less materialistic. In our age, we are held up by the scaffolding of ease and complacency and cannot walk without the crutches of material luxury to help us on our way, yet there are people just like us elsewhere in the world who live lives as content as our own, if not more content, with far less. Therefore, it cannot be said that the ease with which we find ourselves is the recipe for contentment. The secret is thus made open and plain for all to see. Human beings can suffice with little to nothing and contentment is found only with Allah ﷻ, Who says:

لَا يُكَلِّفُ ٱللَّهُ نَفْسًا إِلَّا وُسْعَهَا

Allah does not require of any soul more than what it can afford.[9]

We are capable of doing much with very little, as the lives of the Rightly Guided Caliphs bear ample testimony to. It is for each one of us to look at what excesses we rely on in our day-to-day lives and see where we can lose some needless comforts and make great gains of character in the process. Sayyidunā ʿAlī ﵁ was the ruler of a vast empire, and yet we find that he continued to live the life of a simple man throughout the six decades of his life, eating little, praying much, and limiting his involvement with the world. So set was Sayyidunā ʿAlī ﵁ on this path that Yazīd ibn Miḥjan ﵁ narrates,

---

8 Aḥmad ibn Muḥammad ibn Aḥmad al-Maydānī, *Majmaʿ al-Amthāl*, Vol. 2, p.454.

9 *Al-Baqarah*, 286.

كُنَّا مَعَ عَلِيٍّ عَلَيْهِ السَّلَامُ بِالرَّحْبَةِ فَدَعَا بِسَيْفٍ فَسَلَّهُ فَقَالَ: مَنْ يَشْتَرِي هَذَا فَوَاللَّهِ لَوْ كَانَ عِنْدِي ثَمَنَ إِزَارٍ مَا بِعْتُهُ.

> We were with Sayyidunā ʿAlī in the army and he called for a sword and unsheathed it, saying, "Who will buy this? By Allah, if I had the price of a garment I would not sell it."[10]

This is the height of *zuhd* (detachment/asceticism) and scrupulousness by someone such as he who had the world at his feet, yet he struggled to such an extent that he had to sell a sword he did not want to sell. How could he not have such high moral fortitude and self-discipline when he grew up in the house of our Noble Master ﷺ?

In another narration, Abū Maṭar ؓ states,

رَأَيْتُ عَلِيًّا عَلَيْهِ السَّلَامُ مُتَّزِرًا بِإِزَارٍ مُتَرَدِّيًا بِرِدَاءٍ وَمَعَهُ الدِّرَّةُ كَأَنَّهُ أَعْرَابِيٌّ بَدْوِيٌّ حَتَّى بَلَغَ سُوقَ الْكَرَابِيسِ فَقَالَ فِي قَمِيصٍ بِثَلَاثَةِ دَرَاهِمَ فَلَمَّا عَرَفَهُ لَمْ يَشْتَرِ مِنْهُ شَيْئًا فَأَتَى آخَرَ فَلَمَّا عَرَفَهُ لَمْ يَشْتَرِ مِنْهُ شَيْئًا فَأَتَى غُلَامًا حَدَثًا فَاشْتَرَى مِنْهُ قَمِيصًا بِثَلَاثَةِ دَرَاهِمَ، ثُمَّ جَاءَ أَبُو الْغُلَامِ فَأَخْبَرَهُ فَأَخَذَ أَبُوهُ دِرْهَمًا ثُمَّ جَاءَ بِهِ، فَقَالَ: هَذَا الدِّرْهَمُ يَا أَمِيرَ الْمُؤْمِنِينَ، فَقَالَ: مَا شَأْنُ هَذَا الدِّرْهَمِ قَالَ: كَانَ ثَمَنُ الْقَمِيصِ دِرْهَمَيْنِ فَقَالَ: بَاعَنِي رِضَايَ وَأَخَذَ رِضَاهُ

> I saw Sayyidunā ʿAlī wearing a linen garment, cloaked with a robe, and he had a walking stick as if he were a Bedouin wayfarer until he reached the garment market and said, "A shirt for three dirhams."
>
> When he recognised the person, he did not buy from him. Then another came and, when he knew him, he did not buy anything from him either. Then a young boy came to him and Sayyidunā ʿAlī bought a shirt from him for three dirhams. Then the boy's father came, and the boy told him what had occurred. His father took a dirham and brought it to Sayyidunā ʿAlī and said, "A dirham, O Commander of the Faithful!"

---

10 Aḥmad ibn Ḥanbal, *Kitāb al-Zuhd*, 702.

Sayyidunā 'Alī said, "What is the significance of this dirham?"

He said, "The price of the shirt was two dirhams."

He said, "I bought it happily and he was satisfied with the sale."[11]

Here we see the garb of the Commander of the Faithful, wearing a simple wrap and cloak and walking with a staff, buying garments for three dirhams in the marketplace. There was no difference to how he dressed in the time of the Prophet ﷺ, the time of his predecessor Caliphs, nor in the time when he himself was the Caliph. Abū Mulaykah ؓ narrates,

لَمَّا أَرْسَلَ عُثْمَانُ إِلَى عَلِيٍّ رَحْمَةُ اللَّهِ عَلَيْهِ مَا فِي التَّعَاقُبِ وَجَدَهُ مُتَّزِرًا بِعَبَاءَةٍ مُحْتَجِزًا بِعِقَالٍ وَهُوَ يَهْنَأُ بَعِيرًا لَهُ.

When Sayyidunā 'Uthmān sent for Sayyidunā 'Alī, he found him wrapped in a cloak and tied with a headband as he was taking care of his camel.[12]

Even when buying clothing, he did not buy expensive clothes and sought simplicity and asceticism in his dress. 'Umar ibn Qays ؓ narrates,

قِيلَ لِعَلِيٍّ عَلَيْهِ السَّلَامُ: لِمَ تُرَقِّعُ قَمِيصَكَ؟

قَالَ: يَخْشَعُ الْقَلْبُ وَيَقْتَدِي بِهِ الْمُؤْمِنُ

It was said to Sayyidunā 'Alī, "Why do you patch your shirt?"

Sayyidunā 'Alī said, "The heart is humbled, and the believer emulates it."[13]

---

11 Aḥmad ibn Ḥanbal, *Kitāb al-Zuhd*, 692.
12 Aḥmad ibn Ḥanbal, *Kitāb al-Zuhd*, 696.
13 Aḥmad ibn Ḥanbal, *Kitāb al-Zuhd*, 699.

We can therefore understand that if clothes could be mended, even patched, then he would prefer this over buying something new and being wasteful even in such a small matter. Were he to buy clothes, then he would buy only what was required to cover himself and would not buy for comfort or for show. Even then, he would clothe someone else in better clothing than himself if given the opportunity. One such story of his generous character and simple manners is narrated by Abū al-Nawār ؓ, a cotton trader,

أَتَانِي عَلِيُّ بْنُ أَبِي طَالِبٍ وَمَعَهُ غُلَامٌ لَهُ فَاشْتَرَى مِنِّي قَمِيصَي كَرَابِيسَ ثُمَّ قَالَ لِغُلَامِهِ: اخْتَرْ أَيَّهُمَا شِئْتَ فَأَخَذَ أَحَدَهُمَا وَأَخَذَ عَلِيٌّ عَلَيْهِ السَّلَامُ الْآخَرَ فَلَبِسَهُ ثُمَّ مَدَّ يَدَهُ ثُمَّ قَالَ: اقْطَعِ الَّذِي يَفْضُلُ مِنْ قَدْرِ يَدَيَّ، فَقَطَعَهُ وَكَفَّهُ فَلَبِسَهُ ثُمَّ ذَهَبَ.

Sayyidunā ʿAlī ibn Abī Ṭālib came to me and he had a servant with him. He bought two cotton shirts from me, then said to his servant, "Choose whichever you prefer."

The servant took one and Sayyidunā ʿAlī took the other and put it on. Sayyidunā ʿAlī then extended his hand and said, "Cut from it whatever is left over from my hand." So he cut it off and Sayyidunā ʿAlī picked it up, wore it, and then left.[14]

Are there finer examples of kindness and good manners than the Prophet ﷺ and the Four Caliphs? Sayyidunā ʿAlī ؓ not only bought two similar shirts from the same seller to split between himself and the slave accompanying him, but he gave him preference over himself and allowed him to choose first! We can also see from this how simply he dressed in that he had it cut to size there and then in the marketplace; there was no tailoring or tapering, nor any seamster, he had the clothes cut by those present at the time and put it back on.

14 Aḥmad ibn Ḥanbal, *Kitāb al-Zuhd*, 708.

It is also worth noting that we can see from the narration in discussion and others that Sayyidunā ʿAlī ﷺ would often walk to where he wanted to go, despite having the means to do otherwise. Abū Sinān al-Shaybānī ﷺ narrates that a man said to him,

رَأَيْتُ عَلِيَّ بْنَ أَبِي طَالِبٍ رَضِيَ اللَّهُ عَنْهُ يَمْشِي إِلَى الْعِيدِ.

I saw Sayyidunā ʿAlī ibn Abī Ṭālib walking to Eid.[15]

If there was no requirement to ride, he would walk to wherever he wanted to go. Again, a comparison can be drawn with his time as a young man, when he had laid in the bed of the Prophet ﷺ to confuse the assassins who sought to murder the Prophet ﷺ. He waited three days further to migrate to Medina, returning property to those who had given it to the Messenger of Allah ﷺ for safekeeping. He then famously walked the 200 or so-mile distance from Mecca to the outskirts of Medina until he finally arrived with his feet bleeding due to the rough terrain and poor footwear.[16]

This constant striving extended to his familial affairs as well, and under his leadership, his household also engaged in the same simple lifestyle and shunned the world, choosing to live the simple lives of common Muslims while giving away their worldly wealth to the poor. ʿAlī ibn Rabīʿah ﷺ narrates,

أَنَّ عَلِيًّا عَلَيْهِ السَّلَامُ كَانَ لَهُ امْرَأَتَانِ كَانَ إِذَا كَانَ يَوْمُ هَذِهِ اشْتَرَى لَحْمًا بِنِصْفِ دِرْهَمٍ وَإِذَا كَانَ يَوْمُ هَذِهِ اشْتَرَى لَحْمًا بِنِصْفِ دِرْهَمٍ.

15 Aḥmad ibn Ḥanbal, *Kitāb al-Zuhd*, 705.

16 Dr ʿAlī M. Ṣallābī, *ʿAlī ibn Abī Ṭālib*, Dār al-ʿĀlamiyyah, Riyadh (1431/2010), Vol. 1, p. 83.

Sayyidunā ʿAlī had two wives. If it was one wife's day, he would buy meat for half a dirham; if it was the other's day, he would buy meat for half a dirham."[17]

In this way, both wives and families got by with the sparse amount of food required, ensuring that they could worship Allah ﷻ and carry out their worldly deeds and duties, but not live the excessive lifestyles that have become the norm in much of today's world.

Similarly, Ṣāliḥ Bayyaʿ al-Aksiyyah narrates from his mother (or grandmother), who said,

رَأَيْتُ عَلِيَّ بْنَ أَبِي طَالِبٍ رَضِيَ اللَّهُ عَنْهُ اشْتَرَى تَمْرًا بِدِرْهَمٍ فَحَمَلَهُ فِي مِلْحَفَةٍ فَقَالُوا نَحْمِلُ عَنْكَ يَا أَمِيرَ الْمُؤْمِنِينَ

قَالَ: لَا أَبُو الْعِيَالِ أَحَقُّ أَنْ يَحْمِلَ.

I saw Sayyidunā ʿAlī ibn Abī Ṭālib buy dates for a dirham and carry them in a blanket. The people said, "We will carry them for you, O Commander of the Faithful."

Sayyidunā ʿAlī said, "No. The father of the children has more right to bear the burden."[18]

It is a right to bear the burdens of labour for one's family as well as a duty. As the man of the house, Sayyidunā ʿAlī would not allow anyone else to take the burden from him and assume those rights. Through hardship, one builds character, strength, patience, and an understanding of what this world truly is, a trial that can be passed or failed by the rich or poor alike. Allah ﷻ can choose whether to test us with ease or with hardship and oftentimes our lives

17 Aḥmad ibn Ḥanbal, *Kitāb al-Zuhd*, 696.

18 Aḥmad ibn Ḥanbal, *Kitāb al-Zuhd*, 709.

are filled with both to varying degrees, ever-shifting from one to another; as His slaves, it is up to us to prepare ourselves for the challenges ahead. As Allah ﷻ states in the Qur'an:

الٓمٓ ١ أَحَسِبَ ٱلنَّاسُ أَن يُتْرَكُوٓاْ أَن يَقُولُوٓاْ ءَامَنَّا وَهُمْ لَا يُفْتَنُونَ ٢

وَلَقَدْ فَتَنَّا ٱلَّذِينَ مِن قَبْلِهِمْۖ فَلَيَعْلَمَنَّ ٱللَّهُ ٱلَّذِينَ صَدَقُواْ وَلَيَعْلَمَنَّ ٱلْكَٰذِبِينَ ٣

Alif-Lām-Mīm. Do people think once they say, "We believe", that they will be left without being put to the test? We certainly tested those before them. And in this way Allah will clearly distinguish between those who are truthful and those who are liars.[19]

أَمْ حَسِبْتُمْ أَن تَدْخُلُواْ ٱلْجَنَّةَ وَلَمَّا يَأْتِكُم مَّثَلُ ٱلَّذِينَ خَلَوْاْ مِن قَبْلِكُمۖ مَّسَّتْهُمُ ٱلْبَأْسَآءُ وَٱلضَّرَّآءُ وَزُلْزِلُواْ حَتَّىٰ يَقُولَ ٱلرَّسُولُ وَٱلَّذِينَ ءَامَنُواْ مَعَهُۥ مَتَىٰ نَصْرُ ٱللَّهِۗ أَلَآ إِنَّ نَصْرَ ٱللَّهِ قَرِيبٌ

Do you think you will be admitted into Paradise without being tested like those before you? They were afflicted with suffering and adversity and were so violently shaken that even the Messenger and the believers with him cried out, "When will Allah's help come?" Indeed, Allah's help is always near.[20]

As we are tested both with ease and hardship, it is incumbent upon us to best prepare for them. Sayyidunā 'Alī ؓ had fully internalised this, forgoing access to ease and undergoing great hardship to test himself before he was tested and build resilience against both vice and despair. An example of this resilience-building can be found in his avoidance of eating delicacies. 'Adiyy ibn Thābit ؓ narrates,

أَنَّ عَلِيًّا عَلَيْهِ السَّلَامُ أُتِيَ بِفَالُوذَجٍ فَلَمْ يَأْكُلْهُ.

19 *Al-'Ankabūt*, 1-3.

20 *Al-Baqarah*, 214.

Sayyidunā ʿAlī was presented with fālūdhaj,[21] but he did not eat it.[22]

Likewise, Ḥabbah ؓ narrates,

عَنْ عَلِيٍّ، عَلَيْهِ السَّلَامُ أَنَّهُ أُتِيَ بِالْفَالُوذَجِ فَوُضِعَ قُدَّامَهُ فَقَالَ: إِنَّكَ لَطَيِّبُ الرِّيحِ حَسَنُ اللَّوْنِ طَيِّبُ الطَّعْمِ وَلَكِنْ أَكْرَهُ أَنْ أُعَوِّدَ نَفْسِي مَا لَمْ تَعْتَدْهُ.

Sayyidunā ʿAlī himself explained that fālūdhaj was once brought and placed in front of him, and he said, "You have a pleasant scent, a beautiful colour, and a pleasant taste, but I hate to accustom myself to what my soul is unaccustomed to."[23]

Oftentimes we find ourselves complaining of minor issues as if the weight of the world has come crashing down upon us. Sayyidunā ʿAlī ؓ warned against such a mindset, saying,

مَنْ عَظَّمَ صِغَارَ المَصَائِبِ ابْتَلَاهُ اللهُ بِكِبَارِهَا.

Whoever exaggerates small hardships, Allah tries him with great ones.[24]

It is therefore in our own best interests to avoid weak-mindedness and excessive complaints. Those of our brothers and sisters whom Allah ﷻ has tested with the greatest calamities bear them all without complaint and praise Him not only despite the hardship but because of it. The rest of us feeble believers should learn our lessons vicariously, and guard ourselves against such foolish behaviour. Indeed, it is better for us to not have wealth than it is to become complacent with it, as Sayyidunā ʿAlī ؓ succinctly put it,

---

21 A type of sweet dish.
22 Aḥmad ibn Ḥanbal, *Kitāb al-Zuhd*, 700.
23 Aḥmad ibn Ḥanbal, *Kitāb al-Zuhd*, 707.
24 Aḥmad ibn Muḥammad ibn Aḥmad al-Maydānī, *Majmaʿ al-Amthāl*, Vol. 2, p. 453.

اَلْحِرْمَانُ خَيْرٌ مِنَ الْإِمْتِنَانِ

Deprivation is better than complacency.[25]

This is not to say that we must forgo all our wealth and live in abject poverty, as this can put one in a position of weakness, which can lead one away from Islam as a survival mechanism if allowed to go unchecked. Islam does not advocate people living monastic lifestyles as celibate hermits alone in the mountains, but as Muslims, we should not ever fall into complacency, decadence, and excess.

Other weak-minded traits that Sayyidunā ʿAlī ﵁ advised us to guard against are those of pride and vanity. Vanity can make a person haughty and aloof from others, self-aggrandising and pompous, which also leads to pride; and pride makes a person forget themselves and the reality of who and what they are and can turn one's good deeds into ashes. Sayyidunā ʿAlī ﵁ explains,

مَا لِابْنِ آدَمَ وَالْفَخْرِ: أَوَّلُهُ نُطْفَةٌ، وَآخِرُهُ جِيفَةٌ، وَلاَ يَرْزُقُ نَفْسَهُ، وَلاَ يَدفَعُ حَتْفَهُ.

Why does the son of Adam engage in vanity? His beginning is semen, his end a stinking corpse; he can neither sustain himself nor stave off his death.[26]

When we are between two such poor physical states, what need is there to puff out our chests and announce our momentary blooming in this short, transient life? How can we be proud when we cannot sustain our existence without outside help, cannot go without sleep, and constantly have to relieve our bowels to avoid pain and discomfort? We cannot even stave off

25 Aḥmad ibn Muḥammad ibn Aḥmad al-Maydānī, *Majmaʿ al-Amthāl*, Vol. 2, p. 455.

26 Aḥmad ibn Muḥammad ibn Aḥmad al-Maydānī, *Majmaʿ al-Amthāl*, Vol. 2, p. 454.

our deaths, though many of our most intelligent have wasted their lives in trying. How are we still proud?

Allah ﷻ says in the Qur'an,

وَلَا تُصَعِّرْ خَدَّكَ لِلنَّاسِ وَلَا تَمْشِ فِى ٱلْأَرْضِ مَرَحًا إِنَّ ٱللَّهَ لَا يُحِبُّ كُلَّ مُخْتَالٍ فَخُورٍ

And do not turn your nose up to people nor walk pridefully upon the earth. Surely Allah does not like whoever is arrogant, boastful.[27]

The phrase "لَا تُصَعِّرْ" is derived from "صَعَرَ" which refers to an ailment among camels that results in a tilting of the neck, similar to the effect a stroke has on a person's face and carries the meaning of disdainfully turning away. The phrase "مَرَحًا" implies walking proudly.[28] How can one turn their face away from others in pride when they are from the same origin as them and are headed to the same state? Is it not a strange thing that we were created from the Earth, which is by its nature low to the ground, and yet we walk proudly upon it.

The final part of the aforementioned *āyah* states, "*Surely Allah does not like whoever is arrogant, boastful.*" When Allah ﷻ dislikes such a person, how can such a person continue in his ways knowing this? Sayyidunā ʿAlī ؓ said,

مَنْ رَضِيَ عَنْ نَفْسِهِ كَثُرَ السّاخِطُ عَلَيْهِ

Whoever is pleased with himself, many are displeased with him.[29]

---

27 *Luqmān*, 18.

28 Muḥammad Shafīʿ ibn Muḥammad Yāsīn ʿUthmānī, *Maʿārif al-Qur'ān*, Karachi (1424/2003), 30:18.

29 Aḥmad ibn Muḥammad ibn Aḥmad al-Maydānī, *Majmaʿ al-Amthāl*, Vol. 2, p. 453.

When Allah ﷻ dislikes you, surely the world itself will also dislike you. People who walk the earth carrying air and raising their noses at others are indeed a despicable bunch, and the majority of humanity dislikes and even hates such behaviour.

Sayyidunā ʿAlī ؓ constantly sought to protect himself against such vices of the heart and he therefore constantly built his resilience against them. It was this same resilience against vice that made Sayyidunā ʿAlī ؓ dislike pomposity and excess in decor and celebration. Imam al-Ghazālī ؒ reports in his *Iḥyāʾ*:

وَقَالَ عَلِيٌّ كَرَّمَ اللهُ وَجْهَهُ، لَمَّا رَأَى زِينَةَ النَّبَطِ بِالْعِرَاقِ فِي يَوْمِ عِيدٍ: مَا هَذَا الَّذِي أَظْهَرُوهُ؟ قَالُوا: يَا أَمِيرَ الْمُؤْمِنِينَ، هَذَا يَوْمُ عِيدٍ لَهُمْ. فقال:

كُلُّ يَوْمٍ لَا يَعْصِي اللهَ عَزَّ وَجَلَّ الْعَبْدُ فِيهِ فَهُوَ لَنَا عِيدٌ.

When Sayyidunā ʿAlī, may Allah ennoble his face, saw the decorations of the Nabataeans in Iraq on the day of Eid, he asked, "What is this that they are displaying?"

They said, "O Commander of the Faithful, this is their day of Eid."

Sayyidunā ʿAlī replied, "Every day in which Allah is not disobeyed is our Eid."[30]

Our celebrations should thus be decorated with the obedience of Allah ﷻ. There is no greater method of celebration of the Bounties of Allah ﷻ than increasing our obedience to Him and asking Him to bestow upon us even more goodness. Although there is no harm in showing our happiness through the decoration of our homes, etc., we should remain vigilant that

---

30   Abū Ḥāmid Muḥammad ibn Muḥammad al-Ṭūsī al-Ghazālī, *Iḥyāʾ ʿUlūm al-Dīn*, Vol. 4, p. 289.

we do not go to excess, or worse, emulate the non-Muslim celebrations with gaudy lights and pompous symbolism.

It is incumbent on each of us to avoid the vices of the heart and mind and to put ourselves to the task before we are put to task by Allah ﷻ. Whether the test in life is based on ease or hardship, whether it is based on how we spend our wealth or live without it, life is always testing us. Sayyidunā ʿAlī ؓ once exclaimed,

مَا أَحْسَنَ تَوَاضُعَ الأَغْنِيَاءِ لِلْفُقَرَاءِ طَلَباً لِمَا عِنْدَ اللهِ! وأَحْسَنُ مِنْهُ تِيهُ الْفُقَرَاءِ عَلَى الأَغْنِيَاءِ اتِّكَالاً عَلَى اللهِ.

How excellent it is the humility of the rich before the poor, seeking Allah's favour! And how much more excellent still the poor's disdain of the rich, trusting in Allah.[31]

The word *tīh* here is used in the sense of thinking oneself superior and refusing to allow oneself to be cowed or intimidated by another's wealth or supposed stature.

Wealth is a test, and the rich person who understands this remains humble and seeks Allah's ﷻ favour through charitable giving. Poverty is a greater test and thus the reward for having trust in Allah ﷻ in such a state is naturally greater.

Promoting Generosity and Opposing Greed

الرُّكُونُ إِلَى الدُّنْيَا مَعَ مَا تُعَايِنُ مِنْهَا جَهْلٌ، وَالتَّقْصِيرُ فِي حُسْنِ الْعَمَلِ إِذَا وَثِقْتَ بِالثَّوَابِ عَلَيْهِ غَبْنٌ، وَالطُّمَأْنِينَةُ إِلَى كُلِّ أَحَدٍ قَبْلَ الاخْتِبَارِ عَجْزٌ، وَالْبُخْلُ جَامِعٌ لِمَسَاوِئِ الأَخْلَاقِ.

31 Aḥmad ibn Muḥammad ibn Aḥmad al-Maydānī, *Majmaʿ al-Amthāl*, Vol. 2, p. 454.

Sayyidunā ʿAlī ؓ said:

"Inclining towards the world despite what you see of it is ignorance; falling short of a good deed when you are convinced of its reward is clear loss; placing trust in every person before assessing them is incapacity; and miserliness brings together all moral faults."[32]

These two qualities go hand in hand: opposing greed and promoting generosity. Sayyidunā ʿAlī ibn Abī Ṭālib ؓ did both. It is not merely enough for a Muslim to avoid wrongdoing, nor even enough to simply do right. A Muslim must do both and enjoin others to follow suit. As Allah ﷻ says in Sūrah al-ʿAṣr:

$$\text{وَٱلْعَصْرِ ١ إِنَّ ٱلْإِنسَٰنَ لَفِى خُسْرٍ ٢}$$

$$\text{إِلَّا ٱلَّذِينَ ءَامَنُوا۟ وَعَمِلُوا۟ ٱلصَّٰلِحَٰتِ وَتَوَاصَوْا۟ بِٱلْحَقِّ وَتَوَاصَوْا۟ بِٱلصَّبْرِ ٣}$$

By the passage of time! Surely humanity is in grave loss, except those who have faith, do good, and urge each other to the truth, and urge each other to perseverance.[33]

Time is a currency that is ever being spent, whether we intend to spend it or not. It is finite, and the most valuable thing that we spend in trade every day. Mankind is perpetually at a loss unless he spends his time in 4 things: (1) faith; (2) doing good deeds; (3) urging others towards doing good; and (4) urging others to persevere. Perseverance here refers to both patience in the obvious sense of the word, as well as perseverance in the face of one's desires and wishes to commit sin.[34]

---

32 Ibid.
33 *Al-ʿAṣr*, 1-3.
34 Shāh ʿAbd al-ʿAzīz Muḥaddith Dehlawī, *Tafsīr ʿAzīzī: Pārah ʿAmma*, p.637.

In the above quotation, Sayyidunā ʿAlī ibn Abī Ṭālib ﵁ gives four pieces of advice.

The first is a warning to not fall into the trap of the saying "seeing is believing". The world is a facade that blinds and distracts one from the Hereafter, showing you what you want to see and hiding from you the dangers headed your way, like the Sirens from the Greek myth that sang sweet songs to passing sailors, causing them to wreck their ships on the craggy cliffs of their island coasts. This is especially true in the current world we live in and the future we face, where images, voices, and even videos we see can be faked, and what we see and hear with our own eyes and ears cannot be trusted.

Secondly, he highlighted the folly of knowing something will result in a reward in the Hereafter and still not carrying it out. Each of us knows voluntary acts of good, kindness towards those less fortunate, the remembrance of Allah ﷻ, etc., all will be rewarded in the Hereafter. Why is it that we constantly fail to carry them out, especially when they are easily within our power to do so?

عَنْ أَبِي حَيَّانَ، حَدَّثَنِي مُجَمِّعٌ أَنَّ عَلِيًّا رَضِيَ اللَّهُ عَنْهُ كَانَ يَأْمُرُ بِبَيْتِ الْمَالِ فَيُكْنَسُ ثُمَّ يُنْضَحُ
ثُمَّ يُصَلِّي فِيهِ رَجَاءَ أَنْ يَشْهَدَ لَهُ يَوْمَ الْقِيَامَةِ أَنَّهُ لَمْ يَحْبِسْ فِيهِ الْمَالَ عَنِ الْمُسْلِمِينَ

Sayyidunā ʿAlī was in charge of the treasury. He swept it, washed it, and then prayed in it, hoping that it would be a witness for him on the Day of Requital that he did not withhold money from the Muslims.[35]

Such was the magnanimity of Sayyidunā ʿAlī ibn Abī Ṭālib ﵁ that he had emptied the treasury of wealth to free the Muslims from the burden of poverty and help alleviate them from the difficult test of patience. From this, we can again glean that being poor is not in itself something to celebrate or seek out, but rather it is a difficulty that must be overcome whilst remaining

---

35 Aḥmad ibn Ḥanbal, *Kitāb al-Zuhd*, 695.

patient with the Divine Decree. It is better to have wealth and be less wasteful than it is to lack wealth and be in need of aid.

The idea of sweeping and washing the treasury denotes great respect for the place, both as the location of a sacred duty he was given and as the place upon which he was to pray. It also highlights the emptiness of the treasury chambers at the time. Sayyidunā ʿAlī ﵁ prayed within the treasury chambers to ensure that the earth itself would bear testimony to this act. Sayyidunā Abū Hurayrah ﵁ narrates,

قَرَأَ رَسُولُ اللَّهِ ﷺ هَذِهِ الآيَةَ: {يَوْمَئِذٍ تُحَدِّثُ أَخْبَارَهَا} ثم قَالَ أَتَدْرُونَ مَا أَخْبَارُهَا؟

قَالُوا: اللَّهُ وَرَسُولُهُ أَعْلَمُ.

قَالَ فَإِنَّ أَخْبَارَهَا أَنْ تَشْهَدَ عَلَى كُلِّ عَبْدٍ أَوْ أَمَةٍ بِمَا عَمِلَ عَلَى ظَهْرِهَا تَقُولُ عَمِلَ يَوْمَ كَذَا كَذَا وَكَذَا فَهَذِهِ أَخْبَارُهَا.

The Messenger of Allah recited this āyah, "On that day the earth will recount everything",[36] and then he said, "Do you know what it will recount?"

The Ṣaḥābah said, "Allah and His Messenger know best."

The Prophet said, "Indeed it will bear witness against every servant and maidservant to what they did on its surface, saying that on such a day this person did such and such. This is what it will recount."[37]

The third point that Sayyidunā ʿAlī ibn Abī Ṭālib ﵁ made regarding this is that taking the advice of others all the time before formulating an opinion is a sign of inability. It shows either a lack of sufficient knowledge in the field

36 *Al-Zilzāl*, 4.

37 *Jāmiʿ al-Tirmidhī*, 3353.

in which you are making the choice or a lack of ability to make a decisive decision thus showing an inability to lead.

The fourth and final point he made was that miserliness is the summation of all moral faults. It shows one to be selfish, greedy, spiteful, lacking in moral decency, uncaring of the plight of others, and generally despicable. Greed is a disease of the heart and does not do the one who holds such a sickness within them any favours. Sayyidunā ʿAlī ؓ said,

اَلطَّمْعُ ضَامِنٌ غَيْرُ وَفِيٍّ.

Greed is an unfaithful guarantor.[38]

We cannot rely on our greed to help us through our trials. Those of us who have grown up in capitalist societies and have been taught from an early age that it is "a dog-eat-dog world" and that we should "look after ourselves", have fallen foul of the scam that our greed is trying to sell to us. A person who puts themsleves before others cannot expect others to put them before themselves when they are in need. Sayyidunā ʿAlī ؓ also said,

مَنْ لَمْ يُعْطِ قَاعِداً، لَمْ يُعْطَ قَائِمًا.

Whoever does not give while sitting in comfort, will not receive when standing in need.[39]

We are an interdependent species, and we will always need each other to get by. The ideology of individualism tries to create silos within which each member of society can be isolated and thus better controlled. Greed and selfishness are thus not a guarantor of one's benefit, but a betrayer.

---

38 Aḥmad ibn Muḥammad ibn Aḥmad al-Maydānī, *Majmaʿ al-Amthāl*, Vol. 2, p. 455.

39 Aḥmad ibn Muḥammad ibn Aḥmad al-Maydānī, *Majmaʿ al-Amthāl*, Vol. 2, p. 454.

Fair Treatment of Others

عَنِ الْمُتَّقِي الْهِنْدِيّ، قَالَ عَلِيٌّ بْنُ أَبِي طَالِبٍ رَضِيَ اللهُ عَنْهُ:

اِجْعَلْ نَفْسَكَ ميزاناً بَيْنَكَ وبَيْنَ غَيْرِكَ، وأحِبَّ لَهُ ما تُحِبُّ لِنَفْسِكَ، واكْرَهْ لَهُ ما تَكْرَهُ لَها، ولاتَظْلِمْ كَما تُحِبُّ أنْ لاتُظْلَمَ، وأحْسِنْ كَما تُحِبُّ أنْ يُحْسَنَ إلَيْكَ.

Sayyidunā ʿAlī ibn Abī Ṭālib ﵁ said,

"Make yourself a gauge between you and others. Love for others what you love for yourself, and hate for them what you hate for yourself. Do not wrong others, just as you dislike being wronged. Do good, just as you would love for good to be done to you."[40]

The discussion has thus naturally led to the fair treatment of others. It is a universal rule amongst all righteous-hearted people of the world to love for one another what we would love for ourselves. Proper adherence to this simple principle could do away with many of the problems we see in the world. If we treated every other person as we would wish to be treated, there would be no mistreatment of the weak in society and no exploitation of our peers. Fairness and kindness would be triumphant, and hatred and tyranny would become mere lessons from the past. To be a good leader, it is necessary for one to internalise and act upon this principle in all of one's judgements and dealings. Imam Ibn ʿAsākir ﵀ reported that Sayyidunā ʿAlī ibn Abī Ṭālib ﵁ said,

مَنْ أَرَادَ أَنْ يَنْصِفَ النَّاسَ مِنْ نَفْسِهِ فَلْيُحِبَّ لَهُمْ مَا يُحِبَّ لِنَفْسِهِ.

40 ʿAlā al-Din ʿAlī ibn ʿAbd al-Mālik Husām al-Din al-Muttaqī al-Hindī, *Kanz al-ʿUmmāl*, Vol. 16, p. 172, Hadith no. 44215.

Whoever desires to be fair to people, let him love for them what he loves for himself.[41]

This is the essence of fairness and justice: to be lenient when it is called for, to be just and fair at all times, to put oneself in the shoes of each person and to make a decision based on how one wishes a decision about themselves would be made. Such a methodology would cut out favouritism, nepotism and their ilk and facilitate decisions that were right for all involved.

Imam Ibn ʿAsākir ﵀ also reported that Sayyidunā ʿAlī ibn Abī Ṭālib ﵁ said,

إِنَّ الْمُؤْمِنِينَ قَوْمٌ نَصَحَةٌ بَعْضِهِمْ لِبَعْضٍ مُتَوَادُّونَ وَإِنْ بَعَدَتْ دِيَارُهُمْ وَأَبْدَانُهُمْ وَإِنَّ الْمُنَافِقِينَ قَوْمٌ غَشَشَةٌ بَعْضِهِمْ لِبَعْضٍ.

Indeed the believers are people of goodwill and love for each other, even if their homes and persons are apart; indeed the hypocrites are people of malevolence for each other.[42]

The concept of treating others as we would like to be treated is magnified in the case of our fellow Muslim brothers and sisters. The members of our Ummah should not only be treated as we would like to be treated, but they should also be seen as part of us, as the Prophet ﷺ himself described the Ummah,

تَرَى الْمُؤْمِنِينَ فِي تَرَاحُمِهِمْ وَتَوَادِّهِمْ وَتَعَاطُفِهِمْ كَمَثَلِ الْجَسَدِ إِذَا اشْتَكَى عُضْوًا تَدَاعَى لَهُ سَائِرُ جَسَدِهِ بِالسَّهَرِ وَالْحُمَّى.

41 Ibn ʿAsākir ʿAlī ibn al-Ḥasan, *Tārīkh Madīnah Dimashq*, Vol. 42, p. 517.

42 Ibn ʿAsākir ʿAlī ibn al-Ḥasan, *Tārīkh Madīnah Dimashq*, Vol. 23, p. 465.

You see the believers being merciful, loving, and kind among themselves; they are as one body, if any part of the body is unwell then the whole body shares in its sleeplessness and fever.[43]

This is not to say that the non-Muslim should be treated poorly. Far from it. al-Shaʿbī ﷺ reported,

وَجَدَ عَلِيُّ بْنُ أَبِي طَالِبٍ دِرْعَهُ عِنْدَ رَجُلٍ نَصْرَانِيٍّ فَأَقْبَلَ بِهِ إِلَى شُرَيْحٍ يُخَاصِمُهُ قَالَ فَجَاءَ عَلِيٌّ حَتَّى جَلَسَ إِلَى جَنْبِ شُرَيْحٍ وَقَالَ يَا شُرَيْحُ لَوْ كَانَ خَصْمِي مُسْلِمًا مَا جَلَسْتُ إِلَّا مَعَهُ وَلَكِنَّهُ نَصْرَانِيٌّ وَقَدْ قَالَ رَسُولُ اللَّهِ صَلَّى اللَّهُ عَلَيْهِ وَسَلَّمَ إِذَا كُنْتُمْ وَإِيَّاهُمْ فِي طَرِيقٍ فَاضْطَرُّوهُمْ إِلَى مَضَايِقِهِ وَصَغِّرُوا بِهِمْ كَمَا صَغَّرَ اللَّهُ بِهِمْ مِنْ غَيْرِ أَنْ تَطْغَوْا ثُمَّ قَالَ هَذَا الدِّرْعُ دِرْعِي وَلَمْ أَبِعْ وَلَمْ أَهَبْ.

فَقَالَ شُرَيْحٌ لِلنَّصْرَانِيِّ مَا تَقُولُ فِيمَا يَقُولُ أَمِيرُ الْمُؤْمِنِينَ.

فَقَالَ النَّصْرَانِيُّ مَا الدِّرْعُ إِلَّا دِرْعِي وَمَا أَمِيرُ الْمُؤْمِنِينَ عِنْدِي بِكَاذِبٍ.

فَالْتَفَتَ شُرَيْحٌ إِلَى عَلِيٍّ فَقَالَ يَا أَمِيرَ الْمُؤْمِنِينَ هَلْ مِنْ بَيِّنَةٍ.

فَضَحِكَ عَلِيٌّ وَقَالَ أَصَابَ شُرَيْحٌ مَا لِي بَيِّنَةٌ.

فَقَضَى بِهَا شُرَيْحٌ لِلنَّصْرَانِيِّ قَالَ فَأَخَذَهَا النَّصْرَانِيُّ وَمَشَى خُطًى ثُمَّ رَجَعَ فَقَالَ أَمَّا أَنَا فَأَشْهَدُ أَنَّ هَذِهِ أَحْكَامُ الْأَنْبِيَاءِ أَمِيرُ الْمُؤْمِنِينَ قَدَّمَنِي إِلَى قَاضِيهِ وَقَاضِيهِ يَقْضِي عَلَيْهِ أَشْهَدُ أَنْ لَا إِلَهَ إِلَّا اللَّهُ وَأَشْهَدُ أَنَّ مُحَمَّدًا عَبْدُهُ وَرَسُولُهُ الدِّرْعُ وَاللَّهِ دِرْعُكَ يَا أَمِيرَ الْمُؤْمِنِينَ اتَّبَعْتُ الْجَيْشَ وَأَنْتَ مُنْطَلِقٌ إِلَى صِفِّينَ فَخَرَجَتْ مِنْ بَعِيرِكَ الْأَوْرَقِ.

فَقَالَ أَمَا إِذْ أَسْلَمْتَ فَهِيَ لَكَ!

Sayyidunā ʿAlī ibn Abī Ṭālib once saw a Christian man wearing his lost armour and he took up the matter legally and brought it to the

43 *Ṣaḥīḥ al-Bukhārī*, 6011.

judge, Shurayḥ. Sayyidunā ʿAlī said, "O Shurayḥ, if my dispute was with a Muslim, I would simply sit with him, but he is Christian and the Messenger of Allah said that 'when you share the road with them, make them give way without oppressing them.' This is my armour. I have neither sold it nor given it away."

Shurayḥ said to the Christian, "What do you say about what the Commander of the Faithful has said?"

The Christian said, "It is my armour, but I do not consider the Commander of the Faithful a liar."

Shurayḥ turned to Sayyidunā ʿAlī and said, "O Commander of the Faithful, do you have proof?"

Sayyidunā ʿAlī laughed and said, "Shurayḥ is correct; I have no proof."

Shurayḥ thus ruled in favour of the Christian. The Christian took the armour and began to leave, but then returned and said, "As for me, I testify that this is the ruling of the Prophets. The Commander of the Faithful himself took me to his judge and his judge has ruled against him! I testify that there is no God but Allah and Muhammad is the Messenger of Allah. By Allah, the armour is yours. I followed the army while you were on your way to Ṣiffīn and the armour fell from your luggage."

Sayyidunā ʿAlī said, "If you have embraced Islam, then the armour is yours."[44]

It is this sense of fairness and the righteous way that draws the hearts of the good to Islam. Here Sayyidunā ʿAlī, the ruler of the Empire, took a common man of a different faith to a judge to ensure that the matter was dealt with fairly, and even after it was revealed that the item had been stolen,

---

44   Ibn Kathīr, *al-Bidāyah wa al-Nihāyah*, Vol. ii, p. 107.

he deferred to the judge's decision and gifted the item as a gift to the new Muslim following his acceptance of Islam. If we as Muslims today lived our lives in such a way, the hearts of those who live around us would also be more inclined to Islam. Alas, many of us have little care for our brothers, let alone those who differ from us in creed.

The Misuse of Words

.مَنْ عَلِمَ أَنَّ كَلَامَهُ مِنْ عَمَلِهِ قَلَّ كَلَامَهُ إِلَّا فِيمَا يَعْنِيهِ

Sayyidunā ʿAlī ※ said,

He who knows that his words are part of his actions will rarely speak except about what concerns him.[45]

Words hold great power, and the tongue can be both a tool of great change and influence as well as a weapon causing great harm. Words by their nature hold meaning, and when properly structured they can be fantastically beautiful. When misused, they can cause irreparable damage. It is thus of grave importance for a Muslim to understand that their words will be weighed alongside their other deeds. It is better for us to not speak at all than to utter something that could cause us loss in the Hereafter.

Sayyidunā ʿAlī ※ was the first to act upon his own advice and this is why when we read the authentic sayings of Sayyidunā ʿAlī ※, we find that every word is measured and selected to convey meaning eloquently. There were never any excessive words in his speech, and he only spoke on matters of importance. He had grown up in the noble household of the Messenger of Allah ※ and thus learned rhetoric and eloquence from the greatest teacher. Not a single word was wasted.

---

45 Aḥmad ibn Muḥammad ibn Aḥmad al-Maydānī, *Majmaʿ al-Amthāl*, Vol. 2, p. 454.

There are, however, times when one should speak and times one should remain silent. Imam Fakhr al-Dīn al-Rāzī ﷺ writes that Sayyidunā ʿAlī ibn Abī Ṭālib ﷺ said,

.لَا خَيْرَ فِي الصَّمْتِ عَنِ الْعِلْمِ كَمَا لَا خَيْرَ فِي الْكَلَامِ عَنِ الْجَهْلِ

There is no good in silence when it leads to knowledge, just as there is no good in speaking when it leads to ignorance."[46]

When we know something that will benefit others in some way or increase their knowledge, we should be willing to mention these to them so that they benefit. Should speaking lead to greater ignorance, it should be avoided. This can be applied in several ways: advising people who will do the opposite of the advice is a mistake, saying something that would lead to turmoil is a terrible deed, and arguing for the sake of arguing is wasteful and foolish. The opposites of these examples are also true. Words must thus also be measured for the impact they could have, not merely for the result intended. As Sayyidunā ʿAlī ﷺ also mentioned,

.رُبَّ مَفْتُونٍ بِحُسْنِ الْقَوْلِ فِيهِ

Many a man is trialled by a good word spoken of him.[47]

Sometimes our praise for others can lead to harm, as the recipient becomes infected with pride for which their good is washed away but their self-aggrandisement remains. As Miqdād ibn ʿAmr ﷺ stated,

.أَمَرَنَا رَسُولُ اللَّهِ – ﷺ – أَنْ نَحْثُوَ فِي وُجُوهِ الْمَدَّاحِينَ التُّرَابَ

---

46 Fakhr al-Dīn al-Rāzī, *al-Tafsīr al-Kabīr*, 2:30.

47 Aḥmad ibn Muḥammad ibn Aḥmad al-Maydānī, *Majmaʿ al-Amthāl*, Vol. 2, p. 454.

Allah's Messenger commanded us to throw dust in the faces of those who praise others to their faces.[48]

The advice ensured that praisers were warned away from doing such a thing and that the praiser who received such treatment understood what praise to someone's face was doing to them. It does not benefit the recipient, but rather only causes harm. It is worth considering how often even the well-to-do amongst us make this mistake and praise our pious people to their faces, creating tests for them that could have been avoided had words have been chosen carefully or care had been taken to avoid creating opportunities for them to inadvertently sin. If our words have not been selected and ordered carefully, the results can be equally chaotic.

Words should not only be carefully chosen when speaking to someone face-to-face but should equally be carefully selected when speaking about them to someone else. Backbiting is when one speaks about someone, when they are not present, in a way that is malicious or disliked by that person. Abū Hurayrah ﵁ narrates,

أَنَّ رَسُولَ اللَّهِ ﷺ قَالَ أَتَدْرُونَ مَا الْغِيبَةُ. قَالُوا اللَّهُ وَرَسُولُهُ أَعْلَمُ. قَالَ ذِكْرُكَ أَخَاكَ بِمَا يَكْرَهُ. قِيلَ أَفَرَأَيْتَ إِنْ كَانَ فِي أَخِي مَا أَقُولُ. قَالَ إِنْ كَانَ فِيهِ مَا تَقُولُ فَقَدِ اغْتَبْتَهُ وَإِنْ لَمْ يَكُنْ فِيهِ فَقَدْ بَهَتَّهُ.

The Prophet asked, "Do you know what backbiting is?"

The Ṣaḥābah said, "Allah and His Messenger know best."

He said, "Talking about your brother in a manner which he does not like."

48 Abū ʿAbdullāh Muḥammad ibn Yazīd ibn Mājah al-Rabʿī al-Qazwīnī, *Sunan Ibn Mājah*, 3742.

It was said to him, "What if I actually find that which I mentioned in my brother?"

He said, "If what you assert is found in him then you have backbitten, and if it is not then you have slandered him."⁴⁹

Backbiting and slander take away one's good deeds and give them to the person we are speaking about. It is a great folly to engage in such talk and a sign of weakness of character and personality. Sayyidunā ʿAlī ibn Abī Ṭālib ؓ described it thus:

اَلغِيبَةُ جُهْدُ العاجِزِ.

Backbiting is the labour of the feeble.⁵⁰

To engage in it is despicable and falls far below the standards that Muslims should possess. It is a weak attack on another person's character when the victim is unable to defend themselves and thus is an act of cowardice in the truest sense. Allah ﷻ warns against backbiting and slander in the strongest terms in the Qur'an in the following *āyah*:

يَـٰٓأَيُّهَا ٱلَّذِينَ ءَامَنُوا۟ ٱجْتَنِبُوا۟ كَثِيرًۭا مِّنَ ٱلظَّنِّ إِنَّ بَعْضَ ٱلظَّنِّ إِثْمٌۭ ۖ وَلَا تَجَسَّسُوا۟ وَلَا يَغْتَب بَّعْضُكُم بَعْضًا ۚ أَيُحِبُّ أَحَدُكُمْ أَن يَأْكُلَ لَحْمَ أَخِيهِ مَيْتًۭا فَكَرِهْتُمُوهُ ۚ وَٱتَّقُوا۟ ٱللَّهَ ۚ إِنَّ ٱللَّهَ تَوَّابٌۭ رَّحِيمٌۭ

O believers! Avoid many suspicions, for indeed, some suspicions are sinful. And do not spy, nor backbite one another. Would any of you like to eat the

---

49   *Ṣaḥīḥ Muslim*, 2589.
50   Aḥmad ibn Muḥammad ibn Aḥmad al-Maydānī, *Majmaʿ al-Amthāl*, Vol. 2, p. 454.

flesh of their dead brother? You would despise that! And fear Allah. Surely Allah is the Acceptor of Repentance, Most Merciful.[51]

Allah ﷻ also says,

$$\text{وَيْلٌ لِكُلِّ هُمَزَةٍ لُمَزَةٍ}$$

Woe to every backbiter and slanderer.[52]

From the above verses, it is clear that backbiting and slander are grave sins, likened to the literal eating of one's brother's dead flesh. How despicable and low a thing it truly is!

There are still other ways to misuse one's words, beyond what has already been discussed. Ḥasan ibn Kurayb ؓ narrates that Sayyidunā ʿAlī ibn Abī Ṭālib ؓ said,

$$\text{الْقَائِلُ الْفَاحِشَةَ وَالَّذِي يُشِيعُ بِهَا فِي الْإِثْمِ سَوَاءٌ.}$$

One who says something vulgar and one who publicises it are equal in sin.[53]

This means that quoting someone's vulgarity to pass it on to others without good reason embroils the news-giver in the sin, giving him an equal and complete share of the sin's commission. Passing on the quotation to others for the sake of amusement would fall into this category, giving evidence in a court of law, however, would not.

Another way that our words can be misused is in the act of unjust cursing. ʿUbayd al-Kindī ؓ narrated that Sayyidunā ʿAlī ؓ said,

---

51 *Al-Ḥujurāt*, 12.
52 *Al-Humazah*, 1.
53 *Al-Adab al-Mufrad*, 324.

لُعِنَ اللَّعَّانُونَ.

Those who curse are cursed.[54]

When we wish others ill or invoke curses upon them unjustly, we are invoking curses upon ourselves. As we have seen in the various chapters of this book, words can greatly benefit the speaker, but they can also do untold damage to the speaker's position in the Hereafter. The succinct statement of Sayyidunā ʿAlī ؓ must be kept in mind whenever the thought of cursing someone formulates within us. We should be aware of this double-edged sword.

Lastly, it would behove us to briefly discuss argumentation. Sayyidunā ʿAlī ؓ said,

مَنْ بَالَغَ فِي الْخُصُومَةِ أَثِمَ، وَمَنْ قَصَّرَ فِيهَا ظُلِمَ.

Whoever is excessive in arguing has sinned; whoever falls short in it is oppressed.[55]

Excessiveness in argument is a sign of stubbornness, mean-heartedness, and stupidity. A person who argues for argument's sake rarely thinks through their argument or the reason why they are arguing. Excessive argument builds within us the habit of arguing with others simply to oppose their views, without giving what was said much thought or consideration. To be excessive in argument is a sinful act, but this is not to say that one should *never* argue. There are times when arguments are necessary and proficiency in argumentation is a sign of eloquence and education. A person who falls short in argumentation is oppressed because they are unable to defend themselves. Failure to argue leaves a man weak and thus open to exploitation.

---

54 *Al-Adab al-Mufrad*, 315.
55 Aḥmad ibn Muḥammad ibn Aḥmad al-Maydānī, *Majmaʿ al-Amthāl*, Vol. 2, p. 453.

As we have seen in this section, words have great power and must be used responsibly and well. An intelligent person picks their words carefully and wields them both skilfully and sparingly. It is foolish to be careless, unskilled, and excessive with words, which inevitably affects this life and the next. As Sayyidunā ʿAlī ibn Abī Ṭālib ﵁ eloquently summarised,

إِذَا تَمَّ الْعَقْلُ نَقَصَ الْكَلَامُ.

The smarter you get, the less you speak.[56]

Knowledge and Wisdom

حَدَّثَنَا عَبْدُ اللَّهِ، حَدَّثَنِي أَبِي، حَدَّثَنَا وَكِيعٌ، حَدَّثَنَا عُمَرُ بْنُ السَّعَدِيُّ، عَنْ أَوْفَى بْنِ دَلْهَمٍ الْعَدَوِيِّ قَالَ: بَلَغَنِي عَنْ عَلِيٍّ رَضِيَ اللَّهُ عَنْهُ أَنَّهُ قَالَ:

تَعَلَّمُوا الْعِلْمَ؛ تُعْرَفُوا بِهِ، وَاعْمَلُوا بِهِ؛ تَكُونُوا مِنْ أَهْلِهِ، فَإِنَّهُ سَيَأْتِي مِنْ بَعْدِكُمْ زَمَانٌ يُنْكِرُ الْحَقَّ فِيهِ تِسْعَةُ أَعْشَارِهِمْ، لَا يَنْجُو فِيهِ إِلَّا كُلُّ نُوْمَةٍ، أُولَئِكَ أَئِمَّةُ الْهُدَى وَمَصَابِيحُ الْعِلْمِ.

Sayyidunā ʿAlī ibn Abī Ṭālib ﵁ said,

"Learn knowledge; know it and act upon it. Be among its people, for there will come a time after you in which nine-tenths of people will deny the Truth and only every quiet one will be saved; they are the Imams of Guidance and the Lamps of Knowledge."[57]

Much has been said by Sayyidunā ʿAlī ﵁ on the topic of knowledge. He was known even amongst his esteemed and knowledgeable peers for possessing wisdom and sound judgement far beyond what was expected of his age.

56 Aḥmad ibn Muḥammad ibn Aḥmad al-Maydānī, *Majmaʿ al-Amthāl*, Vol. 2, p. 455.

57 Aḥmad ibn Ḥanbal, *Kitāb al-Zuhd*, 692.

Anas ibn Mālik ﷺ reported that the Messenger of Allah ﷺ stated regarding Sayyidunā ʿAlī's ﷺ position amongst the Ummah,

وَأَقْضَاهُمْ عَلِيُّ بْنُ أَبِي طَالِبٍ.

The wisest of them in judgement is ʿAlī ibn Abī Ṭālib. [58]

It can be said that what Sayyidunā ʿAlī ﷺ warned us about is quite relevant in modern times. Truth has become a subjective idea, especially in the Western world and objective truths are questioned daily. In such a time when falsehood reigns and truth-speakers are not only shunned but persecuted, the ones who save themselves and hold on to the truth are rare to find. In the Western World, many of us have to send our children to learn from people who do not think like us, do not share our culture, and deem what we consider halal to be haram and what is haram to be halal. In this situation, it is difficult for our children to have a firm belief and a solid foundation of Islam. That is why we need to teach our children about Islam and also find opportunities for them to learn about our Deen from Islamic scholars. It is for each of us to ponder over, otherwise, we will be doing our children a disservice when we make decisions based on personal ease or societal pressures without including Islamic teaching at the centre of our children's education. The Imams of Guidance and the lamps of knowledge will be those people who hold on to the truth and protect themselves and their loved ones from this time of falsehood and wickedness.

Sayyidunā ʿAlī ﷺ said,

مَنْ صَارَعَ الْحَقَّ صَرَعَهُ.

Whoever fights the truth, it fells him.[59]

---

58 *Sunan Ibn Mājah*, 154.

59 Aḥmad ibn Muḥammad ibn Aḥmad al-Maydānī, *Majmaʿ al-Amthāl*, Vol. 2, p. 454.

The people of falsehood may seem to have the upper hand, but it is for each of us to latch onto the truth and never let go, for truth always overcomes falsehood; those who oppose it will ever be felled by it. This is not to say that the ignorant people should be treated as adversaries, however, they should be helped to understand through dialogue and discussion. Sayyidunā ʿAlī ﷺ explained,

النَّاسُ أَعْدَاءُ مَا جَهِلُوا.

People are enemies of what they do not know.[60]

Thus, we cannot expect people who do not know the truth to always recognise it when they see it, especially when they have been raised upon its opposite and surrounded by a world that forces falsehood upon them. For example, when people have grown up in insular, monocultural communities, we often find that racism and tribalism spread like wildfire amongst them when presented with someone from outside the group. Likewise, when people have grown up always thinking that the haram is halal, it can take time for them to open themselves up to the truth.

During the civil strife that occurred after the brutal murder of Sayyidunā ʿUthmān ﷺ, al-ʿUtbī ﷺ narrated,

عَن العتبي، قال: قام الحارث بن حوط الليثي إِلَى علي فَقَالَ لَهُ: أترانى أظن طلحة وَالزُّبَيْر وعائشة اجتمعوا عَلَى باطل.

فقال له علي رضي الله عنه: يَا حار إنك ملبوس عليك إِنَّ الْحَقَّ والباطل لا يُعْرَفان بأقدار الرِّجَالِ اعْرِفِ الْحَقَّ تَعْرِفْ أَهْلَهُ واعْرِفِ الباطل تَعْرِفْ من أتاه.

60 Aḥmad ibn Muḥammad ibn Aḥmad al-Maydānī, *Majmaʿ al-Amthāl*, Vol. 2, p. 455.

Al-Ḥārith ibn Ḥūṭ al-Laythī came to Sayyidunā ʿAlī and said, "Do you know that I think Ṭalḥah, al-Zubayr, and ʿĀ'ishah have united upon falsehood?"

Sayyidunā ʿAlī said, "O rebel, you are confused. Indeed, truth and falsehood are not known by the faculties of men. Know the truth and you will know its people; know falsehood and you will know the one who brings it."[61]

It is necessary for each of us to thus know both in detail. We cannot look upon people of varying opinions and objectively know which of them is correct unless we understand what objective truth is and through it learn what falsehood is. It is through the objective truth of Islam that we must view the world and judge it through the prism of the Qur'an and Sunnah. Without an understanding of objective truth, nothing can be said to be objectively false and wrong, no matter how foul it may be.

After this, not only are we as Muslims required to know Islam and thus know the truth, but we must also study and understand the falsehoods that others are upon and through this, learn to protect ourselves from it by knowing its signs. Those who have never understood logic, rhetoric, and politics cannot be expected to recognise the falsehood of a fork-tongued politician when he speaks his riddles, and those who have never studied the various "isms" and ideologies that run rampant in the world do not have a hope in being able to oppose and tackle them.

Knowledge gathering, and the retention of it, is therefore key. Sayyidunā ʿAlī ﷺ said,

اَلْجَاهِلُ الْمُتَعَلِّمُ شَبِيهٌ بِالْعَالِمِ، وَالْعَالِمُ الْمُتَعَسِّفُ شَبِيهٌ بِالْجَاهِلِ.

61 Aḥmad ibn Yaḥyā ibn Jābir al-Balādhurī, *Ansāb al-Ashrāf*, Vol. 2, p. 274.

The ignorant one who learns is like a scholar, the scholar who oppresses is like the one who is ignorant.[62]

Education and knowledge are cornerstones of Islam. An ignorant man who gathers knowledge can attain the status of a scholar; whereas a scholar who acts in ignorance, despite knowing better, can fall to the status of an ignorant. Knowledge and acting upon knowledge increase a person's status in both this world and the Hereafter, whereas failing to act upon gathered knowledge can cause one to fall. One should take care of how knowledge is obtained and how one distributes it. Abū Tufayl ﵁ reported that Sayyidunā ʿAlī ibn Abī Ṭālib ﵁ said,

حَدِّثُوا النَّاسَ بِمَا يَعْرِفُونَ أَتُحِبُّونَ أَنْ يُكَذَّبَ اللَّهُ وَرَسُولُهُ.

Speak to people according to what they know. Would you like Allah and His Messenger to be denied?"[63]

People should be spoken to with words to their level of linguistic and intellectual ability. Sometimes, even our good intentions could mislead a layman on the street who is unaware of the nuances of a difficult subject.

Furthermore, when we ourselves are in the process of gathering knowledge, it is wise to begin with beginner texts or foundational courses, rather than jumping to advanced texts. If a person wants to become a medical professional, he may begin with learning first aid and basic anatomy before moving on to more advanced subjects such as the signs of specific ailments and their cures, and then continue beyond to master niche fields such as heart surgery, etc., after many years of practice. A person who decides to try their luck at heart surgery on their first day will be considered a lunatic. Why is it then that we believe we can jump straight to advanced Hadith studies

62 Aḥmad ibn Muḥammad ibn Aḥmad al-Maydānī, *Majmaʿ al-Amthāl*, Vol. 2, p. 454.
63 *Ṣaḥīḥ al-Bukhārī*, 127.

and interpret the Qur'an when we barely understand the language they are written in?

Once we have worked ourselves up to a suitable level of knowledge, we can then begin to fulfil the roles of scholars and jurists within our community, and here is where wisdom has its part to play. Yaḥyā ibn ʿAbbād ؓ reported that Sayyidunā ʿAlī ibn Abī Ṭālib ؓ said,

إِنَّ الْفَقِيهَ حَقَّ الْفَقِيهِ مَنْ لَمْ يُقَنِّطِ النَّاسَ مِنْ رَحْمَةِ اللَّهِ وَلَمْ يُرَخِّصْ لَهُمْ فِي مَعَاصِي اللَّهِ وَلَمْ يُؤَمِّنْهُمْ مِنْ عَذَابِ اللَّهِ وَلَمْ يَدَعِ الْقُرْآنَ رَغْبَةً عَنْهُ إِلَى غَيْرِهِ إِنَّهُ لَا خَيْرَ فِي عِبَادَةٍ لَا عِلْمَ فِيهَا وَلَا عِلْمٍ لَا فَهْمَ فِيهِ وَلَا قِرَاءَةٍ لَا تَدَبُّرَ فِيهَا.

Indeed that jurist who is truly one of understanding is the one who never allows people to despair of the Mercy of Allah, never grants them concessions to disobey Allah, never lets them feel secure from the punishment of Allah, and never abandons the Qur'an for the sake of anything else. There is no good in worship without knowledge, knowledge without understanding, or recitation without reflection.[64]

Wisdom lies in the balance of these ideas within one's heart and mind. It is knowing that Allah ﷻ is Ever-Merciful whilst knowing that the limits He has set must never be crossed; it is knowing that there is no safety from the punishment of Allah ﷻ except with Him, and knowing that His Divine Revelation is the only path to success. Sayyidunā ʿAlī ؓ also explained that knowledge, understanding, and contemplation must underpin all our actions to ensure that they benefit rather than harm us. Knowledge must be gathered, but it requires understanding and contemplation. The latter can only be gained through deep study, and the former can only be gained through teachers who have learned from teachers themselves. There is no other sure way of ensuring that one understands what they are learning, and unfortunately, one of the greatest failings in modern-day Muslim society

64 *Sunan al-Dārimī*, 305.

is the widespread belief that learning one's religion from reading information taken from the anonymised internet will yield beneficial results with minimum effort. Worthwhile endeavours are achieved through hard work, striving, and help from others, not by taking shortcuts to maximise ease and comfort.

When a student asks a question, it is important to understand one's own limitations and only give answers that they know. As the Arabs say, "Half of all knowledge is saying *I don't know.*" Razī Abū Nuʿmān ﷺ reported,

عَنْ عَلِيِّ بْنِ أَبِي طَالِبٍ رَضِيَ اللَّهُ عَنْهُ قَالَ: إِذَا سُئِلْتُمْ عَمَّا لَا تَعْلَمُونَ فَاهْرُبُوا.

قَالَ: وَكَيْفَ الْهَرَبُ يَا أَمِيرَ الْمُؤْمِنِينَ.

قَالَ تَقُولُونَ اللَّهُ أَعْلَمُ.

Sayyidunā ʿAlī ibn Abī Ṭālib said, "When you are asked about what you do not know, flee."

It was said, "O Commander of the Faithful, how does one flee?"

Sayyidunā ʿAlī said, "Say that Allah knows best."[65]

This is the perfect response to any question when you do not have an answer. It is correct, truthful, and avoids any future issues that may arise from giving the wrong answer. In matters of faith, it is sinful to give the wrong answers, yet often we find ourselves giving answers to show that we are knowledgeable in the field. This is pure ignorance. Knowing one's limitations is the truest sign of self-awareness, and Sayyidunā ʿAlī ﷺ, despite being a sea of knowledge, knew that there were many matters that he did not understand or have the answers to, and on those occasions, it is always best to turn to Allah ﷻ and point others towards doing the same.

---

65 *Sunan al-Dārimī*, 183.

The Folly of Long Hope

عَنْ زُبَيْدَةَ قَالَ: قَالَ عَلِيٌّ عَلَيْهِ السَّلَامُ، وَقَالَ وَكِيعٌ وَحَدَّثَنَا يَزِيدُ بْنُ زِيَادِ بْنِ أَبِي الْجَعْدِ، عَنْ مُهَاجِرٍ الْعَامِرِيِّ، عَنْ عَلِيٍّ عَلَيْهِ السَّلَامُ قَالَ:

إِنَّ أَخْوَفَ مَا أَخَافُ عَلَيْكُمُ اثْنَتَيْنِ طُولُ الْأَمَلِ وَاتِّبَاعُ الْهَوَى، فَأَمَّا طُولُ الْأَمَلِ فَيُنْسِي الْآخِرَةَ وَأَمَّا اتِّبَاعُ الْهَوَى فَيَصُدُّ عَنِ الْحَقِّ، أَلَا وَإِنَّ الدُّنْيَا قَدْ وَلَّتْ مُدْبِرَةً وَالْآخِرَةُ مُقْبِلَةٌ وَلِكُلِّ وَاحِدٍ مِنْهُمَا بَنُونَ فَكُونُوا مِنْ أَبْنَاءِ الْآخِرَةِ وَلَا تَكُونُوا مِنْ أَبْنَاءِ الدُّنْيَا فَإِنَّ الْيَوْمَ عَمَلٌ وَلَا حِسَابَ وَغَدًا حِسَابٌ وَلَا عَمَلَ.

Sayyidunā ʿAlī ibn Abī Ṭālib ﵁ said,

"Two things I fear most from what I fear for you: long hope and following inclinations. Long hope makes you forget the Hereafter, and following inclinations averts you from the truth. Indeed, the World has already passed away and the Hereafter is coming, and each of them has sons. Be of the sons of the Hereafter and not of the sons of the World, for today there is action and no reckoning, and tomorrow there will be reckoning and no action."[66]

Sayyidunā ʿAlī ibn Abī Ṭālib ﵁ warned of two great follies: long hope and following one's inclinations. The idea of having long hopes is a strange one. We all know we are not in this world for a long time and none of us know when our time will end. There is no doubt that people in our immediate circles have "died young" and we have all at least seen or read of children dying all over the world. Yet still as human beings, we fool ourselves with grand plans and big ideas, and even at old age we fail to see the ultimate truth of this world: that it will end. Abū Hurayrah ﵁ narrates that the Prophet ﷺ said,

لاَ يَزَالُ قَلْبُ الْكَبِيرِ شَابًّا فِي اثْنَتَيْنِ فِي حُبِّ الدُّنْيَا، وَطُولِ الأَمَلِ.

---

66 Aḥmad ibn Ḥanbal, *Kitāb al-Zuhd*, 693.

The aged heart remains young in two respects: his love for the world and long hope.[67]

A person given to holding long hopes in their heart becomes unable to see the world for what it is. They are lost in its false wonder and in love with the lie it presents to them. Sayyidunā ʿAlī ﷺ said,

اَلْأَمَانِيُّ تُعْمِي أَعْيُنَ الْبَصَائِرِ.

Wishes blind the eyes of insight.[68]

It is a veil over our eyes that leads to bad decision-making. Sayyidunā ʿAlī ﷺ also said,

مَنْ أَطَالَ الْأَمَلَ أَسَاءَ الْعَمَلَ.

He who entertains long hopes will do wrong.[69]

When we are blinded by long hope, we lack the insight to make correct decisions; when we act on incorrect decisions, we can only expect poor outcomes. There is no use in spending our days counting down to retirement when we do not even know if we will make it to our beds at night. If we plan our short lives in this world as if we are to remain here forever, our actions in this world will be of no value or worth in the Hereafter.

Sayyidunā ʿAlī ﷺ once said,

ألا حُرٌّ يَدَعُ هذِهِ اللُّمَاظَةَ لِأَهْلِها.

---

67 *Ṣaḥīḥ al-Bukhārī*, 6420.

68 Aḥmad ibn Muḥammad ibn Aḥmad al-Maydānī, *Majmaʿ al-Amthāl*, Vol. 2, p. 455.

69 Ibid.

Is there no freeman who will leave this bit of scrap for those who deserve it?[70]

The word *lumāẓah* means the bits of food that remain in the mouth after eating or the residue of anything that is of little quantity to begin with. It is an indication of the very little value and worth this world actually has.

Following one's inclinations is often a result of the folly of long hope, and preferring worldly affairs over the Commands of Allah ﷻ and the Way of the Prophet ﷺ is an act of foolishness. Why should we focus our time and energy on trivial pursuits that do not benefit us and do not help us in achieving our ultimate victory in the Hereafter?

ʿAbdullāh ibn al-Ḥasan ؓ reports that Sayyidunā ʿAlī ؓ said,

لَا يَتْرُكُ النَّاسُ شَيْئًا مِنْ دِينِهِمْ إِرَادَةَ اسْتِصْلَاحِ دُنْيَاهُمْ إِلَّا فَتَحَ اللَّهُ عَلَيْهِمْ مَا هُوَ أَضَرُّ عَلَيْهِمْ وَمَا هُوَ شَرٌّ عَلَيْهِمْ مِنْهُ

People do not abandon something from their religion, intending to benefit their worldly affairs, except that Allah will expose them to something more harmful and evil for them.[71]

Following our inclinations is a trap that not only denies us the chance to benefit but also creates the opportunity for more harm to occur. This is the price of giving up one's religion for the fleeting pleasures of the temporary world. There is no profit to be had, only a multiplication of one's losses. On the same subject, another saying of Sayyidunā ʿAlī ؓ has been recorded, which summarises the deceptive nature of the world and the shortness of our stay upon it. He said,

---

70 Aḥmad ibn Muḥammad ibn Aḥmad al-Maydānī, *Majmaʿ al-Amthāl*, Vol. 2, p. 453

71 Ibn al-Mubārak, ʿAbdullāh, *al-Zuhd wa al-Raqāʾiq*, Dar al-Kutub al-ʿIlmiyyah, Beirut (1425/2004), Hadith 1627.

.اَلدُّنْيَا تَغُرُّ وَتَضُرُّ وَتَمُرُّ، إِنَّ اللهَ تَعَالَى لَمْ يَرْضَهَا ثَوَاباً لِأَوْلِيَائِهِ، وَلاَ عِقَاباً لِأَعْدَائِهِ

.وَإِنَّ أَهْلَ الدُّنْيَا كَرَكْبٍ بَيْنَا هُمْ حَلُّوا إِذْ صَاحَ بِهِمْ سَائِقُهُمْ فَارْتَحَلُوا

The world deceives, harms, and passes. Indeed, Allah the Most High did not approve it as a reward for His friends, nor as a punishment for His enemies.

Indeed, the people of the world are as a caravan; no sooner have they alighted that the driver calls out to them, and they move on.[72]

This is all that the world is. A short pause on the road, not long enough to be considered even a stop. We are here for a moment, and then we continue on our way to one of two destinations: the Garden or the Fire. The world is neither a punishment nor a reward, but merely a testing ground that deceives us into thinking that it is something more; it harms us by wasting our most valuable resource in the form of time; and it leaves us to answer for the mistakes we have made.

The Death of al-Ḥaydar

:عَنْ قَبِيصَةَ بْنِ جَابِرٍ، قَالَ: قَالَ عَلِيُّ بْنُ أَبِي طَالِبٍ رَضِيَ اللهُ عَنْهُ

.مَنْ زَهِدَ فِي الدُّنْيَا هَانَتْ عَلَيْهِ الْمُصِيبَاتِ، وَمَنِ ارْتَقَبَ الْمَوْتَ سَارَعَ فِي الْخَيْرَاتِ

Sayyidunā ʿAlī ﷺ said:

The one unattached to the world deems misfortunes insignificant; the one who anticipates death hastens to do good deeds.[73]

72 Aḥmad ibn Muḥammad ibn Aḥmad al-Maydānī, *Majmaʿ al-Amthāl*, Vol. 2, p. 454.

73 Ibn Abī al-Dunyā, *Kitāb al-Zuhd*, 92.

Death comes to all of us. The only guarantee in life is that it will end. The time, place, and method of death cannot be known, and are from the matters that Allah ﷻ alone knows of. Detachment from the world builds stoicism and resilience within us, as we realise that this world is temporary and the tests within it are insignificant in comparison to the Hereafter; the anticipation of death leads us to spend our lives preparing for it and thus gives us the best opportunity for success in the Hereafter. Sayyidunā ʿAlī ؓ was so acutely aware of death that he detached himself from worldly comforts and gathered good deeds to take forward as provisions.

This mindset was forged during his early life with the Prophet ﷺ, when he grew up in his household and learned the ways of manliness directly from him. Sayyidunā ʿAlī ؓ had even been told how and why he would be killed.

ʿAmmār ibn Yāsir ؓ narrates,

فَيَوْمَئِذٍ قَالَ رَسُولُ اللهِ صَلَّى اللهُ عَلَيْهِ وَسَلَّمَ لِعَلِيٍّ: يَا أَبَا تُرَابٍ لِمَا يُرَى عَلَيْهِ مِنَ التُّرَابِ، قَالَ: أَلَا أُحَدِّثُكُمَا بِأَشْقَى النَّاسِ رَجُلَيْنِ؟

!قُلْنَا: بَلَى يَا رَسُولَ اللهِ

قَالَ: أُحَيْمِرُ ثَمُودَ الَّذِي عَقَرَ النَّاقَةَ، وَالَّذِي يَضْرِبُكَ يَا عَلِيُّ عَلَى هَذِهِ، يَعْنِي قَرْنَهُ، حَتَّى تُبَلَّ .مِنْهُ هَذِهِ، يَعْنِي لِحْيَتَهُ

...On that day, the Messenger of Allah said to Sayyidunā ʿAlī, "O Abū Turāb", on account of the dirt that could be seen on him, "Shall I not tell you about the two most wretched people?"

We said, "Of course, O Messenger of Allah!"

"Uḥaymir of the Thamūd, who hamstrung the she-camel; and the one who strikes you, O ʿAlī, on this", meaning the crown of his head, "until this is soaked with blood", meaning his beard.[74]

Uḥaymir means the "small, red one", and is a nickname of Qidhār ibn Sālif, the brigand from the Thamūd who had orchestrated the murder of the she-camel of Allah ﷻ, on account of his reddish complexion and short stature.

إِذِ ٱنۢبَعَثَ أَشْقَىٰهَا

When the most wicked of them was roused [to kill the she-camel].[75]

Qidhār had fallen in love with a licentious woman by the name of Unayzah, who felt wronged by the existence of the she-camel as she felt her animals were not able to feed properly due to the miraculous creature. She offered herself in marriage to him in exchange for the murder of the she-camel, and Qidhār agreed. He carried out the act by waylaying the mighty creature in a narrow pass on a known route she often took, killing her after first striking her hamstring.[76]

The second person mentioned was ʿAbd al-Raḥmān ibn Muljam al-Khārijī. He too had fallen in love with a promiscuous woman, a *khārijī* by the name of Qatāmah, who sought revenge for the deaths of her family members who had fought against the army of Sayyidunā ʿAlī ؓ. She too offered herself in marriage in exchange for a terrible act: the murder of Sayyidunā ʿAlī ؓ.[77]

---

74 *Musnad Imām Aḥmad*, 18321.

75 *Al-Shams*, 11.

76 Shāh ʿAbd al-ʿAzīz Muḥaddith Dehlawī, *Tafsīr ʿAzīzī: Pārah ʿAmma*, pp. 455-457.

77 Shāh ʿAbd al-ʿAzīz Muḥaddith Dehlawī, *Tafsīr ʿAzīzī: Pārah ʿAmma*, pp. 466-467.

Sayyidunā ʿAlī ﷺ would leave home in the early morning and call people for Fajr as he walked the streets between his home and the masjid. It was his habit to not keep guards around him. On the morning of his murder, he did the same. ʿAbd al-Raḥmān ibn Muljam, his sword dripping with poison, had waited for him in a narrow alleyway in the dark, following the advice of his friends who had been observing the Caliph for some time. As Sayyidunā ʿAlī ﷺ approached, he stepped out of his hiding place and struck him to the head, gravely wounding him.[78]

The blow did not immediately kill him and, as the people seized ʿAbd al-Raḥmān, Sayyidunā ʿAlī ﷺ advised that he be held captive until the results of his attack were known. Were he to survive, then they were to forgive him; were he to die, then the punishment of murder was death. Sayyidunā ʿAlī ﷺ would soon succumb to the poison in his wound, and on the 19th of Ramadan, 40AH, he passed away a martyr and the Rāshidūn Caliphate came to an end.

The comparison that the Prophet ﷺ had drawn between the two most despicable men is plain to see, in the motives of the murders they committed, in the victims themselves, in the method of the murders, and in the wickedness of the murderers.

Of all man's base desires, the lowest is lust. It drives men to behave like beasts and removes their intellect from them; it is acted upon through the use of body parts related to the expelling of filth from the body; it requires one to reveal their private areas to someone else and do that which people dislike to even mention in public. Sinful acts are also of different degrees of vileness; the one engaged in fornication, gluttony, excess, music, etc., is considered to be less evil than the one engaged in tyranny and murder. The one who commits the most heinous crime for the sake of fulfilling his lowest desire is thus the lowest of all. Rights owed to others also have three levels:

---

78 ʿAbd al-Ḥamīd Khān Swātī, *Maʿālim al-Irfān*, Maktaba Durūs al-Qur'an, Gujranwala (2015/ 1436), Vol. 21, pp. 360-361.

(i) the highest are the Rights of Allah ﷻ, our Creator and Sustainer; (ii) the rights of mankind, in the order of our nearest and dearest first and then gradually to mankind in general; (iii) lastly, rights owed to ourselves. The vilest person in terms of breaching rights would be the one who breached all three levels of rights.

Qidhār ibn Sālif was the lowest of the people of the previous nations, for he committed a terrible act of murder to fulfil his basest desire. He also violated his rights by dying a *kāfir*, his people's rights by involving them in his sin and guaranteeing the Wrath of Allah ﷻ upon them, and the rights of Allah ﷻ by slaying the she-camel that He had bestowed on the Thamūd. ʿAbd al-Raḥmān ibn Muljam became the lowest and vilest of our Ummah when he committed the same act for the same reasons.[79]

Following the murder of Sayyidunā ʿAlī ibn Abī Ṭālib ؓ, al-Ḥasan ؓ addressed the people. Abū Razīn ؓ narrates,

خَطَبَنَا الْحَسَنُ بْنُ عَلِيٍّ بَعْدَ وَفَاةِ عَلِيٍّ وَ عَلَيْهِ عِمَامَةٌ سَوْدَاءُ فَقَالَ: لَقَدْ فَارَقَكُمْ رَجُلٌ لَمْ يَسْبِقْهُ الْأَوَّلُونَ بِعِلْمٍ، وَلَا يُدْرِكُهُ الْآخَرُونَ

al-Ḥasan ibn ʿAlī addressed us after the death of Sayyidunā ʿAlī, and he was wearing a black turban. He said, "A man has left you who was not preceded in knowledge by those who came before him, and those who follow him will not surpass him."[80]

Sayyidunā ʿAlī's ؓ funeral prayer was led by his son al-Ḥasan ibn ʿAlī ؓ. He was wrapped in three white cloths and was buried quietly in a simple grave. It is unclear where he was buried, as there are multiple reports regarding the exact location, but it was most likely in Kufa.

---

79 Shāh ʿAbd al-ʿAzīz Muḥaddith Dehlawī, *Tafsīr ʿAzīzī: Pārah ʿAmma*, pp. 463-464.
80 Aḥmad ibn Ḥanbal, *Faḍāʾil al-Ṣaḥābah*, 1026.

When news reached Muʿāwiyah ﷺ of the murder of Sayyidunā ʿAlī ﷺ, he wept. His wife said, "Do you weep for ʿAlī when you fought him?"

Muʿāwiyah ﷺ replied, "Woe to you, you do not know what people have lost of virtue, understanding, and knowledge."[81]

Such was the end of Sayyidunā ʿAlī ibn Abī Ṭālib ﷺ and the simple ascetic life he lived. Amongst the first people to accept Islam, he had grown up in the household of the Prophet ﷺ and had learned to be a man under his tutelage. He was a loyal advisor to each of the Caliphs that preceded him, famed for his wisdom, strength, and asceticism. Undefeated in every duel he fought, unmatched by those who came after him in every noble trait, the likes of him will never be seen again. He was the fourth and final Caliph of the Rāshidūn, and just as his dear friend Sayyidunā ʿUthmān ﷺ had predicted, the world continued to fall apart following his death. Civil wars, strife, and intra-Muslim disputes became more and more commonplace as time moved on. With each passing generation, the Ummah became weaker, influenced by ideologies and thoughts from those outside the fold of Islam. Now, 1400 years removed from these great men, their words and advice remain behind to guide us, a lifeline that each of us must hold on to, lest we drown in the sea of troubles that we find ourselves floundering in.

A Final Word

As human beings, it is in our nature to turn to the wisdom of the ancients in the hope that they may offer us a pathway to success. We know inherently that the giants among men who once strode upon the Earth understood the great secrets and deep wisdom of life that escape us in our modern age of digital illusion and trickery.

81 Dr ʿAlī M. Ṣallābī, *ʿAlī ibn Abī Ṭālib*, Dār al-ʿĀlamiyyah, Riyadh (1431/2010), Vol. 2, p. 628.

As we sail ever forward into stormy seas of technological progress and moral decline, we desperately try to anchor ourselves to the past and the familiar, searching for a safe harbour in the embrace of those who came before. The intellectuals of the Western world continue to turn to their great thinkers and leaders, from Socrates and Plato to Marcus Aurelius and Plutarch, or the secularised philosophers of yesteryear; those of the East find themselves mining the words of Sun-Tzu, Miyamoto Musashi, Confucius, and Buddha, or the hermetic mystics of ancient times. However, while many of them may have some wisdom to share and have benefitted humans to some extent, it cannot be compared to the Divine knowledge Allah ﷻ sent us through His prophets who possessed wisdom directly bestowed upon them by Allah ﷻ. Therefore, instead of being too reliant on ancient philosophers, we should focus on what Allah ﷻ taught us through His prophets, particularly through His last messenger Muhammad ﷺ. As Muslims, we follow the Qur'an and Sunnah first and foremost. The Prophet ﷺ came to us with a perfect message, and he was supported by the best of people. The Prophet ﷺ said,

إِنَّ اللَّهَ تَبَارَكَ وَتَعَالَى اخْتَارَنِي وَاخْتَارَ لِي أَصْحَابًا، فَجَعَلَ لِي مِنْهُمْ وُزَرَاءَ وَأَنْصَارًا
وَأَصْهَارًا، فَمَنْ سَبَّهُمْ فَعَلَيْهِ لَعْنَةُ اللَّهِ وَالْمَلَائِكَةِ وَالنَّاسِ أَجْمَعِينَ، لَا يُقْبَلُ مِنْهُ يَوْمَ الْقِيَامَةِ
صَرْفٌ وَلَا عَدْلٌ.

Allah the Blessed and Exalted has chosen me and has chosen my Ṣaḥābah for me. He has made some of them my deputies, some of them my helpers, and some of them my family. Anyone who curses them has the curse of Allah on him, and of the Angels, and of all people. Allah will not accept any exchange nor compensation from him.[82]

When Allah ﷻ sent us the Prophet ﷺ, he sent with him a host of great men. Each of them is greater than any who came before them or will come after; each of them is a mighty hero and great philosopher, noble leader and genius

82 Sulaymān ibn Aḥmad ibn Ayyūb ibn Muṭayyir al-Ṭabarānī, *al-Muʿjam al-Kabīr*, 349.

thinker, and legend in their own right. Yet even amongst such lofty ranks there were those who excelled beyond their illustrious peers. These are the men whose examples we should be clinging to.

It is hoped by the authors of this humble work that it has helped in some way to inspire our beloved brothers and sisters to turn away from the fools that the people of falsehood turn to, and instead seek inspiration from the greatest men of the greatest generation. If we seek truth, we will find it in the words of al-Ṣiddīq; if we seek fairness, we will find it in the deeds of al-Fārūq; if we seek generosity, we will find it in the ways of al-Ghanī; and if we seek virtue, we will find it in the path of al-Ḥaydar.

May Allah's eternal blessings be upon each of them, and all of their peers and upon the *Ahl al-Bayt*. May peace and blessings forever descend upon the greatest of men, the noble Prophet Muhammad ﷺ, until men no longer walk upon the Earth, deeds are no longer done, and words are no longer spoken. To Allah ﷻ belongs all praise, the first of it and the last of it, both the apparent and the hidden, and He is the One whose help is sought.

سُبْحَانَكَ اللَّهُمَّ وَبِحَمْدِكَ، أَشْهَدُ أَنْ لاَ إِلَـهَ إِلاَّ أَنْتَ، أَسْتَغْفِرُكَ، وَأَتُوْبُ إِلَيْكَ.